Victims of Abuse

Monograph Series of the
Ralph R. Greenson
Memorial Library of the
San Diego Psychoanalytic
Society and Institute

Monograph 3

Victims of Abuse

The Emotional Impact of Child and Adult Trauma

edited by
Alan Sugarman, Ph.D.

International Universities Press, Inc.
Madison   Connecticut

Second Printing, 1996

Library of Congress Cataloging-in-Publication Data

Victims of abuse : the emotional impact of child and adult trauma / edited by Alan Sugarman.
    p. cm. — (Monograph series of the Ralph R. Greenson Memorial Library of the San Diego Psychoanalytic Society and Institute; monograph 3)
    Includes bibliographical references and index.
    ISBN 0-8236-6730-8
    1. Post-traumatic stress disorder. 2. Psychic trauma. 3. Sexual abuse victims—Mental health. 4. Adult child abuse victims—Mental health. 5. Abused children—Mental health. I. Sugarman, Alan. II. Series: Monograph series of the Ralph R. Greenson Memorial Library of the San Diego Psychoanalytic Society and Institute; 3.
RC552.P67V53 1994
616.85'82239—dc20   93-49082
                                              CIP

Manufactured in the United States of America

Contents

vi   Contents

Contributors

Ada M. Burris, M.D.
Senior Instructor, San Diego Psychoanalytic Society and Institute; Associate Clinical Professor of Psychiatry, University of California, San Diego.

Edward L. Fields, M.D.
Senior Faculty, San Diego Psychoanalytic Society and Institute; Associate Clinical Professor of Psychiatry, University of California, San Diego.

John M. Hassler, M.D.
Senior Faculty, San Diego Psychoanalytic Society and Institute; Associate Clinical Professor of Psychiatry, University of California, San Diego.

Don Houts, M.D.
Faculty, San Diego Psychoanalytic Society and Institute; Associate Clinical Professor of Psychiatry, University of California, San Diego.

Selma Kramer, M.D.
Training and Supervising Analyst, Philadelphia Psychoanalytic Institute; Professor of Psychiatry, Thomas Jefferson Medical College; President, Margaret S. Mahler Psychiatric Research Foundation; and Co-editor of *Trauma of Transgression: Psychotherapy of Incest Victims*.

Howard B. Levine, M.D.
Faculty, Boston Psychoanalytic Institute; Faculty; Massachusetts Institute for Psychoanalysis; and Editor of *Adult Analysis and Childhood Sexual Abuse*.

Nadine A. Levinson, D.D.S.
Faculty, San Diego Psychoanalytic Society and Institute; Associate Clinical Professor of Psychiatry, University of California Irvine; and Co-editor of *Female Psychology: An Annotated Psychoanalytic Bibliography.*

Maria T. Lymberis, M.D.
Assistant Clinical Professor, UCLA Neuropsychiatric Institute; Senior Faculty, Los Angeles Psychoanalytic Society and Institute; Senior Faculty, Graduate Center for Child Development and Psychotherapy.

Jack Novick, Ph.D.
Associate Clinical Professor of Psychiatry, Wayne State University and University of Michigan; Faculty and Supervising (C/A) Psychoanalyst, Michigan Psychoanalytic Institute.

Kerry Kelly Novick
Faculty, Michigan Psychoanalytic Institute.

Albert J. Solnit, M.D.
Sterling Professor Emeritus, Pediatrics and Psychiatry and Senior Research Scientist, Yale University Child Study Center; Training and Supervising Analyst, Western New England Institute for Psychoanalysis; Co-author of *In the Best Interests of the Child, Divorce and Your Child, Before the Best Interests of the Child,* and *Beyond the Best Interests of the Child*; and Commissioner of the Department of Mental Health for the State of Connecticut.

Alan Sugarman, Ph.D.
Senior Faculty, San Diego Psychoanalytic Society and Institute; Associate Clinical Professor of Psychiatry, University of California San Diego; and Co-editor of *Borderline Phenomena and the Rorschach Test, The Technique and Practice of Psychoanalysis, Volume II: A Memorial Volume to Ralph R. Greenson,* and *On Living, Hating, and Loving Well.*

Introduction

This monograph grew out of a conference, "Victims of Abuse: The Emotional Impact of Child and Adult Trauma," organized by the San Diego Psychoanalytic Society and Institute in February 1992. The conference was motivated by our concern with the use of the concept of trauma to account for almost every ill that could befall mankind. In particular, the growing popularity of groups such as Adult Children of Alcoholics, or the like, seemed to be trivializing the importance of childhood trauma and blaming all adult problems on one's parenting. Yet the penchant to fall back on such seeming cliches is understandable in the context of growing awareness of certain forms of abuse, such as sexual abuse, being more common than may have been realized in the past.

Thus, the time seemed right to explore these concepts once again from a psychoanalytic perspective. Toward this end, major psychoanalytic clinicians interested in the areas of trauma and abuse were invited to present their current ideas and findings to an audience of mental health professionals. Members of the San Diego Psychoanalytic Society and Institute who had special clinical expertise in these areas were also invited to present their findings in a series of small group workshops at the conference. It is the ideas developed by all these different psychoanalytic practitioners from many different areas of the United States that form the substance of this monograph.

Sugarman's chapter opens the monograph by examining the complex topics of trauma and abuse and placing them in a historical and theoretical context. After that the monograph is divided into two sections, the first on "The Phenomenology and Dynamics of Abuse and Trauma," and the second on "Treatment Challenges with the Traumatized Patient." We begin the first section with Solnit's chapter that examines child abuse from a psychoanalytic perspective. The Novicks then examine the dynamic underpinnings of abuse, emphasizing externalization as a major feature in such phenomena. Kramer's chapter focuses on the residues, both somatic and cognitive, that incest leaves on its victims.

Levinson's and Houts' chapters expand psychoanalytic thinking from an emphasis on childhood traumas to a study of common adulthood traumas—the battered spouse and post-traumatic stress in the workplace, respectively. Burris returns to Kramer's emphasis on somatization as a response to trauma and offers her thoughts on this common phenomenon.

The authors in Part II examine treatment issues raised by traumatized patients. Levine addresses the particularly difficult treatment problems given the fact that these patients tend to repeat or reenact their traumas, and offers advice about how to deal with it. Lymberis examines the complicated area of boundaries in psychotherapy and warns against the tendency of some traumatized patients to provoke their treaters into symbolic reenactments of the original abuse through a variety of boundary violations, the most extreme of which can involve sadomasochistic sexual violations. Fields discusses the counter-transference difficulties posed by patients who have been abused. Hassler's chapter, which rounds out the monograph, offers cases that demonstrate the value of a psychoanalytically oriented psychotherapy in helping patients to resolve their traumas and go on with their lives.

This monograph is not meant to be the final answer to the array of difficulties raised by the traumatized patient. Instead its aim is to be heuristic—to continue the recent attempts of analysts to reconsider the concepts of trauma and abuse and to integrate them into our psychoanalytic framework that usually emphasizes the internal origins of neurosis and character problems. It also attempts to expand the emphasis on sexual abuse or physical abuse during childhood that seems to be the major focus of analysts writing about trauma today, in order to consider other types of trauma, including those occurring during adulthood.

Chapter 1

Trauma and Abuse: An Overview

Alan Sugarman, Ph.D.

One hundred years after Freud's momentous discovery of the psychological vicissitudes of human trauma, psychoanalytic clinicians are once again struggling with how to understand and intervene toward attenuating the effect of these human misfortunes. It seems that every day we are barraged both as professionals and as citizens with news of another instance of traumatization and the need to deal with it. We have come to recognize that trauma affects all age groups and social classes, and that traumatic events can range from the subtle to the extreme. Changing cultural mores about appropriate behavior toward children and toward women are two of the most obvious repercussions of this greater sensitivity.

However, the growing sensitivity to the multitude of ways in which an individual can feel emotionally damaged or psychically scarred carries with it the risk of trivializing this important subject. The recent burgeoning of "victims" groups in which emotionally injured people blame all the difficulties of their lives on having been the children of defective parents of one sort or another, risks both eschewing personal responsibility and reducing the complexity of psychopathology to purely external circumstance. Certainly the impact of parents on children is great; particularly so when severe abuse of one kind or another occurs. Nonetheless, this behavior is filtered through

1

the child's mental mechanisms and organized in ways in which preexisting traits as well as constitutional endowment play a role. Problems with abdicating personal responsibility can be seen in the avalanche of "stress" claims in the legal arena. Too often the psychoanalytically informed clinician sees patients whose character structures are such that they have provoked their job difficulties, overreacted to the job situation, or displaced personal problems into the job place or accident site.

Thus, it seems time to reexamine the concepts of trauma and victimization in order both to help those unfortunate individuals who have suffered genuine trauma as well as to prevent misuse and overgeneralization of these concepts. Such reexamination will require the reevaluation of our definitions of trauma as well as an understanding of the synthesis of the complex interplay of environmental and intrapsychic factors that contribute to the experience of being traumatized. I will suggest below that a developmental approach to the understanding of abuse and trauma is the most helpful in arriving at such a synthesis. Finally, this chapter will address treatment issues raised by such patients in terms of general parameters. Specific details of how to treat different types of traumatized patients will be left to the other contributors of this volume.

HISTORICAL REVIEW

Psychoanalysts' interest in trauma dates to Freud's early affect-trauma model and his conclusion that *"Hysterics suffer mainly from reminiscences"* (Breuer and Freud, 1895, p. 7). With this realization that his hysterical patients shared in common the experience of having been sexually abused, Freud brought the concept of trauma to the forefront of psychoanalytic scrutiny. Expanding on Breuer's work with Anna O, he emphasized that responses to trauma did not usually appear at the time when the trauma took place. Only later, during or after adolescence, could the effect of the trauma be observed when it was revived as a memory (Waldhorn and Fine, 1974). He also introduced the quantitative approach to trauma, an approach still with us today. For Freud, during his early writings, trauma involved a breach in the stimulus barrier so that the psyche was flooded with affect (Waldhorn and Fine, 1974; Blum, 1986). His first technical approach of promoting abreaction of the strangulated affect associated with the memory of the trauma followed logically.

It would be a mistake, however, to assume that Freud dropped his sensitivity to actual trauma as he delineated his topographic model at the point when he realized the ubiquitous role of infantile sexuality leading to fantasy. "The seduction theory was discarded, but the pathogenic significance of seduction and other forms of trauma was retained" (Blum, 1986, p. 8). Freud continued to elaborate his quantitative emphasis on understanding trauma in *Beyond the Pleasure Principle* (1920) when he emphasized that both the intensity of the traumatic stimulus as well as the readiness of the stimulus barrier to cope with it, contributed to the experience of being traumatized.

But Freud (1926) needed the concepts of the structural model to move beyond external sources of trauma. When he described the ego's helplessness as being the major factor in trauma, he added a role for overstimulation arising from internal origins. "The essence of . . . [a traumatic situation] is an experience of helplessness on the part of the ego in the face of accumulation of excitation, whether of external or internal origin" (p. 81). Traumatic or actual anxiety was contrasted with signal anxiety as ego strength and availability of defenses became codeterminants of the effect of the trauma on the psyche. Traumatic events during childhood could be seen as having a greater impact than trauma during adulthood because of the immature ego's lack of resources with which to process such experiences. Freud (1926) also laid the groundwork for a qualitative understanding of trauma in his articulation of a developmental sequence of danger situations ranging from loss of the object to guilt. Such potential sources of trauma moved beyond a solely quantitative emphasis on libidinal overstimulation or ego weakness (or both).

It was Nunberg (1955) who most clearly integrated the understanding of trauma with the structural model, in particular describing inner contributors. Taking an early developmental perspective, he emphasized how disequilibrium between ego development and instinctual development could lead to a state in which the ego was overwhelmed by drive stimuli. Situations wherein either ego development lagged behind instinctual development or situations in which instincts were stimulated excessively would both have the same net result. "In this situation the ego proves incapable of handling the instinctual needs by binding them or by distributing their energy in an orderly manner" (Furst, 1967, p. 29). It is the ego's consequent passivity that results in the individual being traumatized by excessive internal or external stimuli (Nunberg, 1955).

Subsequent analytic exploration of trauma built on this combination of qualitative and quantitative factors as analysts working with traumatized patients came to recognize that the impact of a traumatic experience could not be gauged accurately from the traumatic event alone. Thus, the multifaceted variables contributing to the ultimate experience of trauma received greater scrutiny. Attention turned, in particular, to internal contributors to trauma. Libidinal instinctual contributions (Fenichel, 1945a,b) as well as aggressive instincts (Weiss, 1935) were emphasized as overtaxing the ego. Preoedipal conflicts were noted to cause children to masochistically provoke trauma (Agostin, 1947; Greenacre, 1952; Coleman and Shorr, 1953).

But the environment's contribution to a predisposition to trauma also continued to receive emphasis in studies of earliest infancy (Greenacre, 1952; Hoffer, 1952; Murphy, 1958, 1961). Parental failure to alleviate early states of infantile helplessness, or failure to stimulate early autonomous ego functions such as perception, were shown to create fixation points that affect how subsequent experience is processed and contribute to whether later experiences are experienced as traumatic. Optimal frustration was shown to promote ego development while excessive frustration or trauma only overwhelmed the ego's synthetic capacities and set the stage for dissociation (Loewenstein and Ross, 1992). Much of this early work failed to differentiate adequately between concepts of frustration and trauma, tending to equate the two when speaking of the infant (Stern, 1953a,b; Kramer, 1955). Furst (1967) questioned this assumption that the two were the same but concluded reasonably that such theoretical confusion did not render the notion that early infantile events played a significant role in later trauma any less true.

DEFINITIONAL PROBLEMS WITH THE CONCEPT OF TRAUMA

As is true of many advances in clinical psychoanalysis, greater attention to and understanding of a particular phenomenon has led to attempts to reconceptualize and redefine it in order to take into account new findings. This is clearly the case when understanding the concept of psychic trauma. At the most basic definitional level one must be clear about the phenomenological referents of the term. Discussions of the phenomenon of trauma tend to condense the dynamic sequence of variables which together comprise the phenomenon so that psychic trauma may appear to be a more unitary phenomenon than it actually is. Rangell (1967) has clearly differentiated the traumatic experience into various components which make up the dynamic sequence that we call trauma. These components include: (1) the precipitant of the traumatic process (an internal or external stimulus); (2) the traumatic process involving a breach of the stimulus barrier with a consequent loss of ego mediation; (3) the traumatic effect of this process manifested in a state of psychic helplessness which results in, (4) the release of painful and unpleasurable affect. Only by keeping in mind these components can we develop a thorough psychoanalytic understanding of trauma.

But there are other aspects which must also be attended to in order to understand this prominent human experience in its full complexity. Thus, the first component of the traumatic occurrence, its precipitant, brings to the forefront quantitative issues about the magnitude of stimulation necessary to be considered traumatic. All analysts have had the experience of treating some patients who suffered massive over- or understimulation as children without showing the degree or type of psychological repercussions that would be expected, while seeing other patients who have been exquisitely injured and warped by what seem "objectively" to be far less intense or painful occurrences. A variety of concepts have been introduced in order to make sense of these puzzling differences between individuals. Later, I will discuss developmental and genetic influences. At present, however, economic or quantitative factors will be reviewed.

Kris (1956) differentiated strain from shock trauma in a preliminary effort to address such seeming disparities. Shock trauma referred to those single events such as childhood seduction that overwhelmed the ego's capacity to cope with the stimulation. In contrast, he emphasized more long-standing and ongoing pathological experiences of childhood that both colored the experience of a shock trauma and subsequently integrated it into ongoing psychic development. "Strain refers to long-acting pathogenic determinants, distorted patterns of development, and also to predisposition and to vulnerability. Strain may potentiate shock trauma, and shock inevitably creates strain in its aftermath. Strain may appear to have only deferred or relatively silent effects, unlike the overwhelming impact of shock trauma" (Blum, 1986, p. 12). Often the childhood ego's attempt to adapt to external events that could cause trauma leads to regressive increases in impulses or modification of defenses that strain the ego. It is this state of ego strain and the child's continued ability to adapt to it, or not, that determines whether true strain trauma in which the ego becomes overwhelmed will occur (Sandler, 1967).

Khan (1963) continued this emphasis on the less blatant but possibly more insidious contributions to trauma with his concept of cumulative trauma. Thus, he pointed out that, "Various strains and stresses felt by the child in the context of his ego dependency upon the mother result in some degree of trauma" (Sugarman, 1975, p. 107). The mother's anaclitic function includes serving as a protective shield against overwhelming and noxious external stimuli. Her partial success at performing this function often prevents shock trauma from being experienced throughout any one particular occurrence—instead, the trauma accumulates over time and often becomes evident only in retrospect, within the psychoanalytic situation. Premature and selective ego development then occurs which interferes with the child's ability to form healthy object relationships along with causing other pathological compromise formations.

Other definitional disagreements about how to conceptualize trauma revolve around whether to define trauma by the magnitude of the traumatic precipitant or to focus on subjective elements in order to arrive at a diagnosis of trauma. Analysts emphasizing the quantitative factor in traumatization (e.g., Cooper, 1986) continue to emphasize the flooding of the individual's ego by a cataclysmic event resulting in the typical primitive mechanisms available to the ego for coping and adaptation. This approach to trauma is showing an important resurgence around efforts to understand multiple personality disorders (Loewenstein and Ross, 1992).

Other analysts emphasize the subjective aspect of traumatization (Brenner, 1986; Dowling, 1986). They use the clinical finding that what is traumatic for one individual may not be for another, to conclude that "it is the meaning which an external event has for an individual which accounts for its traumatic effect on him" (Brenner, 1986, p. 200). Such an approach is based on psychoanalytic experience with traumatized patients which has shown that it is the psychological meaning that the individual attaches to his or her trauma that gives it its particular and unique pathological significance. Brenner's (1986) conclusion that "an event is traumatic because of the way in which it impinges on the traumatized individual's pre-existing psychic conflicts" (p. 197) highlights the necessity of examining trauma in terms of its intrapsychic structural context.

MECHANISMS FOR COPING WITH TRAUMA

Psychoanalytic experience has demonstrated that the ego has a limited repertoire of mechanisms with which to handle massive psychological trauma and emotional helplessness (Furst, 1986; Rothstein, 1986a). These mechanisms include: repetition, massive repression, dissociation (Kris, 1956; Loewenstein and Ross, 1992; Roth, 1992); isolation (Kris, 1956); regression, somatization (Kramer, 1990); avoidance of repetition, and defensive sadomasochistic identifications (Asch, 1976; Rothstein, 1986a; Etezady, 1991; Sugarman, 1991a).

   Repetition is probably the coping mechanism that has received the most attention in the psychoanalytic literature (Stern,
1988). The traumatized individual tends to reenact variations
of the original trauma or traumas, which is often the impetus
for him or her seeking treatment, and which often proves the
most difficult traumatic symptom to alleviate, particularly when
it is well integrated into the character structure. Various concepts have been used to explain this tendency to recapitulate the
traumatic experiences, particularly the repetition compulsion
(Furst, 1986). But from a structural standpoint it is more consistent to speak in terms of the ego's defensive attempt to turn
passive into active in an attempt at mastery. This defense is one
of the ego's earliest (A. Freud, 1936) and plays a significant
role in ego and superego development (A. Freud, 1936; Spitz,
1958). It is likely to be this role in ego formation that leads to
the fixation to trauma seen in the traumatized patient (Furst,
1986). Dowling (1986), from another perspective, emphasizes
that the extreme emotional helplessness engendered by trauma
makes it become an organizing event that both integrates past
and present psychological experiences while forming a tem-
plate into which subsequent experience is fit. This organizing
aspect of trauma contributes to its repetitious quality also.
   The degree to which traumatized patients attempt to use
repression is so extensive and rigid that its presence should
raise the diagnostic question of unresolved trauma when it is
seen. One woman in her early thirties, for example, consulted
with an analyst and reported that she went through life without
any thought in her head other than concrete directives such as
"turn left at the corner." Fantasy was a concept without experi-
ential referent for her and the request to associate seemed for-
midable at the beginning of treatment. Only well into the treatment did she recapture memories of her repressed childhood
molestation by her beloved grandfather and realize how she was
reenacting those activities with her husband instead of thinking
about them. Thus, she demonstrated the price of such massive
repression in her repeated unconscious provocations of the
original trauma.
   Some argue that dissociation is an inherent part of trauma
(Loewenstein, 1991; Putnam, 1991; Spiegel, 1991). "Dissociation is defined as an active inhibitory process that normally

screens internal and external stimuli from the field of consciousness. . . . Under normal conditions, dissociation enhances the integrating functions of the ego by screening out excessive or irrelevant stimuli" (Young, 1988, pp. 35–36). These advocates tend to be clinicians treating a relatively narrow spectrum of patients. Other analysts find that formulations involving invariant consequences need to be treated with caution. Traumas such as parent loss do not seem inevitably to cause dissociation. Kris (1956), for example, treating a wide range of patients, emphasized the relationship between dissociation and isolation, using these concepts to consider the complex issue of how the analyst fosters recall of past trauma in order to promote insight and mastery within the analytic situation. He found that isolation of affect was used more commonly than dissociation to cope with these traumas.

Regression is a typical reaction to severe trauma. It can be quite persistent when it occurs early in the child's development (Furst, 1986), when shocking loss of such functions as toileting can occur rapidly after traumatization. Work at the Hampstead Nurseries with children undergoing sudden separation from their parents during World War II found that ego regression as a response to separation trauma required psychotherapeutic efforts in order to attenuate it. And even adults can show prominent ego regression in the face of severe trauma.

Somatization is another common reaction to childhood trauma. Some have suggested that somatization is an infantile precursor to dissociation as a defense against excessive stimuli (Young, 1988). Certainly one cannot ignore the clinical finding that patients with psychosomatic symptoms have a remarkable history of severe trauma including sexual or physical abuse (or both), parental death, parental alcoholism, and divorce in their histories. Thus, Kramer (1990) has used the concept of somatic memories in describing the psychological repercussions of incest. Others have emphasized the defensive focus on the body to avoid awareness of uncomfortable affects including depression (Kohut, 1971; Thompson, 1991) or aggression (Ritvo, 1984; Sugarman, 1991b) that arise from early traumata.

The defensive sadomasochistic identifications that arise from efforts to cope with early trauma are well described in the analytic literature (Berliner, 1940, 1947, 1958; Brenman, 1952; Asch, 1976; Glenn, 1984). The regular pattern of early trauma, particularly pain, in the life of masochistic patients has been noted in leading them to seek out painful experiences in later life (Valenstein, 1973). "If the affect, especially those primal and primitive aspects associated with the early self and self-object experience, take a predominantly painful direction, then a set is established wherein pain, i.e., painful affect, connotes the original self-object, and more succinctly later the self and/ or object" (p. 374).

Consequently suffering becomes inextricably bound up with the libidinal tie to the mother. Later its presence feels unconsciously essential in order to avoid object loss. Cooper (1984), likewise, views these victimized individuals as struggling with the problem of self-definition and separation-individuation. "The object is perceived as excessively cruel and refusing, the self is perceived as incapable with genuine self-assertion in the pursuit of gratification, and the gratification obtained from disappointment takes precedence over genuine libidinal, assertive, or ego functional satisfactions" (p. 52).

THE DEVELOPMENTAL CONTEXT OF TRAUMA

In the developmental approach to understanding and treating trauma the psychological meaning that the traumatized individual attaches to his or her trauma gives it its particular and unique pathological significance for the patient. This is well stated by Dowling (1986) when he says that, "The traumatic experience of the primal scene, or of any other scene, is an experience of meaning" (p. 212). Consequently the developmental stage during which the trauma occurs, as well as the developmental conflicts and interferences that have gone before it, become major influences on the meaning of an event. The continuing impact of the trauma on subsequent development and the equally important role of subsequent development on the trauma, are also very significant.

Because of this interrelationship between trauma and development, the earlier that the trauma occurs the more debilitating will be its impact. Studies of the relationship between development and psychopathology have demonstrated "that earlier disturbances generally have more global and less reversible consequences" (Tyson, 1986, p. 20). Discrete early interferences have a broad impact on subsequent development because of the branching nature of the developmental process. Conditions that disrupt the mother–child relationship during the first 18 months of life, for example, interfere with object relationships, self-esteem, the sense of reality, and identity (Greenacre, 1967). Parent loss is almost always debilitating because it shatters the child's belief in their parents' omnipotence (Samuels, 1988). The younger the child the more necessary is this illusion of parent omnipotence for the maintenance of narcissistic equilibrium and to facilitate ego development. Premature and overly painful disillusionment taxes the young child's ego functioning, interferes with healthy self-esteem, and inhibits the differentiation of reality from fantasy.

Thus, phase specificity also plays a role in determining whether an event is traumatic as well as the nature of the subsequent traumatic process (Furst, 1967). Events are often traumatic because of the ways in which they resonate with the child's developmental stage (Greenacre, 1952). Being exposed in person to the birth of one's sibling with the accompanying sight of blood and intensified expressions of maternal emotion will mean something very different to the one-year-old than it will to the oedipal child.

At other times, an event becomes traumatic because it is out of phase with the child's stage of development. Premature genital stimulation, for example, can be traumatic (Furst, 1967). Clinical experience suggests that children who achieve puberty unduly early are far more traumatized by the upsurge in drives and changes in body ego than those who achieve puberty late.

Development can, at times, also have an ameliorating impact on trauma. Tyson (1986) has pointed to the weakness of psychoanalytic thinking in explaining relative psychological health. He presented an example of a child of oedipal age who had suffered profound losses including the loss of his mother during the first year of his life, and yet had managed to traverse the developmental path into the oedipal period with no worse than a neurosis that responded well to analysis. In this case the relationship with the father and the new stepmother helped the child to cope with this trauma well enough to avoid the profound ego deficits and relational disturbances that would be expected. Such relationships often help development to continue in the face of trauma. For example, the relationship with the surviving parent as well as the nature of the relationship with the deceased parent have been found to be important facilitators of adaptation to the trauma of loss with children who have experienced the death of a parent (Altschul, 1988).

But this emphasis on development, in particular its earliest stages, should not be taken to minimize the role of adult development. "Analytic experience indicates that such massive trauma need not have occurred in childhood to have severely damaging effects" (Blum, 1986, p. 19). Studies of Holocaust survivors, soldiers suffering from war neuroses, or other survivors of disasters during adulthood indicate that the trauma can happen across the developmental spectrum. A fruitful area of study lies in the need to integrate our recently articulated knowledge of adult development with trauma. In particular, the relationship of the traumatic event to the stage of adult development during which it is experienced should offer findings similar to those deriving from studies of childhood trauma. Injuries disrupting reproductive capacities, for example, are likely to be more traumatic during young adulthood with its developmental task of beginning a family than during later stages.

The concept of retrospective trauma (Sandler, 1967) is also a helpful one in understanding the occurrence of trauma during adulthood. Often apparent traumas during adulthood take on their traumatic impact because they revive the memory of an earlier experience or an earlier fantasy that becomes traumatic under the current, adult circumstances. One patient suffered a prolonged traumatic reaction to an automobile accident, for example, when her subsequent recuperation revived experiences of passive helplessness associated with her childhood molestation. This phenomenon of retrospective trauma is another factor demonstrating the importance of a qualitative approach to understanding trauma.

TREATING THE TRAUMATIZED VICTIM

Patients who have suffered severe trauma pose numerous treatment challenges that will be discussed in subsequent chapters. These difficulties are receiving increasing emphasis as therapists once again try to understand the complex interweaving of internal factors and environmental experiences that contribute to their patients' difficulties (Rothstein, 1986b; Levine, 1990a; Kramer and Akhter, 1991). Many of these patients simply are not suitable to be treated with psychoanalysis proper. If the trauma has been severe or early enough it may disrupt ego development sufficiently to preclude the capacities necessary to work in analysis. The patient may lack the ability to form some minimal treatment alliance; access to and an ability to put into words inner subjective experiences such as emotions; a capacity for introspection involving a split between an observing ego and an experiencing one; a willingness to attempt to confine one's impulses to verbal expression rather than enactment; and enough ego strength to avoid severe regression in the face of the powerful feelings, memories, and wishes that will be evoked by such a process. Treatment options for these patients who are not suitable for analysis may range from the supportive end of the spectrum to the more ambitious end wherein psychoanalytic psychotherapy is used as a preparatory phase for analysis. Much further attention to those patients who are incapable of using an insight-oriented approach to treatment is needed. But that will not be the focus of this volume.

For even those patients who are able to use a more exploratory approach pose significant difficulties. Levine's (1990b) description of patients who were sexually abused as children holds true for patients suffering from other types of trauma, also.

The treatments are frequently long and stormy, beset by prolonged periods of distrust and intense negative or erotic transferences. They are often characterized by strong tendencies to enactment and impulsive action and by such phenomena as primitive dissociative reactions, blurring of the boundaries between fantasy and reality,

and reliance on archaic defense mechanisms, such as projection, projective identification, splitting, and denial,
which are more usually associated with the treatment of
borderline, narcissistic, and other primitive personality
disorders [pp. 197–198].

One sees these same sorts of problems with children who,
for example, have suffered the loss of a father. Their problems
with modulating their aggression and apparent superego lacu-
nae have led them to be described as suffering from "father
hunger" (Herzog, 1982).

The transferences formed by patients who have suffered
prominent trauma are inevitably difficult because of the organizing impact of the trauma, particularly its effect on self and
object representations. Adult patients who lost a parent during
their formative years tend to show notable resistance to the
development of the transference (Altschul, 1968; Fleming and
Altschul, 1988). Such patients tend to deny feeling involved
with the therapist in order to unconsciously preserve the relationship through avoiding a full-fledged mourning process. At
other times they are simply too fearful to invest in other human
beings and risk being abandoned once again.

Patients who have suffered abuse of a sexual or aggressive
nature pose other complications in their insistence on repetition. Their repetition compulsion can be so powerful that they
lose the boundary between fantasy and reality (Levine, 1990b)
and border on a transference psychosis as the transference loses
its "as if" quality. One such woman, who had suffered prolonged and painful maternal emotional unavailability as well as
sexual overstimulation (without manifest abuse) by her father
during childhood, lapsed into an early and rigid sadomasochistic transference wherein the analyst was experienced both as
the cold, unavailable mother as well as the father who seemed
to promise special intimacy only to renege on his promise. But
efforts to link her self-destructive acting out to feeling disappointed with the analyst would only lead to plaintive acknowl-
edgments of "You're right, but if you know it hurts me so much,
why don't you change?" It took several years of analysis before
this woman developed some semblance of an observing ego. It

is this difficulty that led Bigras (1990) to warn against too classical, silent, and neutral an analytic attitude because it can be
experienced by the patient as a revived edition of his or her
early maternal deprivation. On the other hand, Levine (1990b)
points out the danger that being too supportive or forthcoming
with such patients can stimulate anxiety over boundary violations and escalate their sadomasochistic provocations.

Not surprisingly, countertransference is the other technical
arena that poses difficulties with these patients. In treating children who have suffered the loss of a parent, countertransference-based reluctance to bring up the parent's death for fear
of hurting the fragile child has been reported (Garber, 1988).
I have noted a similar reluctance to make a firm recommendation for the analysis that such a child might need so clearly for
the same reasons. At the other extreme can be the counterpho-
bic tendency to overwhelm the child immediately and insensi-
tively with comments about the lost parent. One 10-year-old
boy was seen in consultation after refusing to follow through
with the treatment which he needed because the first consultant
had immediately confronted him about his pain over his father's death at the beginning of the first consultation hour before he had built even a semblance of a treatment alliance.

Countertransference problems in treating such children
also revolve around how much the therapist should function as
a developmental object. It is common for these children to
utilize the treater as a functional equivalent of the lost parent.
More than other children they are curious about our personal
lives and insist on personal revelation with an intensity born of
desperation. Countertransference tendencies to become more
of a real person arise in such situations; indeed, often one needs
to be more revealing (Garber, 1988). Situations wherein the
child feels too disappointed at being unable to effect some sort
of replacement of the dead parent with the therapist can disrupt the treatment (Hummer, 1988). And of course these difficulties with enactment and repetition create severe countertransference strains in therapists attempting to treat victims of
childhood sexual abuse. Many of these patients are so intent
on reenacting the sexual abuse that they provoke or demand
enactment of the sexual transference (Smith, 1984; Levine,

1990b). In fact, it is not uncommon to find these patients reporting a history of having been sexually exploited by a number of therapists. The gratification of other types of wishes are also provoked from their therapists and these, too, can symbolize the original abuse.

But the sadomasochistic transferences of these patients stimulate more in the therapist than a wish to gratify libidinal impulses. Their anger over what they experience to be the therapist's lack of caring when appropriate limits are maintained can be persistent and provocative enough to stimulate countertransference sadism. Forgetting sessions with the patient, being insensitive with one's words or tone of voice, lapses in the timing of interventions, and excessive confrontation are some of the hallmarks of the countertransference which abused patients can stimulate. It is not uncommon for the therapist to begin to question his own competence and choice of livelihood when treating these patients. They are adept at recreating within the therapist an experience of their own helplessness, humiliation, and despair at the time of the trauma. Equally problematic can be the tendency to deny these countertransference feelings to oneself because of one's guilt over one's rage toward the patient. Such countertransference experiences are inevitable with these patients and can be useful sources of information for formulating one's interventions if the extremes of enacting or denying them can be avoided.

CONCLUSION

In conclusion, the understanding and treatment of trauma is a complex topic, one that is beginning to gain the attention that it warrants. Clinicians today are far more sensitized to the need to be aware of potential trauma as a contributor to the symptoms and character traits with which their patients present. This volume addresses the developmental approach to the understanding and treatment of trauma. The remaining chapters will explore this area with more detail and suggest a variety of treatment strategies for helping these unfortunate individuals.

Helping the "victims" of such trauma regain their developmental momentum in order to arrive at an identity separate from their trauma is an arduous but necessary task when treating them.

REFERENCES

Agostin, T. (1947), Prodromal traumatic cycles in adulthood. *Psychoanal. Quart.*, 13:467–478.

Altschul, S. (1968), Denial and ego arrest. *J. Amer. Psychoanal. Assn.*, 16:301–317.

——— (1988), Trauma, mourning, and adaptation: A dynamic point of view. In: *Childhood Bereavement and Its Aftermath*, ed. S. Altschul. Madison, CT: International Universities Press, pp. 3–15.

Asch, S. (1976), Varieties of negative therapeutic reaction and problems of technique. *J. Amer. Psychoanal. Assn.*, 24:383–408.

Berliner, B. (1940), Libido and reality in masochism. *Psychoanal. Quart.*, 9:322–333.

——— (1947), On some psychodynamics of masochism. *Psychoanal. Quart.*, 16:459–471.

——— (1958), The role of object relations in moral masochism. *Psychoanal. Quart.*, 26:358–377.

Bigras, J. (1990), Psychoanalysis as incestuous repetition: Some technical considerations. In: *Adult Analysis and Childhood Sexual Abuse*, ed. H. B. Levine. Hillsdale, NJ: Analytic Press, pp. 197–218.

Blum, H. P. (1986), The concept of reconstruction of trauma. In: *The Reconstruction of Trauma: Its Significance in Clinical Work*, ed. A. Rothstein. Madison, CT: International Universities Press, pp. 7–27.

Brenman, M. (1952), On teasing and being teased: And the problem of moral masochism. *The Psychoanalytic Study of the Child*, 7:264–285. New York: International Universities Press.

Brenner, C. (1986), Discussion of the various contributions. In: *The Reconstruction of Trauma: Its Significance in Clinical Work*, ed. A. Rothstein. Madison, CT: International Universities Press, pp. 41–56.

Breuer, J., & Freud, S. (1895), Studies on Hysteria. *Standard Edition*, 2:1–251. London: Hogarth Press, 1955.

Coleman, M. R., & Shorr, J. E. (1953), Ego development through self-traumatization. *Psychoanal. Rev.*, 40:225–242.

18 Victims of Abuse

Cooper, A. M. (1984), The unusually painful analysis: A group of narcissistic masochistic characters. In: *Psychoanalysis: The Vital Issues*, Vol. 2, ed. G. H. Pollock & J. E. Gedo. New York: International Universities Press, pp. 45–67.

———— (1986), Toward a limited definition of psychic trauma. In: *The Reconstruction of Trauma: Its Significance in Clinical Work*, ed. A. Rothstein. Madison, CT: International Universities Press, pp. 41–56.

Dowling, S. (1986), Discussion of the various contributions. In: *The Reconstruction of Trauma: Its Significance in Clinical Work*, ed. A. Rothstein. Madison, CT: International Universities Press, pp. 205–217.

Etezady, M. H. (1991), Victims of incest. In: *The Trauma of Transgression: Psychotherapy of Incest Victims*, ed. S. Kramer & S. Akhtar. New York: Aronson, pp. 149–166.

Fenichel, O. (1945a), The concept of trauma in contemporary psychoanalytic theory. *Collected Papers*, 2:49–69. New York: W. W. Norton, 1954.

———— (1945b), *The Psychoanalytic Theory of Neurosis*. New York: W. W. Norton.

Fleming, J., & Altschul, S. (1988), Activation of mourning and growth in psychoanalysis. In: *Childhood Bereavement and Its Aftermath*, ed. S. Altschul. Madison, CT: International Universities Press, pp. 277–307.

Freud, A. (1936), *The Ego and the Mechanisms of Defense*. New York: International Universities Press.

Freud, S. (1920), Beyond the pleasure principle. *Standard Edition*, 18:3–64. London: Hogarth Press, 1955.

———— (1926), Inhibitions, symptoms and anxiety. *Standard Edition*, 20:77–174. London: Hogarth Press, 1959.

Furst, S. S. (1967), Psychic trauma: A survey. In: *Psychic Trauma*, ed. S. S. Furst. New York: Basic Books, pp. 3–50.

———— (1986), Psychic trauma and its reconstruction with particular reference to postchildhood trauma. In: *The Reconstruction of Trauma: Its Significance in Clinical Work*, ed. A. Rothstein. Madison, CT: International Universities Press, pp. 29–39.

Garber, B. (1988), Some common transference-countertransference themes in the treatment of parent loss. In: *Childhood Bereavement and Its Aftermath*, ed. S. Altschul. Madison, CT: International Universities Press, pp. 145–163.

Glenn, J. (1984), Psychic trauma and masochism. *J. Amer. Psychoanal. Assn.*, 33:357–386.

Greenacre, P. (1952), The prepuberty trauma in girls. In: *Trauma, Growth, and Personality*. New York: W. W. Norton, pp. 204–223.
———— (1967), The influence of infantile trauma on genetic patterns. In: *Psychic Trauma*, ed. S. S. Furst. New York: Basic Books, pp. 108–153.
Herzog, J. M. (1982), On father hunger: The father's role in the modulation of aggressive drive and fantasy. In: *Father and Child*, ed. S. W. Cath, A. R. Gurwitt, & J. M. Ross. Boston: Little, Brown, pp. 163–174.
Hoffer, W. (1952), The mutual influences in the development of the ego and the id. *The Psychoanalytic Study of the Child*, 7:31–41. New York: International Universities Press.
Hummer, K. M. (1988), Termination and endings. In: *Childhood Bereavement and Its Aftermath*, ed. S. Altschul. Madison, CT: International Universities Press, pp. 187–236.
Khan, M. M. R. (1963), The concept of cumulative trauma. *The Psychoanalytic Study of the Child*, 18:286–306. New York: International Universities Press.
Kohut, H. (1971), *The Analysis of the Self*. New York: International Universities Press.
Kramer, P. (1955), On discovering one's identity. *The Psychoanalytic Study of the Child*, 10:47–77. New York: International Universities Press.
Kramer, S. (1990), Residues of incest. In: *Adult Analysis and Childhood Sexual Abuse*, ed. H. B. Levine. Hillsdale, NJ: Analytic Press, pp. 149–170.
———— Akhter, S., eds. (1991), *The Trauma of Transgression. Psychotherapy of Incest Victims*. Northvale, NJ: Jason Aronson.
Kris, E. (1956), The recovery of childhood memories in psychoanalysis. *The Psychoanalytic Study of the Child*, 11:54–88. New York: International Universities Press.
Levine, H. B. (1990a), Clinical issues in the analysis of adults who were sexually abused as children. In: *Adult Analysis and Childhood Sexual Abuse*, ed. H. B. Levine. Hillsdale, NJ: Analytic Press, pp. 197–218.
———— (1990b), *Adult Analysis and Childhood Sexual Abuse*. Hillsdale, NJ: Analytic Press.
Loewenstein, R. J. (1991), An office mental status examination for chronic complex dissociative symptoms and multiple personality disorder. *Psychiat. Clin. N. Amer.*, 14:567–604.
———— Ross, D. R. (1992), Multiple personality and psychoanalysis: An introduction. *Psychoanal. Inq.*, 12:3–48.

Murphy, W. F. (1958), Character, trauma, and sensory perception. *Internat. J. Psycho-Anal.*, 39:555–567.

——— (1961), A note on trauma and loss. *J. Amer. Psychoanal. Assn.*, 9:519–532.

Nunberg, H. (1955), *Principles of Psychoanalysis*. New York: International Universities Press.

Putnam, F. W. (1991), Dissociative disorders in children and adolescents: A developmental perspective. *Psychiat. Clin. N. Amer.*, 14:519–531.

Rangell, L. (1967), The metapsychology of psychic trauma. In: *Psychic Trauma*, ed. S. S. Furst. New York: Basic Books, pp. 51–84.

Ritvo, S. (1984), The image and use of the body in psychic conflict: With special reference to eating disorders in adolescence. *The Psychoanalytic Study of the Child*, 39:449–469. New Haven, CT: Yale University Press.

Roth, S. (1992), Discussion: A psychoanalyst's perspective on multiple personality disorder. *Psychoanal. Inq.*, 12:112–123.

Rothstein, A. (1986a), Conclusion. In: *The Reconstruction of Trauma: Its Significance in Clinical Work*, ed. A. Rothstein. Madison, CT: International Universities Press, pp. 219–230.

——— (1986b), *The Reconstruction of Trauma: Its Significance in Clinical Work*. Madison, CT: International Universities Press.

Samuels, A. (1988), Parental death in childhood. In: *Childhood Bereavement and Its Aftermath*, ed. S. Altschul. Madison, CT: International Universities Press, pp. 19–36.

Sandler, J. (1967), Trauma, strain, and development. In: *Psychic Trauma*, ed. S. S. Furst. New York: Basic Books, pp. 154–174.

Smith, S. (1984), The sexually abused patient and the abusing therapist: A study in sadomasochistic relationships. *Psychoanal. Psychol.*, 1:89–98.

Spiegel, D. (1991), Dissociation and trauma. In: *American Psychiatric Press Annual Review of Psychiatry*, Vol. 10, ed. A. Tasman & S. Goldfinger. Washington, DC: American Psychiatric Press, pp. 261–275.

Spitz, R. (1958), On the genesis of superego components. *The Psychoanalytic Study of the Child*, 13:375–404. New York: International Universities Press.

Stern, M. M. (1953a), Trauma and symptom formation. *Internat. J. Psycho-Anal.*, 31:202–218.

——— (1953b), Trauma, projective technique and analytic profile. *Psychoanal. Quart.*, 22:221–251.

——— (1988), *Repetition and Trauma: Toward a Teleonomic Theory of Psychoanalysis*. Hillsdale, NJ: Analytic Press.

Sugarman, A. (1975), Book review of *The Privacy of the Self*, by M. M. R. Khan. *Bull. Menninger Clinic*, 39:106–108.
—— (1991a), Developmental antecedents of masochism: Vignettes from the analysis of a three-year-old girl. *Internat. J. Psycho-Anal.*, 72:107–116.
—— (1991b), Bulimia: A displacement from psychological self to body self. In: *The Psychodynamic Treatment of Anorexia Nervosa and Bulimia*, ed. C. Johnson. New York: Guilford Press, pp. 3–33.
Thompson, T. L. (1991), Psychosomatic phenomena. In: *Beyond the Symbiotic Orbit*, ed. S. Akhtar & H. Parens. Hillsdale, NJ: Analytic Press, pp. 243–260.
Tyson, R. L. (1986), The roots of psychopathology and our theories of development. *J. Amer. Acad. Child Psychiatry*, 25:12–22.
Valenstein, A. F. (1973), On attachment to painful feelings and the negative therapeutic reaction. *The Psychoanalytic Study of the Child*, 28:365–392. New Haven, CT: Yale University Press.
Waldhorn, H. F., & Fine, B. D. (1974), *Trauma and Symbolism*. New York: International Universities Press.
Weiss, E. (1935), Agoraphobia and its relation to hysterical attacks and to traumas. *Internat. J. Psycho-Anal.*, 16:59–83.
Young, W. (1988), All that switches is not split. *Dissociation*, 1:31–41.

PART I

Phenomenology and Dynamics of Abuse and Trauma

Chapter 2

A Psychoanalytic View of Child Abuse

Albert J. Solnit, M.D.

A psychoanalytic view of child abuse emphasizes the relationship between external events and subjective experience. The psychoanalytic view is not a narrow one since subjective experience is significantly influenced by antecedent events that influence the child who is being abused and the child abuser. This presentation concentrates on the child's experience, although awareness of the motives and behavior of the abuser can be factored into the dynamics of such tragic events. In the larger picture, familial, cultural, legal, and historical contexts should be included.

To give but one brief example: during testimony many years ago before a U.S. Senate Committee chaired by Senator Walter Mondale, a 45-year-old woman testified on her experience as an abused child who had been put into a series of foster homes. Her father was alcoholic and repeatedly physically abused her and her siblings while drunk, begging for forgiveness the next day as he coped with his guilt, his hangover, and his need to remain gainfully employed. She said, reflectively, that she would have been better off to stay home with her alcoholic, abusing father and her mother who could not protect the children—those bruises and risks to life and limb, in retrospect, would have been better than to have the "bones" of her spirit repeatedly fractured by her experiences in the twelve foster homes she lived in from the age of 10 until she was emancipated at the age of 18.

It is desirable and necessary that there be laws governing the organization of our society's values and responses to child abuse. But, as is true of our clinical and theoretical knowledge, legal methods and rules of evidence are understandably limiting and crude when they are used to try to sort out complaints, to conduct investigations and evaluations, and to bring justice to bear in determining the best interests of each child who comes to the law's attention because of abuse. Often the junction of legal and clinical responsibility and processes may be harmonious; but just as often they may be an awkward fit that requires each to acknowledge its boundaries, its limitations, and to find a way for the two to work together in the best interests of children whose parents, for one reason or another, have failed to meet our societal standards of providing adequate care, protection, and guidance. Both fields, legal and clinical (psychoanalytic), seek to know what happened, who was involved, and what the consequences were.

It should be emphasized that the law uses police detective skills to ask questions; and clinicians, especially those guided by psychoanalysis, use clinical skills to clarify, understand, and treat. When lawyers, detectives, and policepersons try to become clinicians, they are at risk of obscuring what needs to be clarified legally; when clinicians devise methods, use dolls and games, and examinations that encourage them to act as detectives, lawyers, and policepersons, they are at risk of being incompetent as clinicians in addition to their lack of expertise in the area of law enforcement.

One last presumption: though psychoanalytically it is useful to assume that the past influences the present and future, understanding the past is not sufficient to adequately explain the present and future. For example, do those who have been abused as children invariably become abusive adults? In fact, more than half who were abused do not become abusive parents (see Kaufman and Zigler, 1987).

Tragically, the violent, physical abuse and murder of children by adults, often parents, is as old as recorded human history. Sad as it may seem, most of us would not want to live in a society that was able to prevent every single instance of child abuse because that could only be carried out in a prisonlike state. At the same time, all of us would like to prevent as much child abuse as is possible to prevent in a relatively free society in which the democratic values of family privacy and the pluralism of differing life-styles are protected and supported.

Historically, in the United States, the famous case of Mary Ellen in the late nineteenth century (Coleman, 1924; Bremner, 1971) was not the first incidence of child abuse to receive national attention; "nor was it evident . . . that there were not laws to protect children from parental abuse; but because of the unusual publicity it received, it shocked many people into a greater awareness of this serious human problem, and it sparked the beginning of a massive crusade against child abuse" (Hiner, 1979). Precipitated by the reactions to what happened to Mary Ellen in New York City, realizing that children should have at least as much protection as domestic animals, the New York City Society for the Prevention of Cruelty to Children was organized in December 1874. Ironically, it was the American Society for the Prevention of Cruelty to Animals which responded effectively to the previously thwarted efforts of a New York charity worker, Mrs. Etta Angell Wheeler, to remove and protect Mary Ellen from her abusing parents.

Much as in the new era of concern about abused or battered children in the 1960s and 1970s, the crusade in the 1870s was dedicated to making certain that existing laws prohibiting cruelty to human beings would be enforced and that children would be protected. The movement grew quickly, for the nineteenth century, though not as quickly as it again grew when rediscovered in the 1960s. By 1905 there were 400 societies working to prevent cruelty to children or to intervene protectively when it was discovered. "In 1908, E. Fellows Jenkins, secretary and superintendent of the New York Society for the Prevention of Cruelty to Children, estimated that 'almost ¾ of a million of children' (Jenkins, 1905, 1908) had been involved in the investigation of that society alone" (Hiner, 1979, p. 233).

The rediscovery of the abused or battered child was ushered in by a radiologist, Dr. John Caffey, who initially reported

it in 1946 as a new syndrome in which subdural hematomas in
infants were often associated with atypical fractures of the limb
and ribs (Caffey, 1946, 1950). It was not until 1962 when C.
Henry Kempe and Ray Helfer referred to "The Battered Child
Syndrome" that the medical profession and the public allowed
itself to undo its denial of child abuse and to overreact by treating that continuing tragic human condition as though it were a
new discovery (Kempe and Helfer, 1962). "The Battered Child
Syndrome" became a "newly discovered" human behavior that
was to be blotted out by new laws that mandated how and by
whom the reporting would be required and how the reporters
were to be protected.

The roots of human violence that culminate in parents
and other adults physically assaulting children, especially young
children, represent a part of our biosocial heritage that has
gone awry. Violence is aggression that has broken out of the
socialization channels that the community accepts and supports
when adult aggression is modified and transformed in the service of providing safe, affectionate care for children. Because
our society assumes that parents will nurture and safeguard
children, it has constitutionally guaranteed parental autonomy
in providing care for their children. Such guarantees also protect the integrity of family life associated with the privacy, intimacy, and richness of emotional exchange in a healthy family.

The child is entitled to feel wanted in the continuing care
of affectionate parents who provide him with emotional nurturance and stimulation, guidance, and a safe social–physical environment. In connection with the violent, physical, and sexual
abuse of children by adults, especially their parents, we are
confronted with a breakdown of an acceptable standard of parental care. Our society no longer tolerates physical abuse of
children by parents. Beyond the violation of humanitarian considerations, such abuse represents a threat to the well-being of
a community and to the values we place on children in our
society. The violence that is unleashed when adults assault children and the imminent threat of damage to children when
adults fail to safeguard them from physical harm, represent
the activation of potential violence toward children of which
each and every adult is capable. This human potential is highly

charged and highly unacceptable as adult behavior, which clari-
fies to a significant extent why adults either deny the existence
of child abuse or overreact in order to demonstrate that they
are opposed to children being the victims of such inhumane
and cruel behavior.

PSYCHOLOGICAL ROOTS

The human infant is relatively helpless at birth. Helplessness is
a magnet for nurture, for attention, and for action; it is also a
painful reminder to the adult of his own earlier helplessness,
and perversely can invite the adult's attack (violence). The pro-
tracted helplessness and dependency of the young child dictate
a biological and psychological requirement for survival; they
also represent, inevitably, the needs of the helpless child to be
cared for by an adult. Newborns may not survive if adults are
not aggressive and loving enough, that is, if the adult is severely
neglectful in protecting and nurturing the child. Infants may
not survive if the adult's aggression becomes transformed into
violent behavior. Such destructive effects may be evoked either
by the adult's incapacity to invest the child with affectionate
care and expectations or because the adult loses control and
becomes violent and assaultive. Such loss of control may be the
repetition of earlier experience, having its origins in the past
when the adult as a child was the object of violent destructive
assaults by his or her own parent or parents.

Close biological and psychosocial ties become the basis for
survival and assure the unique development of each child. The
parent–child relationship is the matrix for the child's emerging
socialization as a member of the family. The family, in turn, is
a basic social unit of the community. In the context of institu-
tionalized social behavior in the community, children and adults
form group relationships across families; and we are able to
compare the standards of child care within the family to those
that represent the standards of the community.

The child mediates, as he is able, the outside pressures to
produce or conform to the social demands or opportunities. At
the same time he is responding either directly or indirectly to

his own inner pressures and tensions. Before the young child becomes able to mediate these competing, interacting demands, an adult, the parent, is the mediator. This adult protects the child from too much or too many environmental stimuli or demands. As an affectionate regulator, the parent buffers the inner drives and tensions by soothing attention and by providing gratifications that enable the dependent child to reduce the fluctuating tensions. In psychoanalytic terms, the parent is an auxiliary ego for the young child who is not yet sufficiently mature to have such self-regulatory capacities. Among the child's most dynamic sources of power are his impulses, his drives, and his unfolding capacity to become a unique person who borrows attitudes and behaviors from many models and yet retains his own individuality, whether dramatic, ordinary, or uncommon. As he mobilizes his inner resources and responds to the pressures of the social environment, the child helps to change and form the emotional climate of his own world. The child's behavior is derivative of inner impulsive energies interacting with the demands and channeling impact of the social environment, largely organized for young children by their parents and siblings.

From the viewpoint of psychoanalysis and child development, the violence of the individual represents a social derivative of biological, psychological, and cultural interaction. It is, however, necessary to clarify the difference between subjective and behavioral aspects of violence. Violent feelings and thoughts are not the same as violent behavior. Thus, as the poet Stephen Spender (1976) suggested:

The thought perhaps—the wish to kill,
That I can understand, but really
To do the deed. Ah, no, that beats me.

When violent subjective states are curbed and transformed into nonviolent, socially constructive behavior, child care can be sound, leading to healthy, safe development. Conversely, when the adult's aggression is expressed without the binding, modifying influence of affection (or sublimated sexuality), the child frequently becomes the target of violent assaultive damaging behavior associated with serious bodily injury.

FAMILY AND DEVELOPMENTAL PERSPECTIVES

In the family, the child is safeguarded from violent assaults and the imminent risk of serious bodily injury by the care and guidance of ordinary devoted parents who provide protection against outside dangers, and act as buffers for the child's own violent impulses through their affectionate guidance and concern. The parents and child influence each other toward social accommodation and satisfaction by virtue of their primary, mutual parent–child relationship, the basis of family integrity, and by feeling valued as individuals and as a family.

The nuclear family, however, is changing in its structure and functions though it is still the mainstay of social organization and support for children and adults. Certain social indicators characterize some of the main changes, especially the divorce rate, the number of children raised in single-parent families, and those raised in families in which both parents work. For example, in the United States, 45 percent of the mothers of children aged 3 to 6 years of age and more than one third of the mothers of children under the age of 3 worked in 1975, and most worked full time (Kamerman and Kahn, 1976). Are these changing indicators associated with child abuse? Are parents less able to protect and nurture their children in such a changing social environment?

Child rearing can be seen as a matter of parents regulating the nurturance, the stimulation, and the frustration that their children receive. A closer consideration of the meaning of nurturance reveals its importance at every phase of development. The human child is born helpless and perishes if he or she is not nourished, protected, soothed, and stimulated by an older person capable of providing such care on a continuing basis. What begins as biological helplessness leads to social and psychological attachment as a result of the interaction of the infant and the maternal person or persons. The infant progresses from biological dependency to psychological and social attachment in which the child craves affection, approval, and predictable dependable responses from the caretaking adults. This craving, or "social addiction," is the "stuff" out of which social development emerges as a result of identifications with the primary psychological parents. Through these close relationships, the child acquires and internalizes parental attitudes and expectations. These identifications are the core of the unique personality of each child.

In a sense we are endowed and challenged by this psychological and social "addiction" for the rest of our lives. The gradual transformation of the addiction leads to the need for social closeness, friendship, companionship, and eventually to the reestablishment of another family group. It also is a source of the need for privacy and independence. As with many of the lines of development, passive experiences such as being fed or bathed become the "instruction" or preparation for actively taking care of oneself and later of others. Many of our neurotic and developmental deviations stem from the failure to turn passive experiences into active, self-initiating capacities, unique to the individual, but influenced to a significant extent by how the child identifies with his parents and older siblings.

These identificatory processes may entrap the child in conflict or may be his pathway to a unique and well-functioning personality. How the parents nurture and how they serve as advocates for health care, schooling, and participation in the life of the community are all vital influences on the developing child's personality and sense of self.

If parents are depressed or suffer from the long-term effects of deprivation in their own childhood, they may lack the capacity to stimulate, nurture, protect, guide, and support their children. They transmit to their children what they themselves had suffered. In this way, certain deficits and deviations may be transmitted from one generation to the next through the dynamics of the family interactions. When such parents turn what they experienced passively into an active mode of behavior, doing to their children what had been done to them in their childhood, they and their children also may be entrapped in the repetition of a past interactional pattern that distorts and limits their normal development and capacities.

Of course, a significant number of such parents resolve their difficulties by making as certain as they can that their children will not suffer what they suffered. They interrupt the transmission of the identification with the aggressor and master the residue of their past deprivation or abuse by doing for their children what had not been done for them. They are active in providing sustained affectionate care and guidance, safety, and assistance in helping their children come to grips with the real world in a socially constructive and satisfying way. To a significant extent, the later outcome of childhood deprivation can be influenced by the alternatives available to the child, adolescent, and young adult in the form of attractive, voluntary opportunities for sound health care, education, and employment that can make a difference in how the child becomes a future parent. Similarly, the continuity of cultural ties, social options, and pride in one's family or neighborhood represent support for individual mastery of earlier deficits, deprivations, or disruptions of primary psychological relationships.

Because privacy is essential in creating the intimacy necessary for family integrity and fostering the development of primary psychological relationships in the family, our society's democratic values are consistent with psychoanalytic knowledge about the needs of the developing child and parent. A free society can provide legal and societal guarantees to safeguard family life. What are the grounds for putting these guarantees aside?

Since there is little or no agreement on what constitutes emotional and psychological neglect, the dividing line between respecting and intruding into family privacy should be physical abuse of the child or neglect that represents an imminent risk of serious bodily injury to the child. Other forms of child neglect should be a challenge and invitation to create attractive, accessible voluntary services; not the basis for intruding into the privacy of the family. Such respect for privacy meets with our value preferences in a free, democratic society. These preferences also converge with children's developmental needs for affectionate closeness, continuity, and the establishment of the primary psychological relationships between parents and children.

Subjective feelings can influence parental behavior and increase the complexity and sensitivity of these mutual relationships. A young child's behavior is or can be experienced differently by various adults or by the same adult at different times according to differing moods. For example, an adult can respond to the same manifest behavior of the particular child as playful at one time, as irritating and provocative at another time, and as demanding and tyrannical at another. Such complexity is commonly observed between parents and their young infant during fussy periods, especially the paroxysmal fussiness of the first months of life when a variety of parental responses can take place. One parent or set of parents experiencing their child's fussy behavior as normative, will rock, soothe, and stay with the child patiently; another parent experiencing such behavior as illness in the child will call the pediatrician or discuss it with the visiting nurse; yet another parent or set of parents experiencing the fussy behavior as violently and provocatively demanding reacts to it violently, feeling the need to "survive" by not allowing the "tyrannical" baby to "destroy" them. Obviously, in the case of younger children the chemistry of violence is one that incorporates the behavior of the child and the parent's tolerances of and reactions to the child's behavior.

REDISCOVERY IN THE PRESENT

Specific instances can be even more complicated. An autistic psychotic child, age 6, engaged in violent self-mutilating behavior and at other times in attacks upon household materials, and occasionally, on his parents and siblings. The parents understood these acts as the behavior of a sick child. They tried to curb it through a well-structured and simplified environment, through the elimination of environmental hazards, and through the use of psychological and pharmacological treatment. They were able to mitigate all but the violent self-destructive behavior in which the child cut himself with any piece of glass he could find and break to form a sharp edge or point. The mother described how the child could detect pieces of glass in the yard that had been overlooked despite the family's extensive effort to eliminate the hazard. The boy had an extraordinary sensitivity to bright, flickering lights, which such pieces of glass exhibited when the sun was out. Finally, the parents adopted the recommendations contained in a paper the National Society for Autistic Children (NSAC) distributed in 1975 on behavior modification, which carefully delineated the way in which to use painful aversive conditioning as a teaching method—not a treatment—to rapidly bring under control behavior threatening a child's safety or his survival in an optimum environment. The paper of the NSAC (now the Autism Society of America) indicated such aversive conditioning may involve spanking and electric shock. (Presently, the association recommends "parental choice" regarding aversive conditioning.) These parents were able to help their son in the least detrimental way. Thus, the question of physical abuse in childhood can be seen as a relative one that requires an awareness of the complexity involved.

As mentioned earlier, after World War II the condition of the battered child was first called to our attention by a pediatric radiologist, Professor John Caffey (1946, 1957) of Columbia University, College of Physicians and Surgeons. Why such an obvious condition could first be noticed as a radiological syndrome is an acknowledgment of how we can individually and collectively deny what we do to children. It is protective of children for adults to be reminded regularly that as much as adults need and cherish children, they also resent and fear them as competitors, replacements, and as consumers of limited resources of affection, energy, privacy, space, food, and valued materials. Following a world war, ironically, we were able to "rediscover" adults' inhumanity to children only if it was first presented in a radiological journal as an esoteric report of a new and puzzling syndrome.

As the awareness of child abuse spread, like a delayed virus, the studies revealed what appeared to be a large number of undetected cases of abused children. Some workers perceived or interpreted these findings to represent an epidemic of violent injuries and destruction of young children by their parents. The theory of delayed virus infection, as in multiple sclerosis, is heuristically useful; that is, parents who, as children, were deprived, abused, and battered carry a "virus" that may be activated as a pathogenic virus—or may produce an antibody to prevent the repetition—when those individuals have their own children. If the virus is activated by the child's particular pattern of behavior and development, then there is a high risk of the parent's past experience being repeated, but now with the child as the object of the adult's violent behavior. Conversely, the child's behavior and the parent's "immunizing antibody" reaction to having been violently abused as a child may ward off the risk of battering or physical abuse being transmitted from one generation to the next.

Continuing historically into the 1950s and 1960s, laws requiring the reporting of child abuse and neglect and protecting those who report them against legal risk, swept through this country with unprecedented speed. They were designed not only to safeguard our children and to express in unmistakable terms our opposition to child abuse (i.e., to ward off the tendency toward denial and to represent our collective conscience about such matters), but also to reduce the legal vulnerability of those adults who were encouraged or mandated to report suspected cases of neglect or abuse. Unfortunately, these reporting laws emphasized how to assuage the conscience of our adult society. Although the reporting laws provided immunity against legal risk, they rarely, if ever, provided more preventive, therapeutic, or protective resources for such children and their families.

Indignation translated into such legislative action was a mixed blessing. The positive aspects of it were that we all became more aware of the problem. We were encouraged to develop an orderly way of reporting child abuse, and we began to plan for and institute protective, educational, rehabilitative services. But such legislative impulsivity can beget chaos. The negative aspects have been that family privacy has frequently been coercively invaded following false reports based on lifestyle differences and on prejudice against minorities, single-parent families, and low-income families. The concept of emotional neglect has been used as a basis for coercive inquiry when there is no consensus of how to define emotional neglect operationally in order to distinguish emotional disturbance from emotional neglect. Finally, the epidemic of reporting has not been matched by proportionate, appropriate services to help the child and family; instead, we often permit the state to point the finger of suspicion or accusation when the state does not have adequate resources to help the child and his family. This lack of services has often contributed to a greater risk for such children. Thus, inquiry and identification are a threat and a promise; if the promise cannot be kept by appropriate and sustained services, there is the threat of more risk of violence to the vulnerable child.

Mandatory reporting or reporting of neglect and abuse that guarantees legal immunity has swelled the number of complaints for neglect and abuse that must be investigated by the state. There continues to be an alarming increase in the reporting and in the efforts to investigate such reports. In most, if not all, states (Nagi, 1975; Cohen and Sussman, 1975), this epidemic of reporting has thrown out a wide net bringing in, along with the reports of serious life-threatening cases of physical abuse, instances of suspected neglect and false reports that do harm and are not helpful.

In most states a quarter or more of the reports on neglect and abuse do not involve any physical or sexual abuse and do not involve the imminent risk of serious bodily injury (see Monthly Reports of Connecticut Department of Children and Youth Services, April and May 1979). Investigations into those erroneously reported constitute an unwarranted intrusion into family privacy, weakening the integrity of the families involved. At the same time, such a deployment of resources utilizes the limited resources that create a pattern of providing too little, too late for those children already abused or those who are at serious risk of imminent physical injury.

Our epidemic of mandatory reporting spreads a net that does not distinguish sufficiently clearly between those who can be helped through identification and those who may be harmed by it. It does not put sufficient emphasis on how to strengthen the family by voluntary support services. The registries and reporting figures satisfy the alarmists, but do not necessarily create or effectively encourage or support services.

TRUTH TELLING: THE CHILD AS WITNESS

When assumptions are made about what children can tell us about their preferences and their experiences, a controversy exists concerning truth telling by children, even younger children, if they are asked how the adults on whom they depend care for them, especially in regard to involving them in sexual activities. In the last ten years or more there has been increasing concern about young children who may have been sexually molested or abused by adults, often one of their parents. The most common focus of this concern is about little girls (usually 2 to 6 years of age) and either their fathers or their mothers' boyfriends. In association with this increasing concern, especially as dramatized by allegations that day care workers and noncustodial fathers have been sexually abusing young boys and girls, there has been a determined effort to be more aware of this threat to child health.

The law wisely assumes that the child, especially the younger ones, cannot take an oath swearing to an appropriate higher authority (usually the parents for younger children) to "tell the truth, the whole truth, and nothing but the truth."

In the United States there has been a great increase in allegations of noncustodial fathers sexually abusing their young children, mostly little girls, during visitations. These have been reported especially in connection with efforts on the part of the custodial mother to eliminate visitation by the father or to insist it be monitored. It also has been associated with efforts by fathers to take legal action to change the custodial arrangements from the mothers to themselves or from individual to joint custody arrangements.

During this period in the United States and elsewhere in the Western world, there have been efforts to educate young children to resist and to report on sexual molestation attempted or carried out on them by adults. As a result of such efforts, we have noted the introduction of educational programs into schools and home settings based on the following assumptions or convictions: (1) that children can be taught to distinguish good from bad touching; and that they could report bad touching to a trusted adult; (2) that children always tell the truth if they are asked about adults involving them in sexual activities.

As our clinical experience and studies of these allegations and conditions have increased, it has become apparent that these two assumptions or convictions should not be taken for granted. First, young children often cannot distinguish between what adults refer to as good and bad touching. The latter is intended to alert the young child to touching that is sexually stimulating, erotically arousing, and designed to satisfy adult, not child, needs. Second, young children often cannot answer direct questions about sexual or erotic arousal by an adult because they do not understand the question cognitively; because the question frightens them or makes them so anxious that they try to reduce the anxiety or fear by their answer rather than to try and comprehend the question. In other words, they often try to guess and learn what the interviewer wants them to say, to please the interviewer, and reduce the felt threat of such questions by adults.

This line of questioning becomes all the more alarming when there has been a divorce and the child feels he or she has lost one parent. In our clinical studies at the Child Study Center of Yale University, such children, in psychotherapeutic sessions, become aware that they are frightened of such questions because they fear a wrong answer will lead to losing both parents; while each such child is trying to please the adult-interviewer by giving answers that are suggested by the questions. They often feel that if they can give the "right" answer the adults they have pleased (police officers, social workers, judges, or clinical psychologists, nurses, psychiatrists, and pediatricians) will not send them away from the only parent they have left; and even magically, if they give the answers they think the interviewers want them to give, their parents will come together again as they had been before, when they were married and taking care of their children, as father and mother, as husband and wife.

The word *truth* or the phrase "search for truth" clearly implies that truth is a dynamic, unfolding, never-ending goal and that the search for it will never end. We can hope for refinements, revisions, elaborations, and transformations if we persist in our approximations and as we accept the detours that are necessary in pursuing our goals. Paradoxically, the search for truth requires a tolerance for ambiguity, speculation, and apparent contradictions. In the process of searching for truth, we are also attempting to reconcile the so-called objective view with the subjective experience. Maturational and developmental considerations are especially vital when we explore how children search for truth. For example, a 4-year-old normal child may not yet understand that a toy remains the same size even though it appears to be smaller the further away it is from a person looking at it. As the child matures and develops, his intellectual (cerebral-cognitive) capacity increases, his experience accumulates, and he or she can learn to understand that the size of the retinal image is combined with the sense of the distance that the toy or other object is from the observer to enable the observer to know and explain how large the object is.

Children who are the focus of custody hearings, legal cases involving child abuse, visitation and other court matters, must be interviewed tactfully to elicit useful information and avoid psychological damage. Young children may be reliable witnesses if you know how to evaluate what they communicate. The best way to elicit useful information from young children is not to ask direct questions. Rather, adults should begin by winning the child's trust. Invite them to talk about things in a friendly, nonjudgmental way. Then you might ask the child tactfully, often indirectly, to throw some light on what happened.

Programs to teach children to resist and report sexual abuse may make some erroneous assumptions about children's ability to be reporting witnesses. Just as young children often cannot distinguish between what adults refer to as "good" and "bad" touching, they often confuse what they feel and think with what they perceive the adult wants them to say. Thus, young children often cannot answer direct questions about sexual abuse because they don't understand or are frightened by such questions. This line of questioning becomes all the more alarming to the child when there has been a divorce and the child feels he or she has lost one parent.

Since there has been little or no agreement on the criteria for what constitutes sexual abuse unless it is physically obvious, there has been a strong tendency by the concerned adults, who with other adults are manifestly opposed to the abuse of children by adults, to ask the child what has happened—to have the child tell the truth about sexual seduction, molestation, and abuse if the question is raised by either children or by adults.

More recently, in England, there have also been glaring examples of denial, now alternating with experience of false reporting. In a small town in northern England, Cleveland, there were one or two, perhaps several, cases of sexual abuse reported and documented. This was followed by an "epidemic" of more than a hundred such cases, mostly falsely reported, as the result of a zealous pediatrician, very opposed to adults sexually abusing children. She devised a test in which the opening of the anal sphincter, while the child held his or her breath and bore down, that is, using the Valsalva phenomenon, was measured and the degree to which the anus opened, dimpled, and suggested penetration, led to a physical measurement of the opening. This became the criterion for the diagnosis of sexual abuse. Also, children were asked to confirm this presumption, and apparently many went along with the suggestion of the sexual abuse team.

This epidemic was duly evaluated and exposed by a Royal Commission, and it is carefully reported in a White Paper, "Report of the Inquiry Into Child Abuse in Cleveland (England) 1987" (1988). This report is also known as the "Butler-Sloss Report."

In the April 13, 1991, issue of the *Lancet* there is a reflective commentary that states:

> Child sexual abuse is not a subject that readily lends itself to clear guidelines. Considerable sympathy for those who zealously attempt to root out practices that offend our deepest moral sensibilities is matched by equally strong feelings about the disruption of normal happy families on the strength of unsubstantiated evidence. Small wonder that [protective] social workers [and others] involved in such cases seek refuge in apparent certainties—e.g., the dogma that what children report can be regarded as the literal truth or the belief that there are irrefutable physical signs of abuse that can be demonstrated by adequately trained pediatricians [The *Lancet*, p. 890].

In a recent report by the Royal College of Physicians ("Physical Signs of Sexual Abuse in Children" [1991]), it is made clear "that medical evidence in most cases can by itself neither exclude nor establish the diagnosis with certainty" (The *Lancet*, p. 890). This commentary concludes with two statements worthy of our attention:

> "Although we have a right—even a duty—to intervene in very private matters if moral conventions are being overturned, we should think carefully about the appropriate balance between protecting children and allowing families the moral space in which to live their own lives in their own way without snooping, surveillance, or arbitrary interference. In striking such a balance society must necessarily come down on the side of supporting what is healthy rather than rooting out what is diseased [The *Lancet*, p. 890].

> One thing is clear, we have struggled long enough with the existing system to acknowledge that it cannot be made to work effectively in a large proportion of cases [The *Lancet*, p. 890].

In clinical studies at the Yale Child Study Center, psychiatrists have observed that there is a vast misunderstanding about what it means when you ask a child to answer a question. Children under the age of 8 or 9 don't fully understand the concept of truth, although they may know, for example, what it is to lie.

CONCLUSION

In truth, this paper has not been completed, because our studies must continue if we are to keep up with, or not lag too far behind, the relatively rapidly changing manifestations of man's inhumanity to man as it shows up regularly, too often in our lack of kindness to children. However, we have learned that just as children may not be able to understand truth telling, so it is with us adults, especially the professionals who are advocates for children. It may be kinder to say we don't know what is the truth than to become detectives, policepersons ferreting out an alleged crime and finding out who did it. Even when we shouldn't ask children direct questions about truth, even when we can't be sure whether or not the child has been sexually exploited or abused by an adult, we have other criteria by which we can determine the best interests of the child (Ceci and deBruyn, 1993). This is so despite the inquiry and evaluation being conducted without confidentiality safeguards and even when the parents do not bring the child for evaluation voluntarily as we apply our clinical methods and knowledge. Best interests and least detrimental alternatives should be our aim, along with doing our best to find the truth without doing harm, and to accept the limitations of what is truth and how we are able to approximate it.

REFERENCES

Bremner, R., et al., eds. (1971), *Children and Youth in America: A Documentary History*, Vol. II, 1866–1932, Parts One through Six. Cambridge, MA: Harvard University Press.

Caffey, J. (1946), Multiple fractures in the long bones of infants suffering from chronic subdural hematoma. *Amer. J. Orentgenol.*, 56:163.

———— (1950), *Journal of Pediatric X-ray Diagnosis*, 2nd edition. Chicago: Year Book Publ., Inc., p. 684.

———— (1957), Some traumatic lesions in growing bones other than fractures and dislocations: Clinical and radiological features. *Brit. J. Radiol.*, 30:225.

Ceci, S. J., & deBruyn, E. (1993), Child witness in court: Growing dilemma. *Children Today*, 22:5–9.

Cohen, S. J., & Sussman, A. (1975), The incidence of child abuse in the United States. (An unpublished paper submitted to the Office of Child Development.)

Coleman, H. S. (1924), *Humane Society Leaders in America*. American Humane Association.

Connecticut Department of Children and Youth Services (1979), Monthly Reports, April and May.

Hiner, R. N. (1979), Rights, punishment and abuse of children. *Bull. Menninger Clinic*, 43:233–248.

Jenkins, E. F. (1905), The New York Society for the Prevention of Cruelty to Children. *Ann. Amer. Acad. Polit. & Soc. Sci.*, 26:774–777.

—— (1908), The New York Society for the Prevention of Cruelty to Children. *Ann. Amer. Acad. Polit. & Soc. Sci.*, 31:492–494.

Kamerman, S. B., & Kahn, A. J. (1976), European family policy currents: The question of families with very young children. (Preliminary draft of a working paper, Columbia University.)

Kaufman, J., & Zigler, E. (1987), *The American Journal of Orthopsychiatry*, 57:186–192.

Kempe, C. H., & Helfer, R. (1962), The battered child syndrome. *J. Amer. Med. Assn.*, 17:181.

Lancet, The (1991), Child sexual abuse and the limits of responsibility. Volume 337, April 13, p. 890.

Nagi, S. (1975), Child abuse neglect programs: A national overview. *Children Today*, 4:13–18.

Report of the Inquiry into Cleveland 1987 (1988), Reported to Parliament by the Secretary of State for Social Services by Command of Her Majesty, July.

Spender, S. (1976), Adaptations of lines of Ibsen in Peer Gynt. In: Preface to *The Deadly Innocents*, by M. Gardiner. New York: Basic Books.

Chapter 3

Externalization as a Pathological Form of Relating: The Dynamic Underpinnings of Abuse

Jack Novick
Kerry Kelly Novick

Child abuse is currently so much talked about that we might tend to think that, like AIDS, it is a late twentieth century phenomenon. *The New England Journal of Medicine* of December 6, 1990 (Jellinek, Murphy, Bishop, Poitrast, and Quinn, 1990) stated, "Over the past two decades the incidence of child abuse and neglect has increased dramatically, with 2.2 million cases reported in 1987" (p. 1629). There is no doubt that there has been a dramatic increase in our awareness of and sensitivity to child abuse. In many states, mental health workers are now required to take courses on abuse. But there is some question whether the actual incidence of child abuse has increased. In a recent survey of the literature on sexual abuse the psychohistorian Lloyd deMause predicated the universality of incest. He asserted that "it is incest itself—and not the absence of incest—that has been universal for most people in most places at most times. Furthermore, the earlier in history one searches, the more evidence there is of universal incest, just as there is more evidence of other forms of child abuse" (1991, p. 125). In his seminal 1974 paper, deMause presented a wealth of data

45

to demonstrate that "the further back in history one goes . . . the more likely children are to be killed, abandoned, beaten, terrorized and sexually abused" (1974, p. 1). Kahr (1991) found evidence for widespread abuse of children throughout history and concluded: "Thus I submit that the actual extent of abuse in history has been more grave than we can even understand" (p. 207).

More traditional historians have arrived at similar conclusions. John Boswell, in his book *The Kindness of Strangers* (1988), detailed child abandonment throughout the history of Western civilization, citing rates even in prosperous countries of between 20 and 30 percent. Greven, in his recent book *Spare the Child* (1991), focused on the religious roots of child physical abuse, demonstrating, as Alice Miller did earlier (1983), that a range of abusive practices was sanctioned as good for the child. Biblical authority was found, for instance, in Proverbs 23:14, "Thou shalt beat him with the rod,/And shalt deliver his soul from hell."

Nineteenth century intellectuals and reformers were well aware of the extent of child abuse; writers such as Dickens vividly. portrayed abuse and exploitation of children. Freud's traumatogenic theory of adult neurosis was part of this nineteenth century sensitivity to child abuse. Contrary to the assertions of Masson (1984) and others, Freud never repudiated or suppressed the fact of childhood sexual abuse but modified his seduction theory and placed the reality of sexual abuse in the framework of a more comprehensive theory based on his new discoveries of the intrapsychic world of fantasies, wishes, and conflicts (Hanly, 1987; Shengold, 1989).

Mental health writers seem now to have come full circle. Rather than having made new discoveries which invalidate or supersede psychoanalytic insights, they have returned to the nineteenth century awareness of child abuse, and many propose methods of treatment remarkably close to the cathartic method first employed by Freud to abreact the affects associated with trauma. Just as an exclusive focus on the intrapsychic led many to neglect environmental factors, there is a danger that emphasis on the concrete events of sexual or physical abuse may lead us to negate the dynamic underpinnings and sequelae.

Years of accumulated psychoanalytic knowledge have led us to the understanding that each person processes external events to give them unique internal meaning and psychic representation (Solnit, chapter 2, this volume).

The complex interplay of external and psychic realities has been a central psychoanalytic concern from our very beginnings. Even Freud's early seduction theory was not a simple one of cause and effect between a reality event and symptom formation but posited a transformation of repressed memories by "deferred action" (Schimek, 1987; Novick and Novick, 1994). In a chapter entitled "Did it Really Happen?" Shengold (1989) looked at this issue from the perspective of the sexually abused child. He noted that this burning question for the victim of soul murder has a long philosophical history and is a current controversy in psychoanalysis with the poles represented by Masson (1984), who denied the pathogenic power of fantasies, and Spence (1982), who denied the importance of historical truth. Many psychoanalysts approach one or the other extreme. For example, deMause (1991) said that Abraham, Jung, Melanie Klein, and Kernberg tend to avoid the topic of childhood sexual abuse in contrast to Freud, Ferenczi, and many women analysts who accept memories of incest as real. Our position was well expressed by Shengold when he concluded, "it does make a difference whether something actually happened but this does not deny the pathogenic power of fantasy" (1989, p. 38). In this paper our emphasis is on the complex matrix of relationships which allows for the occurrence of abuse. Since abuse is trauma which could be avoided, there are two questions which are central. First, how is it possible for parents to allow abuse to occur? And, second, what role does the child's personality play in the occurrence and sequelae of abuse?

We think that at least part of the answer lies in the conceptualization of abuse as a symptom of a pathological relationship between parent and child, a relationship which in itself is assaultive and intrusive, whether or not concrete instances of physical contact occur. Such pathological relationships all revolve around issues of power and submission; in fact they can be described as sadomasochistic. Sadomasochism has been at the center of psychoanalytic interest since Freud's early discoveries, and clinicians have continued to struggle with the many theoretic and technical issues involved. We have written about sadomasochism from a developmental point of view, emphasized the complexity of these phenomena and said that sadomasochism can be best understood as the result of a multidetermined epigenetic sequence of pain-seeking behaviors which start in infancy. In our sample of masochistic patients we identified externalization by the parent as a major determinant of the pathology.

In a paper published in 1970 we described externalization of aspects of the self representation as a defense "aimed at avoiding the narcissistic pain consequent upon accepting devalued aspects of the self" (p. 84). On the basis of child analytic material we concluded that:

> [C]hildren who are the objects of parental externalizations . . . show a severe narcissistic disturbance with mental pain and conflict rooted in the acceptance of the devalued self and the inability to integrate positive aspects with the conscious self representation. There is a primary impairment of the integrative function of the ego, the maintenance of self esteem and the development of an adequate self representation. . . . The extensive use of externalization relates to a pathological balance in the family, a closed system in which all members of the family play interdependent roles. A change in any one member of the family directly affects each of the others and produces a complete disruption of the family equilibrium [Novick and Kelly, 1970, pp. 92–93].[1]

We have come to think that externalization by the parent is in itself a form of psychological assault on the personality of the child and is central to the pathological relationship in which abuse can occur. In this paper we will present a series of child, adolescent, and adult cases, each of whom was sexually abused.

---

[1] In a recent unpublished paper, Samuel Weiss of Chicago presented a wealth of child analytic material to arrive at a similar conclusion (Weiss, 1991).

We will use this material to try to understand the nature of their relationships in the past and the present, and, on that basis, to make appropriate technical suggestions.

Mrs. N was 45 years old when she sought help to leave an abusive marriage. She presented as a helpless, victimized person, unhappy in all her relationships and suffering from multiple physical complaints. In the first interview, she recounted that, some years earlier, she had broken down when her new boss accused her unjustly of unethical behavior at work. Unable to stop crying, she was eventually hospitalized and was put on antidepressant medication. Although her response clearly indicated an extreme reaction, the therapist first remarked that she must have felt justifiably angry and betrayed at that time, and then wondered whether such a thing had ever happened to her before.

She then said that she had been sexually abused by her mother's brother. The events had occurred repeatedly between ages 4 and 6. When Mrs. N finally told her mother, she was slapped and called a liar. It soon emerged that the uncle was also abusing his daughter. Mrs. N's aunt, his wife, packed up her children and left immediately. The extended family was in turmoil; the maternal grandmother went into mourning and joined the mother in blaming Mrs. N for causing the whole disaster. From that point on, the grandmother singled out Mrs. N by giving her different presents than the other grandchildren, presents like costume jewelry and see-through blouses, more appropriate for a sexually active adult than a school-aged girl.

After a period of analysis, Mrs. N progressed sufficiently to leave her inadequate, cross-addicted and violent husband and initiate divorce proceedings. Her family reacted in a way which confirmed Mrs. N's memory of their response to the childhood abuse. Her parents and her siblings blamed her for the break-up of her marriage, accusing her of being selfish, destructive, and sexually uncontrolled. With the support of her analyst, Mrs. N asked her older relatives about her parents' histories and discovered that both her mother and her uncle had been sexually abused as children. Mrs. N's mother was said to have been sexually promiscuous before and after her marriage.

This sounds like the typical history of a multigenerational dysfunctional family in which abuse has occurred. When faced with histories like these, there is so much pathology that it is sometimes hard to know where to start understanding or intervening. For instance, we have not even mentioned the role of Mrs. N's father and the interference of his pathological jealousy with her appropriate adolescent intellectual and social ambitions. However, we would suggest that looking at parental externalizations can help us to clarify the pattern of pathological transmission of abuse from one generation to the next. Externalization is an abuse in itself, as it violates the child's selfhood. This is the mechanism of what Shengold (1989) and others have called "soul murder."

What was externalized onto Mrs. N? Both her mother and grandmother appeared unable to take responsibility for and integrate their own sexuality and attributed to Mrs. N their illicit and uncontrolled sexual wishes and the helpless, victimized aspect of their own self representations. This pattern of attributing unwanted parts of the self to the child began long before the actual sexual abuse occurred. The crucial parental function of protecting the child was counteracted by the process of externalization. Thus, in this case the sexual abuse occurred against the backdrop of long-standing abuse in the form of mother's externalizations.

The treatment material allows us to explore the ramifications of this abuse in the development of Mrs. N's personality and pathology. Mrs. N was a very bright, competent person who had become a successful midlevel manager, despite the active opposition of her husband and her parents. At work she provided her employers with detailed, complex, analytic operational reports, but, from the start of her analysis, she presented herself in treatment as a helpless, overwhelmed, and victimized person who had no capacity to protect herself from a long series of physical and emotional exploitations by authority figures. Initially she saw her analyst as one more idealized person, who would provide her with suggestions and solutions, in effect, control and regulate her life. Mrs. N's parents had indeed been unable or unwilling to meet her basic need for psychological and physical protection. Did her apparent confusion and inadequacy represent a primary deficit which the analyst should attempt to repair? The analyst's feelings were the clue that the desired interventions were not simply a helpful human response to Mrs. N's basic needs, but rather an interaction forced and subtly molded by Mrs. N's externalizations. Mrs. N was very grateful and highly complimentary; instead of the usual sense of low key gratification from doing a good enough job in a difficult and frequently frustrating line of work, the analyst began to feel like a wise, all-knowing guru. There was an increasing awareness of the impulse to rationalize an unusually active technique, which covered up a tinge of guilt for crossing some habitual boundary and anger at feeling pressured to do so. In fact Mrs. N had recreated an abusive relationship by becoming the helpless, dependent child her parents had externalized onto her and maintaining that role by allocating her high level ego capacities to the analyst. By identifying with her externalizations (Sandler called this "role responsiveness" [Sandler, 1976]), the analyst became a participant in her perpetuation of her abuse. This was part of the patient's lifelong defensive effort to "normalize" parental abuse.

Mrs. N's mother buttressed her externalization of guilty sexual excitement onto Mrs. N by allowing the abuse to occur. Mrs. N defended against her perception of her mother's inadequacy by allocating all blame to her uncle. This had continually to be reinforced by generating abusive relationships with all subsequent men. We would suggest that some such pattern explains the typical finding that someone other than the mother often inflicts the concrete abusive acts.

Confirmation of this view came in Mrs. N's furious response to the analyst's attempt to focus attention on the defensive nature and purpose of the relationship she was trying to create in treatment. Not surprisingly, the analysis then entered a tumultuous period of complaints, accusations, threats to leave or kill herself. Although Mrs. N had always attributed her problems to the sexual abuse, the experience of reenacting an abusive relationship in the transference made her aware that her difficulties sprang from the abusive externalizing relationship with her parents. In the treatment she realized that she had not only internalized the parental externalization of helplessness and damage, but had also identified with the family style of defensive externalization. She had learned to deal with her conflicts by externalization. Gradually her attribution to the analyst of qualities and responsibilities which really were hers was understood as a forcible violation of the analyst's role, similar to her experience when her childhood self had been burdened with helplessness which contradicted her actual competence, guilty responsibility when she was an innocent victim, and grown-up sexual demands when she was a little girl.

This work allowed for exploration of what had led her to accept the externalizations and then to perpetuate them. For instance, when the analyst did not respond to her demand for an interpretation, but asked Mrs. N to think about her dream, she became enraged. She accused the analyst of being malicious and withholding. Her stream of criticisms continued to the point where the analyst became aware of the provocation to respond in kind and was therefore able to interpret her anticipation of mutual fury. The underlying fear of abandonment came through in her preemptive withdrawal. This led to memories of hiding alone in the barn to avoid being attacked and rejected by her parents. Threatened by her intelligence, they frequently called her stupid. This memory brought her back to the transference dilemma, in which she feared that having her own associations to her dream would threaten the analyst's competence.

Such sequences recurred whenever she was called upon to use her mind in the analytic work. Thus it became clear that she felt she had to externalize her own excellent ego capacities and identify with externalized parental incompetence in order to maintain attachment, defend against mutual destructive rage if she repelled the externalizations of others, and deny parental inadequacy and pathology. It was this work in the transference which helped her to integrate her ego functioning with the rest of her personality. This enabled her to end her abusive marriage and withstand her family's furious manipulative reaction to her assertion of autonomy. Externalization is intimately linked with an inability to tolerate the separate existence of another. So, for children who are targets of parental external-izations, separation becomes defined and experienced as a hos-tile act. This can be very clearly demonstrated when we turn to work with adolescents, whose developmental task is to define a separate identity.

Mary, whom we have described in detail elsewhere as suf-fering from a severe sadomasochistic disorder (Novick and Novick, 1987, 1991a,b; Novick, 1984, 1990), came into analysis at the age of 18, following a serious suicide attempt. What is relevant here from her treatment is that both her suicide at-tempt and the occurrence of two years of sexual abuse by her older brother were the result of extreme long-standing pathol-ogy in her relationship with her parents. The most striking feature of the initial presentation was the disparity between the family's description of Mary as a high-achieving, well-behaved person, generally well-adjusted and happy, with many friends, and the analyst's perception of Mary sitting with her teeth clenched and her legs trembling while she held in a rage that she later described as so powerful that it would overwhelm everyone. Through the first year of analysis, the parents' denial of Mary's lifelong distress emerged. Long periods of unhappi-ness in childhood seemed to have gone unnoticed, as did her severe menstrual dysfunction, which was ignored for some years until frequent fainting spells from loss of blood necessi-tated medical intervention. Her mother, an overly conscien-tious housewife, was ever vigilant about household matters. However, the intrusions of Mary's older brother into her bed-room and the noises of scuffles and sexual activity apparently aroused no suspicion. The mother denied any knowledge of the continual sexual abuse when Mary was between the ages of 13 and 15. Mary's inability to remain away from home at univer-sity was not seen as indicative of any problems.

At the end of a year of analysis, Mary was still alive, but the analyst's main concern was that she might become psychotic or kill herself. The parents, however, expressed their pleasure at her progress and their feeling that she was back to being a normal girl and suggested that she stop treatment. The paren-tal denial of her distress had been obvious from the beginning of her treatment; more subtle but increasingly apparent was their denial of everything individual about her. For instance, she had never had a birthday celebration of her own, but had always "conveniently" shared her party with a family member, whose birthday was a week later. The gifts she received bore no relation to her tastes or interests. Each year, the approach of her birthday intensified her conflicts; indeed, her suicide attempt had been made just after her eighteenth birthday. Mary's mother always said that she and Mary were just alike. As the scale of her denial of Mary's individuality became apparent, the analyst and Mary began to understand that the mother was attributing to Mary her own actual or wished for characteristics, irrespective of Mary's own personality. As the work of analysis freed Mary to begin developing along her own lines, it became inescapably clear that she was in fact very different from her mother in temperament, cognitive style, energy level, interests and talents. The mother reacted irrationally to each of Mary's progressive moves: for example, when Mary moved to her own apartment, her mother became busy cleaning the attic and would not come downstairs for hours when Mary made a weekend visit home; Mary's independent decision about her hairstyle precipitated her mother's tears and running out of the house. With Mary's continued growth the family's pretense of normality crumbled. Her mother's condition deteriorated; she became severely depressed and suicidal, eventually entering treatment. The parents separated and the father precipitately left his secure and prestigious position to move to another locale.

This disruption of her family's pathological equilibrium confirmed the understanding that her growth involved rejecting her parents' externalizations (Novick and Kelly, 1970; Weiss, 1991). In 1970 we described a subtype of externalization called generalization. This is a mode of thinking typical of early childhood, in which a person ascribes to the object characteristics similar to his own. "As a defense, generalization is frequently used to stave off the painful affects attendant upon separation and represents a fantasy fusion of self and object representations" (p. 79). Thus we could see that the mother's externalization was an attempt to deny separateness. Her abuse of Mary for her own emotional needs superseded her maternal protective function and made Mary feel that she could neither turn to her mother for help, nor turn away from her to help herself, without risking complete abandonment.

During the termination phase of Mary's analysis, the pressure of imminent real separation brought to the fore her own feelings connecting externalization with leaving and being left. She brought into the transference the push to be the same as her depressed mother. She told the analyst, "When I'm happy, I feel I'm not with you. To be unhappy is to be like you, to be with you, to sit quietly and depressed with the whole world right here in this room." This material allowed work on Mary's motives for accepting her mother's externalizations and then using externalization herself as a mode of attachment to the analyst. With Mrs. N we saw how, in an adult, externalization interfered with integration; Mary helped us to understand how externalization interfered with the adolescent task of identity formation. Now we will look at material from the analysis of a child to see what happens earlier.

When Kyle first came for evaluation at 5 years, 1 month, she was hard to see behind the curtain of her long hair, and she was also emotionally invisible, playing in an automatized and boring way. She could not remember her games from one session to the next, and, although she was a very bright, verbal child, seemed to have difficulty in school and in treatment maintaining or following a logical sequence; for instance, in a game of going to school, she could not decide whether the dolls should get into the car before they arrived at school, or arrive and then get into the car. After some time in treatment, it became apparent that her superficial way of relating, playing, and thinking reflected a massive defense against being surprised or attacked. She began to talk of her need for a "boo warning," so that she could prepare herself for any eventuality.

Kyle had been brought for treatment because of her parents' concern over her apparent fascination and fearful excitement at sexual matters, and a lag in reading readiness. Mother and daughter quarrelled continually and seemed to be locked in a sadomasochistic interaction. The parents presented as a possibility that Kyle had been molested by her half-brother

Richard, nine years older. In fact her mother had witnessed many instances in which Richard grabbed Kyle's buttocks and nipples, licked her genitals, and climbed into her bed at night from infancy on.

After six months of treatment, Kyle began to play out with little dolls Richard's visits to her bed when she was younger. By this time, Richard had been sent away for residential treatment, for which Kyle felt guilty responsibility. Day after day in the sessions she set out the configuration of the bedrooms and the dark of nighttime, but initially warded off any attempt by the analyst to talk about what was happening, even to the dolls. She also began to have nightmares, bouts of enuresis, and became increasingly restless. Her newfound capacity to be present emotionally and cognitively receded in treatment and her teachers reported renewed intermittent "tuning out" at school. Her games took on a sinister component of gory genital damage to all the little girl dolls. At this point interpretation addressing the relations and confusions among her own excitement and masturbatory impulses, her wetting, and fears and fantasies of castration began to take hold. Kyle was learning to read and wanted to make a "word-book" in her session. Her choice of words to illustrate each letter included "a for asshole, b for beat it, f for fatness, h for hitting Kyle, l for lick, m for mommy mad, t for tapping you," and so on. Kyle began to talk of Richard's excited behavior and we could clarify the real and fantasied effects of his intrusions and her attempts to reenact these in the transference. Kyle's primary and secondary defensive interference with ego functions of integration, memory, and impulse control was typical of children who have suffered abuse in the preschool years. Abuse interferes with all ego functions, particularly reality testing and maintaining differentiation between self and other. Kyle was truly unsure at the age of 6 whether the children dressed in Halloween costumes were really monsters. In games and in interactions with the analyst it was often hard to tell who was doing what to whom. Not only was Kyle confused, but there were times when the analyst was made to feel confused.

After 1½ years of treatment Kyle had made great improvements, particularly in her ego functioning. She almost never presented the withdrawn, confused, unintegrated appearance of the early days. Her massive defensive disruption of her synthesizing function and memory had yielded to interpretation and verbalization, and her relationships and cognitive functioning reflected these gains. But, as Kyle continued to reject the externalizations of helplessness, confusion, and lack of self-protection, the family began to show signs of disruption, with parental discord increasing markedly.

The concrete sexual abuse had taken place in the context of a long and complex history of family dysfunction, in which externalization played a prominent role. Kyle's father had first married a very disturbed woman, who abused their children physically and sexually and eventually committed suicide. He then married Kyle's mother, who, at the age of 19, weighed 200 pounds and had been sexually abused by her half-brother in early childhood. Subsequent interviews with father substantiated the inference that he related to women as damaged and defective. The line of externalization came also from the maternal grandmother, who was preoccupied with the idea that her daughter should be exactly the same as she, to the point where she urged Kyle's mother to dye her hair to match. By the beginning of the treatment, Kyle's mother was slender and had begun graduate work, while Kyle was overweight, confused, and sexually abused.

The analyst worked with the mother throughout Kyle's treatment, and, during the period of Kyle's working through her feelings about the events with Richard, mother had been able to reduce the overstimulation of scary movies, outings which were inappropriately exciting, intrusive and confusing lack of privacy in bedrooms and bathrooms. And yet her unconscious participation in exposing her daughter to abuse persisted, for example, in her buying for Kyle a dress which said "Tickle me" all over it. In the interview when this outfit's message was called to her attention, the mother talked extensively about maternal grandmother's pressure on her to be like her. The analyst asked about the maternal grandmother's reaction to mother's childhood sexual abuse; the grandmother had been vague and denied that it could really have happened. In a similar way, although fully aware that Richard was impulsive

and had suffered sexual abuse, the mother nevertheless denied
the clear indications that Richard was abusing Kyle. At this
point the analyst interpreted the mother's need to protect the
maternal grandmother from her own rage and reproach by
doing to Kyle what maternal grandmother had done to her,
that is, externalizing her own helplessness, confusion, and uncontrolled excitement onto the child. The interpretation
seemed to have a strong impact. Within two weeks, Kyle's
mother had resumed her own analysis, and seemed genuinely
to have changed the tone of her interactions with Kyle.

In therapy Kyle was able to use her restored ego functions
to acknowledge her anger at her mother and complain about
her being controlling, bossy, and smothering. Both Kyle and
her mother began to reject the externalizations which had
maintained the marriage. This work and the impact of the
mother's treatment further disrupted the previous pathological
family equilibrium. The parents were on the verge of divorce;
under this threat of abandonment, the mother could not continue her support of her own and Kyle's progressive development and Kyle's treatment was interrupted. Soon after termination of Kyle's treatment, the parents nevertheless decided on
divorce and Kyle insisted on coming to tell the analyst. She
drew a picture of her family, all with sad faces and tears, and
then crossed out the image of herself. Kyle felt obliterated and
disregarded.

Using material from adult, adolescent, and child analyses,
we have tried to show that instances of concrete sexual abuse
occur in the context of and subsequent to the establishment of
an abusive externalizing relationship. This understanding of
abuse as a broader relationship issue allows us to look beyond
particular events both historically and clinically. In each of the
cases we have described, parental externalizations violated the
patient's selfhood long before the sexual abuse. We would like
now to use infant observational material to examine the early
stages of an externalizing relationship.

For the last ten years, we have been part of a research
program, with Drs. Donald Silver and B. Kay Campbell, studying the development of relationships between adolescent mothers and their babies. We have followed eighty-five pairs through

their two-year stay in a residential center, which provided schooling, therapy, medical and social supports for the mothers and medical and day-care services for the babies. Research data included periodic videotaping as a developmental record, therapy notes, cottage observations, medical and social history records, and case conference discussions. Here we will describe interactions between one mother and her baby between the ages of 3 and 15 months.

Mother, whom we will call S, was one of twins, who were both sexually abused by a relative in childhood. She witnessed a murder when she was a little girl and her beloved older brother was sent to prison for the murder of a neighbor girl at the time S became pregnant. As soon as the pregnancy became known, her extremely religious family rejected her completely. S said her mother was a controlling and manipulative person, and S was described in the cottage as hostile, irritable, and demanding. During a feeding situation at 3 months, her baby Eric was a healthy, active, related infant. Observations at this time noted S's love for her baby, but there was concern at her rough handling and apparent use of him for her own needs. For instance, she had difficulty sleeping and kept the baby awake with her until late into the night, when she would take him into her bed in order to go to sleep.

Sequence 1

Three months old. S and Eric were in a feeding situation. S was affectively engaged with her baby, who drank her in with his gaze. He sucked vigorously, then played with the teat with his tongue and lips. S reacted to this by attributing mischief to him and began to tease him with the teat, brushing it on his lips and cheek. She remarked: "Feeding time at the farm," that is, he was a pig. S's affect varied from cheerful engagement to solemn distraction or withdrawal, as well as a teasing provocation.

Sequence 2

Nine months old. S had been instructed, "Be with your baby." She filled the floor with toys, and engaged Eric in hectic play.

He began repeatedly to explore toys with his hands, eyes, and mouth, only to be immediately interrupted by mother's presentation of a new stimulus. He could not complete a play sequence without disruption, could not experience competent, effective play. S offered him a toy bunny, but then she grabbed it back, saying, "Don't eat bunny," then bit it herself. When Eric put a rattle into his mouth, S pulled it away, asking "Can I have some?" Throughout there was intrusion and interruption in his nascent ego functioning; his age-appropriate assertion and exploration were misinterpreted, and greed and oral aggression were attributed to him.

Sequence 3

One year old. Again S had been instructed to "Be with your baby." At the beginning of this play sequence she pushed him to perform on a toy piano. When he began to try it himself, she fetched a beach ball and began a game. At the beginning of the game, there was a joyful interaction between them, with Eric crowing in delight and S praising his performance. Then she happened to hit him on the head with the ball. She apologized, but then repeatedly bounced it off his face and head on purpose. S also began to call him derogatory names, like "Fat belly, old man, slobbery," and so on. Eric began to look bewildered, but tried to continue the game. S persisted in hitting him with the ball. Eventually Eric looked away, confused, then hit himself in the head.

This is a crucial sequence. For Eric there was a shift of affect from joyful achievement to resigned acceptance of his mother's externalization of badness.

Sequence 4

Fifteen months old. Eric and his mother were at the table for snack. He was now very competent at self-feeding. This snack should have been pleasurable for him, as he was being offered sweet cupcakes and there was no nutritional pressure. Nevertheless, the sequence began with S trying to make him eat, feeding him as if he was a helpless baby, which he resisted. The next segment, moments later, illustrated the escalating tension between them. Eric responded angrily and with distinct aversion of his gaze and S sighed in angry discouragement. In the third sequence there was continuing refusal to look at his mother; Eric only fed himself when angrily blotting her out. S tried unsuccessfully to enter his field of vision, and reacted with helpless anger to his stubborn refusal to comply.

In these sequences, covering a year of Eric's life, we see him change from a happy, engaged infant to an angry withdrawn toddler. His joyful competence was no longer evident; instead we saw a retreat to either bewilderment or sulkiness with his mother. Material from S's therapy revealed the oral demanding nature of her aggression, a quality she attributed to Eric from his birth. She succeeded in externalizing this aspect of herself onto Eric, as he became a biter in the nursery. S tried to control the externalized aggressivity by keeping him an incompetent infant, but this he was still resisting as a toddler, as was seen in the earlier eating sequence.

We have tried to demonstrate that concrete sexual abuse often occurs in the context of a preexisting abusive relationship with the parent. By its nature externalization constitutes an abuse since it violates the child's existing and developing personality. When a patient describes instances of abuse, an underlying pathological relationship may be assumed. Whether or not concrete abuse occurred or is remembered, an abusive relationship from childhood may first be picked up by the operation of externalization in the transference. In a phenomenon as perverse, pervasive, and complex as child abuse, it is obvious that externalization is only part of the explanation. Externalization is a general term for a variety of mechanisms, and, when a child is the object of externalization, he too becomes an externalizer, with that process gathering layers of determinants and functions through the course of development. Externalization is a mechanism leading to and forming part of the adult sadomasochistic character, which is a frequent clinical outcome of childhood sexual abuse. By the time the patient enters treatment, externalization has become a dominant mode of relating.

In what we have called the "externalizing transference" (Novick, 1982) the patient attributes to the analyst a part of his own mental apparatus and then forms a relationship on that basis. Mrs. N focused her attention on the uncle as the abuser, but the underlying abusive externalizing relationship with her mother emerged only when the analyst took up her externalizations in the transference. The analyst was alerted to the externalizations by his own affective responses. Children externalize in an obvious way, calling the analyst messy, smelly, stupid, or disgusting. Adults may be more subtle, but, when the analyst feels violated in his professional or personal *self*, when he feels over time that he is being gaslighted (Calef and Weinshel, 1981), misunderstood, misinterpreted, ignored, rendered ineffectual and helpless, furious yet guilty, when he feels trapped in a static situation, where interventions are repeated without insight or growth, yet any attempt to alter the interaction is met with vigorous resistance, then he should consider the possibility that the patient has established an externalizing transference, based on childhood abuse by an externalizing parent.

Technically, once the externalizing transference has been recognized, the various motives and effects must be dealt with. As we see with Mrs. N, the adolescent Mary, and Kyle the schoolchild, the patient has internalized the externalization in order to remain attached and not feel abandoned, to contain rage at the externalizing mother, to keep the relationship from disintegrating in a mutual explosion of fury, and to maintain a feeling of being essential to the mother. This omnipotent conviction is validated in the reaction of the parents when the child begins to reject the externalization, as we saw in each of our cases.

Externalization does not operate alone, but calls upon and leads to other defenses. Two are particularly important: turning aggression against the self and denial. Turning aggression against the self, a crucial element in the whole range of self-destructive actions, including provoking or tolerating abuse, is a defense which builds upon the internalization of an external-ized aspect of the parent. In normal development, the self representation emerges out of and contains the body representation. Integration starts with the experience of pleasure in one's body at the hands of a loving parent. Externalization interferes with the sense of ownership and integration of body and self. These patients experienced their bodies as owned and controlled by their mothers, and so aggression toward the mother was defended against and expressed by attacks on the body. When Mary tried to kill herself, she was trying to murder the mother inside her.

Denial operates first to avoid the perception that the mother is an abuser. Second, denial is used to avoid the pain and disappointment of acknowledging that mother is neither an idealized saint nor a persecuting monster, but rather an inadequate parent, unable to fulfill the ordinary good-enough protective functions. Shengold's (1991) recent study of the pathogenic impact of parental weakness is relevant in this regard.

Work on these motives for defense must be accompanied by attention to the severe damage they have done to all the functions of the ego. Mrs. N's integrative capacity was severely compromised by her need to externalize; Mary's compliance with her mother's externalizations interfered with all her ego functions, but especially those needed for independent action; because of her internalization of her mother's externalizations, Kyle could not use her memory or her reality testing. In Eric's case the externalization led to a corruption of his psychic economy and self-regulation shifted from a base in pleasure to one in pain and anger.

The goal of the therapeutic interventions at this stage of treatment is to help create conditions for the reinternalization of the externalized parts of the self. Then the patient can experience an internal conflict, and face the pain of dealing with developmental issues which had been avoided by living within the narrow confines of an unchanging externalizing relationship. Rage, sadness, loss, and mourning come into the center of the treatment.

The clinical phenomena we have been describing in terms of externalization and internalization are often formulated, particularly by those influenced by Kleinian theory, as examples of "projective identification." Although the distinctions warrant separate and full examination, it is important to note here that our usage is not simply a matter of taste or politics, but involves substantive conceptual objections to labeling complex interactions as "projective identification." The term was complex when first introduced by Melanie Klein (1946) and later additions by authors such as Bion (1958), Rosenfeld (1965), Meltzer, Bremner, Hoxter, Weddell, and Wittenberg (1975), Ogden (1979), Grotstein (1981), and others have given the term such an array of meanings, some of them contradictory, as to render it useless. Grotstein (1981) listed at least twelve varieties of projective identification. Kernberg (1987), whose writing has made the concept of projective identification palatable to American psychoanalysts, said that its "meaning has become blurred; it has been used to mean too many different things by too many different people under too many different circumstances" (p. 93).

Projective identification is a pivotal concept in the Kleinian account of normal and pathological development, and, as such, is a cornerstone of Kleinian technique. Many analysts have also thereby applied the concept to diagnostic differentiations. We are reluctant to use a concept which implies a specific diagnostic category, points to a particular developmental phase, and legislates for a specific technique. In contrast, the classical concept of externalization is mainly descriptive of a mental process with no additional developmental, diagnostic, or technical implications.

Projective identification seems to be used in a way which condenses a sequence of defenses and reactions within both the subject and object. This may not only be confusing but also risks oversimplification. Important steps can be missed, some with crucial technical implications. For example, in our films of Eric, labeling the interaction as "projective identification" would miss the rage which arises between the projection and the identification, or, as we prefer to term these processes, *externalization* and *internalization*. There is clinical gain from being able to follow with the patient each step of the sequence. Technically it is crucial to help the patient recover the feeling of rage which follows externalization and precedes internalizing or identifying with the externalized aspect of the other.

Finally, in a field where clear thinking and free communication are both clinical and theoretical goals, we find it preferable to use a verb (to externalize) to describe the process rather than a noun. It is more direct and more elegant to say: "A externalizes something onto B; B becomes angry and then may internalize it." If we say: "By a process of projective identification A has projectively identified B with something and B in turn has identified with it," we lose the opportunity both to trace the affective steps in the sequence and to assign active responsibility for these processes.

When the externalizing transference is first linked to childhood abuse, patients often experience relief, clarity, and hope. Therapies which stop at this point of discovery avoid the conflict and resistance which inevitably ensue. Initial good feelings rarely last, as defensive confusion, doubt, and displacement of rage to others, including the therapist, are soon invoked. Considering the many determinants and functions that accrue to the role of the victim, it is not surprising that lasting change is strongly resisted.

What then can provide an impetus and motivation for change? Despite differences in age, background, and experiences of the three patients we have described, Mrs. N, Mary, and Kyle all lived lives devoid of pleasure. Pain and suffering characterized their relationships, their achievements, and their activities. Nothing was done for pleasure, nothing gave them pleasure, indeed the goal of their functioning was not pleasure but omnipotent control of others. In a paper on omnipotence and masochism (Novick and Novick, 1991a) we described two distinct systems of self-esteem regulation. One is the omnipotent system, which stems from early and persisting experiences of helplessness, frustration, and rage. We said that those who live by the omnipotent system manifest a desperate clinging to pain, because "pain is the affect that triggers the defense of omnipotence, pain is the magical means by which all wishes are

gratified, and pain justifies the omnipotent hostility and re-
venge contained in the masochistic fantasy" (pp. 323–324). In
looking at abused patients we would emphasize that a major
mechanism of the omnipotent system is externalization.

Mrs. N, Mary, and Kyle were victims of externalization in
childhood and they became externalizers, with the fantasy that
they could use an externalizing relationship to control the actions and feelings of others and deny and avoid reality perceptions and constraints. When we recognize the externalizing
transference and help patients reinternalize parts of themselves, they can then take pleasure in functioning, pleasure in
reality-attuned interactions with others, and begin to experience pleasure as an alternative basis for the regulation of self-
esteem. In other words, therapeutic work on the patient's externalizations helps restore a normal system of self-regulation, one
in which self-esteem comes from competent, realistic, empathic,
and loving interactions with oneself and others. It is only when
the patient has available this pleasure-based alternative to the
externalizing, omnipotent system, that he can experience an
internal conflict between the two systems. The therapeutic work
must address the price paid for living in the omnipotent system
and restore the patient's capacity to choose.

The essence of the two systems is captured in our images
of Eric. We see him at 9 months, crowing with delight at his
skill in catching the ball. At 15 months, we see him transformed
into the initiator of hostile interactions. He turns away from his
mother, looks right through her, gazes at the ceiling, at the
cameraman, while she sighs in helpless frustration and rage.
Through externalization, S has turned Eric into her angry,
sadistic self. She and Eric are tied together in a sadomasochistic
relationship forged and maintained by externalizations. If
someone like Eric comes later to treatment, a central goal would
be to help him reject externalizations and rediscover the joyful
ball-player part of himself.

REFERENCES

Bion, W. (1958), On hallucination. In: *Second Thoughts*. New York:
    Jason Aronson, 1967, pp. 65–85.

Boswell, J. (1988), *The Kindness of Strangers. The Abandonment of Children in Western Europe from Late Antiquity to the Renaissance.* New York: Pantheon Books.

Calef, V., & Weinshel, E. M. (1981), Some clinical consequences of introjection: Gaslighting. *Psychoanal. Quart.*, 50:44–66.

deMause, L. (1974), The evolution of childhood. In: *The History of Childhood*, ed. L. deMause. New York: Psychohistory Press, pp. 1–73.

——— (1991), The universality of incest. *J. Psychohistory*, 19:123–164.

Greven, P. (1991), *Spare the Child. The Religious Roots of Punishment and the Psychological Impact of Physical Abuse.* New York: Alfred A. Knopf.

Grotstein, J. S. (1981), *Splitting and Projective Identification.* New York: Jason Aronson.

Hanly, C. (1987), Review of *The Assault on Truth: Freud's Suppression of the Seduction Theory*, by J. Masson. *Internat. J. Psycho-Anal.*, 67:517–521.

Jellinek, M., Murphy, J. M., Bishop, S., Poitrast, F., & Quinn, D. (1990), Protecting severely abused and neglected children. An unkept promise. *New England J. Med.*, 323:1628–1630.

Kahr, B. (1991), The sexual molestation of children. Historical perspectives. *J. Psychohistory*, 19:191–214.

Kernberg, O. (1987), Projection and projective identification. In: *Projection, Identification, Projective Identification*, ed. J. Sandler. Madison, CT: International Universities Press, pp. 93–115.

Klein, M. (1946), Notes on some schizoid mechanisms. In: *Envy and Gratitude and Other Works 1946–1963.* New York: Delacorte Press/Seymour Lawrence, 1975, pp. 1–24.

Masson, J. (1984), *The Assault on Truth: Freud's Suppression of the Seduction Theory.* New York: Farrar, Straus & Giroux.

Meltzer, D., Bremner, J., Hoxter, S., Weddell, D., & Wittenberg, I. (1975), *Explorations in Autism.* Perthshire: Clunie Press.

Miller, A. (1983), *For Your Own Good. Hidden Cruelty in Child Rearing and the Roots of Violence.* New York: Farrar, Straus & Giroux.

Novick, J. (1982), Varieties of transference in the analysis of an adolescent. *Internat. J. Psycho-Anal.*, 63:139–148.

——— (1984), Attempted suicide in adolescence: The suicide sequence. In: *Suicide in the Young*, ed. H. S. Sudak, A. B. Ford, & N. B. Rushforth. Boston, MA: John Wright, PSG, pp. 115–137.

——— (1990), The significance of adolescent analysis for work with adults. In: *The Significance of Child and Adolescent Analysis for Work with Adults*, ed. S. Dowling. Madison, CT: International Universities Press.

———— Kelly, K. (1970), Projection and externalization. *The Psychoanalytic Study of the Child*, 25:69–95. New York: International Universities Press.

———— Novick, K. K. (1991a), Some comments on masochism and the delusion of omnipotence from a developmental perspective. *J. Amer. Psychoanal. Assn.*, 39:307–328.

———— ———— (1991b), Deciding on termination. In: *Saying Goodbye: A Casebook of Termination in Child and Adolescent Analysis and Therapy*, ed. A. G. Schmukler. Hillsdale, NJ: Analytic Press.

Novick, K. K., & Novick, J. (1987), The essence of masochism. *The Psychoanalytic Study of the Child*, 42:353–384. New Haven, CT: Yale University Press.

———— ———— (1994), Postoedipal transformations: Latency, adolescence, and pathogenesis. *J. Amer. Psychoanal. Assn.*, 42:143–169.

Ogden, T. (1979), On projective identification. *Internat. J. Psycho-Anal.*, 60:357–373.

Rosenfeld, H. (1965), *Psychotic States*. New York: International Universities Press.

Sandler, J. (1976), Countertransference and role responsiveness. *Internat. Rev. Psychoanal.*, 3:43–47.

Schimek, J. (1987), Fact and fantasy in the seduction theory: A historical review. *J. Amer. Psychoanal. Assn.*, 35:937–965.

Shengold, L. (1989), *Soul Murder: The Effects of Childhood Abuse and Deprivation*. New Haven, CT: Yale University Press.

———— (1991), A variety of narcissistic pathology stemming from parental weakness. *Psychoanal. Quart.*, 60:86–89.

Spence, D. (1982), *Narrative Truth and Historical Truth*. New York: W. W. Norton.

Weiss, S. (1991), The universal resistance to child analysis. Paper presented to Michigan Psychoanalytic Society, October.

Chapter 4

Further Considerations on Somatic and Cognitive Residues of Incest

Selma Kramer, M.D.

During the past twenty years, there has been an increase in the number of published reports on the psychoanalytic treatment of children and adults who had experienced maternal or paternal incest during their childhood or adolescence. Still, relatively few authors seem to concern themselves with reports of such psychoanalyses. In the main, they have been Shengold (1967, 1974, 1979, 1980), who reported physical, sexual, and psychological abuse by parents as "soul murder" of their children; Margolis (1977, 1984), who wrote about consummated incest in an adolescent male; Silber (1979); and Kramer (1974, 1980, 1983, 1987), who wrote about maternal incest and its treatment.

In this chapter, I continue my exploration of the long-term consequences of incest by examining two phenomena that I believe are the residues of parental sexual abuse. The first phenomenon includes the varieties of physical sensation and disturbances in sexual functioning which, I feel, result from "somatic memories." The second pertains to the general and specific learning problems that patients who were incestuously involved with their parents often demonstrate. As background I shall begin by briefly reviewing some relevant conclusions drawn from previous work with this population of patients.

69

While sexual abuse in childhood is disturbing for the child's development independent of whether the abuser is a stranger or a family member, incest is particularly disruptive when committed by a parent. In such instances, the child easily loses the capacity to trust authority figures. In addition, the sense of guilt and responsibility for the act, which the child is apt to feel by virtue of its self-centeredness, is reinforced by at least two additional factors. The first relates to the child's sensitivity to the parent's role as arbiter of right and wrong, which makes the child particularly susceptible to any remarks or behavior of the abusing parents intended to induce or reinforce a sense of guilt in the child. (Of particular relevance here is the process by which the abusing parent displaces his or her own sense of guilt onto the child, as was first described by Ferenczi in 1933.) The second factor promoting guilt is that bodily excitement arising from the sexual act is occurring with an object who is still tinged with unresolved oedipal feelings and hence is particularly forbidden, and that there is pleasure to the child when the genitals are stimulated, nonetheless. Victims of incest must face three questions: (1) Did it occur? (2) Did I let it occur? and, (3) Did I enjoy the experience?

Within this range of general response to parental incest are important differences that result from whether the incestuous parent is the mother or the father. It has been my experience that mothers who engage in incest with their children have more serious psychopathology than do fathers who commit incest.

It appears that two factors exist in the mother–child relationship for maternal incest to occur: First, the child is unwanted, unrewarding to the mother, not satisfying to her narcissism, even from birth (Browning and Boatman, 1977). In addition, since the mother–child symbiosis is parasitic and is not resolved, the mother is unable to permit the child to individuate.

Litin, Griffin, and Johnson (1956) and Brandt Steele (personal communication) suggest that a tight, unresolved symbiosis exists, in cases which I call maternal incest, between the child and the mother who herself had problems in separating from her own mother and also had sexual conflicts which interfered with her marriage. Steele says, "It is the adult using the unwitting, obedient child to solve maternal needs, and exploitation and distortation of the normal, mutual interaction."

I found that where there was more than one child, the mother sexually stimulated only the one child who was unwanted or was perceived by her as inferior, a disappointment, so imperfect as to be dehumanized. She showed contempt by expressing most hurtful verbal hostility, derided and used the one child (Kramer, 1974).

This sexual abuse started early as an outgrowth of the mother's too zealous attention to the hygiene of their children's peritoneal areas. The "cleansing" continued for much too long and was converted by the mothers into masturbation of their children. Two of my patients, Donald (Kramer, 1974) and Casey (Kramer, 1980), stopped their mothers only when they reached adolescence, fearful that their mothers' attentions would produce orgasm. The abuse of a third patient, Abby (Kramer, 1980), stopped only after the child had been brought to treatment. I have come to believe that because the abuse started so early and involved their mothers when they were at the center of their children's universe, before intrapsychic separation of self and object had been achieved, the consequences for these children were extensive and severe, leading to the particular disturbance in reality testing that underlies what I have termed "object coercive doubting" (Kramer, 1983).

In contrast fathers are seldom sexually abusive until the child is well into latency or adolescence. The later onset means that the child's reality testing is usually much better established and will therefore be significantly less affected by the incest and its consequences than in those instances where the sexual abuser was the mother and the incest began much earlier. The constellation of residues that I wish to focus on first, is found in patients of both sexes who were incestuously involved with either parent. The most noteworthy constellation I refer to as "somatic memories" of incest. These are bodily sensations that occur well into adulthood and are most often accompanied by great displeasure, aversion, or physical pain during foreplay, intromission, or coitus. Occasionally, in contrast to hyperesthesia, these patients reported reacting to touch in the opposite way, with muted feelings, frigidity, and anorgasmia. Some patients reported feeling furious during lovemaking, a fury that was at first incomprehensible, especially since they themselves had either initiated or consented to the sexual overtures. Reliving incestuous phenomena in the transference caused these patients to experience and complain of hyperacusis, hyperosmia, and sensitivity to touch (e.g., my couch was "scratchy"). One patient was panicked by male strangers whom she saw on the way to my office, afraid that I would allow them to touch her body.

Steele (personal communication) agreed that somatic sensitivity and other sexual problems in adults may derive from childhood sexual abuse. Steele's views are consonant with those of Katan (1973), who also noted that her patients had problems in integrating libidinal and aggressive drives and frequently turned their aggression against themselves.

Frequently interrelated with the somatic memories are problems in learning, in retaining what has been learned, and in "showing what one knows," for example, by reciting in school, doing well on tests, and the like. These patients may also demonstrate muting of their affects, as well as problems in perceiving affects in themselves or in others. At times, this muting of affects may progress to a picture not unlike that of a clinical depression.

None of my patients initially told me that incest had occurred. Most did not remember. In fact, one patient had amnesia for the first eight years of her life. As treatment progressed and memories of the incest emerged, they were tolerated by means of intermittent denial, disavowal, or splitting. Reconstruction was necessary in every case to represent to the patient the story he or she had told me but could not really perceive or accept. Reconstruction also verified the patient's reality, in contrast to the parental denial of the incest. The somatic memories represent, I feel, a breakthrough caused by incomplete repression.

CLINICAL EXAMPLES

Case 1

Casey came to analysis at age 20 because she "did not know where to go in life." She had trained for ballet, but now, although she had been told she had a successful career ahead of her, she found it impossible to become a professional dancer. She "froze up" on the stage and could not tolerate being touched or, especially, lifted by her partner. She also feared performing in public; she would become confused and forget her routine. It soon became obvious in the analysis that she feared that being successful would mean leaving home.

Casey was the younger of two sisters; there was also a brother ten years younger. Her mother had not wanted to be pregnant with Casey, but when the pregnancy was accepted, the mother wished for a boy. Instead, she gave birth to a girl with a minor birth defect. Casey and her mother had been overly close, "enmeshed." Casey manifested splitting of the self and maternal object representations, which allowed her to retain a "good" representation of her mother, while relegating "badness" to teachers, onto whom all evil was placed. The self was "good," nonhostile, noncompetitive, nonsexy; her peers, whom she envied but could not relate to, were "bad." They did the exciting things she wished to do but could not. Only after the two sides of self and object were fused could she remember what she had known but could not let herself acknowledge or tell me, that her mother, as far back as Casey could remember, had masturbated her until Casey reached puberty. Even now Casey had to stop her mother from touching her clothed body. Casey's analysis was slow, and, to her, distressing, for it meant that she had to see things in her relationship with her mother that were painful. She was reluctant to forego the security of allowing her mother to make plans for her, to comfort her when Casey was troubled, to spend money on her. For a long time the analysis and the analyst were the intruders, threatening the sanctity of the distorted mother–child relationship. More than once Casey blurted out, "You want me to become independent, to give up what I count on!" At the same time she felt that I was as seductive as was her mother because I encouraged free association, which in Casey's mind, was something dirty and bad. Only when the actual seduction and its vicissitudes had been analyzed could Casey go through the development process necessary for her to be a separate and appropriately sexual individual.

Casey had suffered a severe narcissistic injury as a result of her mother's use of Casey's genitals as a dehumanized part of herself, and also because of her mother's frequent rejection of Casey. This intrusion interfered greatly with Casey's early development and made her question the "ownership of her body" (Laufer, 1968, p. 115).

Casey lacked a healthy sense of autonomy and self-worth. Instead, she was plagued by self-doubt and shame, demonstrating Erikson's (1959), psychosocial crisis of early childhood: autonomy versus shame and doubt. Mahler and McDevitt (1980) described the toddler's glee in the growing autonomy of the practicing subphase, which is followed by the rapprochement subphase realization of his separateness and vulnerability and threatened collapse of his self-esteem. To obviate this threat, the mother must be emotionally available to the child and yet at the same time must provide the child with a gentle push toward independence. The analysis, not the mother, gave Casey the "gentle push toward independence."

There was more interference from the parents than in the usual analysis of a young adult. Casey's mother complained that she was seeing too little of Casey, especially when Casey returned to school for the basic education denied her because of her training for ballet. In addition, there was considerable resistance on Casey's part because she feared that exploring the maternal incest could mean that both she and her mother were homosexual.

Some months after she had begun to explore the sexual stimulation by her mother Casey said plaintively, "It's one thing to say 'She did it to me' and I can be angry and hate her, but it's another to say 'I wanted it and went out for it'. Did I feel I was to blame? I still feel guilty." Still later she said, "She has a basic flaw, but if I give her up I won't have a mother." Casey had serious problems in college, for her conflicts over what she called "worries about what I am allowed to know" (about the relationship with her mother) intruded into most subjects, especially the humanities. For a long time she used her mother to quiz her, as if doing so could mean that her mother wanted her to learn. After quite a while, she studied with friends. As one might expect, her mother's sad retort was, "You don't need me anymore."

Casey's father was a successful professional tied to his career, glad that Casey's and her mother's preoccupation with each other made his wife less burdensome to him.

When Casey was in her mid-twenties, she had a number of sexual relationships with men whose appearance, intellect, or personality problems were such that certain aspects of Casey's relationship with her mother were replicated all too easily. Casey could not reach orgasm. At the same time, the continuing influence of the mother's masturbation of her was demonstrated when Casey complained that she could not tell whether her body and genitals were being stimulated by her mother or her lover. She said plaintively, "Before, I could not get my mother out of my head. Now I can't get her out of my bed." Both foreplay and intromission caused anxiety because of this confusion.

She complained that her current lover, A, "used her," seemed to "turn on" to her and then to "turn off," much as her mother had. The analysis revealed that she had feared having an orgasm when masturbated by her mother, for doing so would show her mother and herself that she enjoyed their sexual encounters. She had no orgasms with A. For about six months, material about A waned, presumably because Casey perceived that the relationship had no future. During this time there was a decided shift in the transference.

Casey now began to make demands of me in an entirely new way. Whereas earlier she had tried to coerce me to be a partner in the object-coercive doubting, her demands now were that I do what she wanted or that I not make her accede to what she felt was unfair. (These "unfair" demands were those that had been in operation throughout Casey's treatment and dealt mainly with keeping appointments, payment, and such.) Now she broke appointments without notice and announced that she would not pay for them. At the same time, she demanded extra appointments, telling me that she considered it her privilege to get them, even if it meant inconveniencing another patient or me. In contrast to the rather passive acquiescence she had displayed through the earlier phases of treatment, now there was more definiteness, more aggression in her demands, and, I felt, more of a sense of self. I found myself puzzled but not displeased by the change, and I sensed some amusement, which I understood when I envisioned her as a foot-stamping 2-year-old, demanding with a sense of justification that I not leave the city for a week of meetings because "I won't let you go away." "Why?" "Because I say so."

After a period of time, Casey again spoke of A, complaining that he used her and then ignored her. In spite of her complaints, her affect was such that I commented that she seemed not to want me to think that anything in the relationship had been of value to her or fun. Casey retorted, "You're too snoopy. It's none of your business." Although her voice was light, almost jesting, a quality she conveyed made me think that she was consciously withholding something.

She broke off with A after a painful argument. After a few lonely weeks, she met a new man, B, who was both more mature and more appropriate. She told me that sex with him was different from that with A. For several months, during sex with A she had had multiple orgasms from the time of intromission. With B, she had one orgasm with each intercourse, which they had many times a day.

I reviewed the recent material and commented that the "secrets" about which Casey felt I was too snoopy had to do with her increased sexual freedom and her ability to have orgasms. I also noted that there had been a lessening and finally an absence of dreams about hairy spiders or octopi (which the analysis revealed to stem from the sexual exploitation by her mother). Casey was pleased to be capable of this sexual awakening and was especially delighted to have withheld from me the secret of her sexual fulfillment.

I interpreted this as meaning that her body, and her genitals in particular, belonged to her, not to her mother or to me. And her teasing about keeping the secret showed both of us that she had a mind of her own. I could see more clearly that the period in which she was negativistic and demanding, and yet secretive about her increasing possession of her genitals, had seen developmental strides. Whereas earlier Casey could ask (seldom demand) that she be treated as an exception because she had been sexually abused, now she conveyed, "I deserve; I am entitled because I am separate, because I am I."

She conveyed the pleasure of achieving a feeling of secure separateness never sufficiently experienced before. She now seemed to be fired by purpose and normal striving, not by humiliation. That Casey could be teasing and secretive, but had a growing sense of purpose, signaled that she was now handling her aggression more appropriately. Rather than being turned against herself, the aggression now mixed with libido was modulated, directed outward, and useful in helping her to proclaim ownership of her mind and body. The better sense of self, of knowing what was hers, and of possessing her own genitals were signs of progress, although at times they caused resistance in the analysis.

The sense of entitlement, hitherto considered evidence of pathology, may be considered to be a normal stage in the development of autonomy and independence of the body. Anna Freud (1965) suggested the possibility, although she did not designate it as such, as she depicted the overlapping and interrelating lines of development. If it is normal for children to demand because they have a sense of self and are struggling to achieve autonomy, can we not consider the entitlement that we see in some analyses to derive from the resumption of development?

Case 2

D, a 23-year-old, anxious, depressed woman, college educated but "going nowhere,' was referred by her aging analyst when D took a job in Philadelphia. D hated to leave her former analyst, Dr. X, whom she regarded as handsome, charismatic, and sorcererlike. She was angry at him because although she knew that he was to retire soon because of failing health, she could not tolerate the dystonic thought that he might have wanted to rid himself of her. D soon pushed the thought out of consciousness and concentrated on telling me of the many ways in which I was inferior to her former therapist. Her strong, positive, erotic paternal transference to him was obvious, yet for reasons she could not fathom she realized that she was relieved to be in treatment with me and not with him. She was extremely anxious and depressed. I felt that analytic psychotherapy, three times a week, with D sitting up, was the preferred form of treatment.

D was the third of five children, the only girl in a very chaotic family, with parents who prided themselves on being "modern." She felt that she was her father's favorite. Her father was the guru in a commune; they lived with many others in a rambling house with no doors on the bedrooms nor locks on the bathrooms. Sex talk was rampant; exposure to the primal scene was frequent. There was considerable sex play in the attic/bedroom shared by all the children until D was 14 and the eldest boy was 18. As treatment proceeded, the picture of the family became more clear. D's mother seemed helpless to counter her husband's pronouncements on everything they did. Early in D's life, her mother disregarded, as had her husband, the needs of members of the family for privacy, regulation of aggression, establishment of appropriate behavior, and taking responsibility for schoolwork. She obeyed her husband's firm and strange rules about health in general and about food in particular. Health was assured by limitations of food and complete freedom in sex.

When D, at age 9, well before prepuberty, complained to her parents of her brothers' sexual molestation, she was told to stop acting "like an old lady." When at 12 she told her father that a man in the commune had made sexual overtures to her, she was told that she had an overactive imagination. D's hyperacusis, which had always been obvious in the analysis, gradually took center stage, together with the frightening fantasy that my house was swaying. In spite of its solid construction, D felt that the house might collapse. This ominous foreboding was seen in both transferential and extratransferential phenomena. Dreams and associations were to the emotional instability of life on a commune, with its many moves because of irate neighbors. At the same time, hyperacusis was associated to exposure to primal scenes, to fights between adults in the commune, and to excited listening to the approach of vigilante groups. Although both themes were obvious in dreams and associations, the patient could not accept transference interpretations concerning her fear that treatment itself was unstable, that I might "unload" her, as her previous therapist had done, or that I would not protect her from the sexually attacking men. She said angrily, "You don't take me seriously." Her tone was like Chicken Little's predicting "The sky is falling in," although now it conveyed anger rather than agitation.

During a tornadolike weather disturbance, she was troubled by the darkening sky, but especially by the noises of the increasing winds. She said, "Don't you hear the noise? How can you sit there?" I pointed out that her fear was occasioned not only by the noises but that old "inside" fears really caused her upset. At that point, a large limb crashed down from a neighbor's tree shattering the glass of my greenhouse and setting off my burglar alarm. The patient gasped in panic. Afraid that someone had been hurt, I excused myself and went to inspect the damage. When I returned, the patient seemed more relaxed in spite of the violent storm. She smiled and said calmly, "This time you believed me." She could see that I had reacted and by doing so was verifying the truth in her experience. Instead of giving her "psychobabble," I confirmed her reality testing—that she had been frightened by an outside threat, which related at first to her brothers', their friends', and her father's friend's molestation of her.

Soon material centered on her father. On coming to Philadelphia she had decided to take courses in a restaurant school in the hope of opening her own business. Courses on nutrition and food planning provoked a "learning block," for it was in those areas that her father's edicts had controlled the thinking and eating of the entire family. He had them follow one dietary fad after another. The painful recognition of the oddness of her father's dietary pronouncements led her to face his other practices. He had paraded around the house nude to "let toxins be emitted through his pores." He had taught himself acupuncture, and oriental massage techniques. She was afraid of needles and refused acupuncture but she could not refuse the massage since it was "good for you." She also admitted, with shame and guilt, that she had enjoyed the "treatments."

At this time D began to have extreme aversion to her boyfriend's fondling her breasts during foreplay. She complained that I was not taking my proper role and that I should tell her to break off with her boyfriend "since he hurt me." I went first to earlier material about her brother and his friends tweaking her breasts, a painful-pleasurable experience. She was very definite, saying, "No, it's not my brother and his friends." Soon she had dreams and fantasies of being in a zipped-up container that she could not leave. Then someone else was there, keeping her from leaving. She recalled sharing her father's sleeping bag on camping trips and the many massages he gave her. He would start on her back. She wished that I would scratch her "itchy places." Then there was a flustered, pained silence, after which she said, "I kept thinking of my breasts. It was nice, and it was awful." First she associated to nice times, then to awful times with her boyfriend; then she said flatly, "It's my father. He scratched my back and then went to my breasts. I know he massaged my thighs. I felt like screaming with excitement and pain. My mother should have forbidden it. I don't think she approved but no one could stop him, ever."

As D began to "dethrone" and demystify her father, she became able to learn and chose a career in law, a field her father hated! Even at the end of treatment a residue of her experiences with her father (rubbing his pubic area in the bath) emerged when she entered the session gagging. She had opened a bottle of liquid detergent by snipping the top; she became ill at the sight of the white liquid emerging.

Case 3

R came from a poor, uneducated family but had performed brilliantly in school and at the urging of her teachers had attended college and pursued a graduate program in business administration. (Her mother's hope had been that R would become a telephone company operator.) R's superior intelligence enabled her to learn simply by listening to lectures and without having to study (i.e., to show her intention to learn). She had problems reading certain things; she could not tell time, read a road map, or do simple "pencil and paper" arithmetic.

She came to treatment because of recurrent depression, low self-esteem, and great anxiety that occurred whenever, as a student advisor in a prestigious college, she was told by a student of having experienced incest. She was intelligent enough to know that these "reports" stirred something in her and was also well-enough informed to wonder why she had amnesia for the years throughout her prelatency and latency years until puberty.

During her sessions, R was troubled by a hypersensitivity to smell. She often thought that she detected a chemical smell in my waiting room or inner office; she disliked it and became anxious, although she could not say why. Later, when she associated the "chemical smell" to alcohol, she remembered that her parents had been alcoholics throughout much of her early life. After a "cure" through AA, her mother became hyperreligious and attended daily Mass. Like D, R was hypersensitive to being touched, to being carried (she was very petite and at times in their lovemaking her husband carried her to bed), and to her own touch of certain things. The reaction to touch and to being carried could be traced back to "some sort of molestation but by whom I do not know." Her revulsion to touching and to feeling recalled a hitherto repressed preadolescent fear of dogs, cats, and birds. She realized that she was not really afraid that they would bite her, but rather that she would "feel something solid, like a bone under the loose skin of the animal." She felt nauseated and accused me of making her experience feelings she did not want to experience, memories she should not be touching. She complained of the chemical smell again and said, "It's like the smell of semen."

I reconstructed that she was telling me of being touched, being carried against her will, and being made to touch (or to rub) something (a penis). I said she could recall the anxiety and revulsion and that she saw me, her therapist, both as the seductive male and as the indifferent female parent. The patient then remembered that when her mother was angry because her husband had abused her, she would make him sleep with one of the children while she took others to bed with her. He chose the child in a counting-down game that always ended with the selection of my patient. She had often puzzled about

his way of "counting out." She knew now that he had fooled
her with his numbers game and that in his gentler moods he
was devoted and loving but, when drunk, had a fierce temper.
R could not distinguish the noises of her parents' fighting from
noises of their sexual activities. She began to remember hitherto
repressed memories: of being carried to the "other bed," of
being told to touch something, of not knowing whether he
was the nice daddy or the fearsome one. At this point, she
complained once more about the "alcohol-semen" smell, thus
opening by this "somatic memory" memories of the sexual
smells of incest with her father—alcohol and semen.

Case 4

Donald's analysis has been reported in detail elsewhere
(Kramer, 1974). He had been referred at 10 years of age because of his "habits," that is, having to rise and sit down again
a certain number of times in multiples of four. His parents
requested an evaluation after he rose and sat sixty-four times
in the midst of a raging summer storm; his mother worried
what the neighbors might think! Donald was the only child born
to parents who had married rather late. His mother was tied to
her own mother; his father, to his own father. Donald's mother
considered him strange looking from birth and felt that he was
overly large, ugly, and too serious. His father spent a great deal
of time with him, in part to protect him from the mother's
carping.
    When Donald refused to come for treatment, his parents
complied with his wishes. Therefore, I did not see him until he
was 15 when Donald and his parents became terrified by his
mounting temper outbursts. At that time he came willingly, for
he saw himself as a volcano that could erupt at any moment.
He was extremely tall, cadaverously thin, and had severe pustu-
lar acne. He looked to the analysis as a place to get help with
his temper, his separation fears, and his low self-esteem. Donald
knew, but was afraid to acknowledge, that his mother was psychotic. In her interviews with me she revealed a paranoid psychosis. Donald complained about, but could not avoid, his extreme closeness to both parents. His father was his protection

and yet stimulated Donald when they wrestled. His mother was "crazy-clean," yet she flitted into his room in ultra-sheer nighties, always using an excuse to intrude on him. Donald revealed that he had reached puberty early, having had his first nocturnal emission at 9½. He had been plagued by sexual excitement, by obvious bodily changes, by the acne that his mother said was caused by his doing "bad things."

The analysis enabled him to face his mother's psychosis, to separate both emotionally and physically from both parents, and to live much as does the average teenager. He did well in school without needing to involve his parents. And he worked through the years of sexual excitement resulting from the fact that one or the other parent slept in his room from the time he was 7 until he was 14; his excitement alternated with curiosity, as he listened at the wall between bedrooms, and with fury when he recognized primal scene noises from the adjoining room.

The "somatic memory" of maternal incest appeared during a period of severe regression near the end of his analysis when Donald expressed the delusion that I could see his nose and lips get bigger and smaller, that I was refusing to tell him what I knew, but was instead keeping it to myself, smiling sarcastically. Donald was in great psychic pain and pleaded with me to "tell him the truth." We had long before analyzed his own mother's and his upward displacement from his genitals to his face; he had spoken of his anger at mother's perpetual, grimacelike smile, both sarcastic and seeming to "know" what others were thinking (and were saying about her, one of her psychotic mechanisms). After months during which he was agonized, sure that I knew but would not tell him of my awareness of his upward-displaced tumescence and detumescence, I made a reconstruction in which I said that I felt that something had, indeed, happened; that someone had not only known but had caused the size of a part of his body—his penis—to change; that he was aware of that person's sarcasm. With surprise, Donald said: "My mother bathed me until I was past 14. She bathed me *all over*." Donald found these baths to be exquisitely painful (emotionally), shameful, and exciting all at the same time. Since he reached puberty at 9½, he would become erect when she rubbed his penis. We were able to pursue the sexual abuse in the transference: I might have evil and magical qualities that enabled me almost to read his mind; he was able to agree with my assertion that he was sure that I could cause him to have an erection when we talked of sexual matters; finally he was able to acknowledge his pleasure in this fantasy as well as his exhibitionism when he implored me to look at him.

Williams (1987) said "In reconstructing a seduction at an early age which led to a severe neurosis, no conscious recollections can be obtained" (p. 146). For Donald the seduction had persisted until he was past 14. However, although he remembered being bathed, defenses against the entire gestalt included repression, displacement, denial, and projection. Williams (1987, p. 146) referred to Freud, who in writing about the Wolf Man said that "[scenes that] further lay claim to such an extraordinary significance for the history of the case, are as a rule not reproduced as recollections, but have to be divined—constructed—gradually and laboriously from an aggregate of indications . . ." (Freud, 1918, p. 51).

I propose that in certain patients who have suffered childhood sexual abuse, the memory as such is not available or is only partially available. However "somatic memories" of the trauma persist and carry with them some of the actual sensations of fear, anxiety, anger, revulsion, and pleasure that accompanied the childhood seduction; concurrent with the "somatic memories" are learning problems, the nature of which may be specific for the particular child. In maternal incest, the learning problems are involved in pathological, object-coercive doubting.

I. Brenner (1988), studying sensory bridges to object loss during the Holocaust, said that some patients who suffered early object loss could conjure up memories of early sensory experiences that became bridges to the lost objects. I have found that sensory experiences in my patients provided bridges both to objects and to early experiences or to experiences too painful to integrate into the personality. At the same time I found that the learning problems were part of the process of repression that is used to deal with the pain and disorganizing memories of incest.

THE LEARNING PROBLEMS AND INCEST

There are many degrees and kinds of learning problems that arise in patients who did not experience incest. I have not, however, analyzed any case of incest that does not manifest some sort of learning difficulty. Several theoretical formulations are useful to explain this phenomenon.

The very title of Frank's (1969) paper on primal repression, "The Unrememberable and the Unforgettable," connotes the intrapsychic residues of early severe traumas. Frank says that even after secondary process mentation has been firmly established, physiological, environmental, and emotional traumas may overwhelm the higher ego functions, and by promoting regression may create conditions suitable for passive primal repression. Although Frank's clinical material does not include incest, it involves late (adult) residues of profound infantile traumas. The analyst's reconstruction enabled the patient to "know," to "show that he knew," by questioning his parents about his having come close to freezing to death because of parental neglect. Frank feels that passive primal repression encompasses a developmental, rather than a defensive vicissitude, and that a common feature of passive primal repression is the absence of preconscious representation, which results from, among other causes, *mental overstimulation*. I am convinced that both physical and mental overstimulation may result in amnesia and in problems of learning. Just as in the case Frank cited, I feel that memories of incest may be retrieved with the aid of reconstruction in psychoanalysis.

Woodbury (1966) describes defenses against intrusion by the incestuous parent which appears as a shell against both feelings and knowledge. He described altered body–ego experiences, similar to Donald's insistence that I knew what his body was experiencing (penile tumescence and detumescence displaced upward to his lips and nose). Donald was very certain of the changes in the size and firmness of his lips and nose.

Shengold (1967) described autohypnosis as a means of promoting isolation of affect "not only as a defense to deal with the erogenity and excitement involved in [his patient's] sexual

wishes but also to bring about the repetitions of the past traumata in attenuation: the patient could do, with and to others
what had been before done to her—now evading the overstimulation by way of hypnosis" (p. 407). Another patient he described (p. 410) had a general inability to integrate knowledge
because of "the danger of re-experiencing the affects of the
past" arising from the fact that he had shared his mother's bed
from age 3, when his father died, until past puberty.

He also reported a patient's use of massive isolation to
"keep the overstimulation and rage in check." Shengold added
an important caveat, namely, that a special need for denial
should alert the analyst not only to the possibility of psychotic
or borderline ego, but also to the likelihood that he is "dealing
with one of the [people] who have lived through too much" (p.
414).

Elsewhere Shengold (1974, 1979) refers to "vertical splitting" a defense that makes "the good mother preservable only
at the *expense of the compromise of reality testing by denial*" (pp.
107–108; emphasis added).

Repression may be partial, as in a case reported by Finkelhor (1979), whose patient did not forget that her father
masturbated himself on her chest and later took her to the
bathroom and had her soap his penis and masturbate him. She
did not forget or deny the stimulation, but instead repressed
her fury. However, when her fiance rubbed her breast she
slapped him (pp. 185–214). She could acknowledge that her
father's manual stimulation felt good, but that admission made
her feel even worse, at the mercy of the adult and out of control
of her own body and emotions.

Others have reported on the interferences with thinking
and learning in children who have been victims of incest. Ferenczi (1933) was very definite in his description of the child's
inability both to know and to learn. He also alluded to the
introjection of the *guilt feelings* of the adult. In describing patients with problems of doubting similar to those of my patients
who had suffered maternal incest, he wrote:

> I obtained new corroborative evidence for my supposition
> that the trauma, especially the sexual trauma, as the patho-
> genic factor cannot be valued highly enough. Even chil-
> dren of very respectable, sincerely puritanical families, fall

victim to real violence or rape much more often than one had dared to suppose. It is the parents who try to find a substitute gratification in this pathological way for their frustration, or it is people thought to be trustworthy who misuse the ignorance and innocence of the child [p. 161].

He described interferences with the child's thinking and reality testing, as well as with his autonomy, and alluded to the formation of pathological defenses: "These children feel physically and morally helpless, their personalities are not sufficiently consolidated in order to be able to protest, *even if only in* thought, for the overpowering force and authority of the adult *makes them dumb and can rob them of their senses*" (p. 162; emphasis added). Ferenczi described identification with the sexual aggressor and went on to say:

The most important change, produced in the mind of the child by the anxiety-fear-ridden identification with the adult parent, is the introjection of the guilt feelings of the adult which makes hitherto harmless play appear as a punishable offense.

When the child recovers from such an attack, *he feels enormously confused*, in fact, split—innocent and culpable at the same time—*and his confidence in the testimony of his own senses is broken*. Not infrequently the seducer becomes over-moralistic [pp. 162–163; emphasis added].

The many mental mechanisms used to militate against remembering, against knowing, and against revealing what they have experienced has ruled incest victims' lives and colored their object relationships. The victims have low self-esteem, are self-critical, and have myriad doubts about themselves. It is for this reason that I feel (as does Shengold) that it is important that the analyst verify the incest experience as it emerges in treatment. I, for one, have never encountered an adult who has fabricated a story of incest. Most of them have had to repress, deny, isolate, or otherwise defend against knowing for psychic survival or for survival within the family. The learning problem in maternal incest was unique.

The patients coerced the maternal object or her substitute to argue one of the opposing sides of the child's intrapsychic conflict (or its derivative). The lack of adequate selfobject differentiation (or the persistence of the selfobject [Kernberg, 1976]), caused this type of doubting to be considerably different from the doubting of the obsessive–compulsive individual who has separated and individuated, who is troubled by conflict between components of his own psychic structure. My patients used the incompletely differentiated self and object to express and to argue the conflict, a conflict which was usually, but not always about knowing something; but there was almost never any closure to the conflict.

In addition, all three patients showed much conflict about physical separation from their parents. In the course of their analyses it became obvious that my patients controlled their parents' freedom by their supposed need for help with homework and by their separation problems. The parents, to my surprise, were extremely compliant in response to their children's control. Later, when their children resumed development and began to take steps toward independence and autonomy, the parents protested, even complaining to me that analysis was changing the relationship between parent and child. However, these patients' most profound attempts to control were evident in the object-coercive doubting. I speculate that its origin was in the child's uncertainty about what was happening to his or her body and how was it taking place when, at the time of incomplete differentiation, the child's genitals were repeatedly stimulated. The child struggled against his or her intrapsychic resistance against knowing, the latter accentuated by the denial of reality by the mother.

Although colleagues have told me of similar doubting in patients who had experienced paternal incest, I myself have not seen object-coercive doubting except where the mother has sexually overstimulated the child from a time before the differentiation process normally evolved. I have seen in paternal incest patients considerable rumination about "did it occur," but the quality of this self-doubting process is different from that in object-coercive doubting. I keep an open mind about this, however, and remain interested in hearing of material that might corroborate object-coercive doubting in paternal incest victims. Although paternal incest is more common than maternal incest, I find it interesting that I encountered a large number of paternal incest cases only after the analysis of the first two maternal incest cases had been completed. While it would be easy to say that it is happenstance, I really have no explanation for this phenomenon in my practice. I do not rule out a countertransference reaction that could have prevented me from responding to subtle paternal incest cues. My patients' material about maternal incest was not at all subtle.

SUMMARY

I have described two important residues of incest: (1) "somatic memories" and (2) problems in learning. In regard to the former, I feel it is significant that incidents and affects that are otherwise repressed or denied persist in a somatic form. In discussing the related phenomenon of anniversary reactions, Dlin (1985) states that theories of childhood trauma and repression are important but are not enough to explain "the why," "the when it happens," and "why it takes the form it does." He characterizes the mechanisms involved as a trauma that is locked in or fixed, a "somatic time bomb waiting to be touched off by specific triggers" (p. 517). Such are the residues of incest that are activated by life events giving rise to the somatic memories reported by my patients.

The learning problems that I have described are a function, in part, of powerful resistances to remembering the events and feelings connected with the incest. Other contributing factors, especially in the young child, include identification with the abusing parent's distortion of reality and obeying the parental admonition not to know or tell of what has happened between them. In the older child, shame, guilt, and the need to deny sexual pleasure help to reinforce the not knowing. In children of any age, what begins as a defense against specific

memories and their related feelings can become generalized
into a cognitive style.

As a component of their learning problems, many incest
victims demonstrate an inability to trust themselves to know or
to trust others to be honest. This distrust has important technical implications for the analyst in helping these patients to reality test and therefore verify the actuality of the incest (see Shengold [1967], for a related view).

Sachs (1967) offered a relevant perspective when discussing the role of the analyst in helping patients to distinguish
between fantasy and reality and their influences on conflicts,
conflict resolution, and the behavioral residues of acting out.
His description of what may happen when the patient is told
by the analyst that some kind of trauma has, indeed, occurred
is a poignant reminder of how meaningful psychoanalytic treatment can be for adult patients who were sexually abused as
children. "There occurs . . . a release from obsessional self
doubt which has affected some aspects of reality testing [and a
strengthening of] the distinction of fantasy from actual events
after their occurrence. The belief and acceptance of the memory results in an exhilarating feeling of relief . . . at least someone believes me" (p. 422).

Why is it that relatively few psychoanalysts have written
about incest? Freud's changing attitudes about incest in the
pathogenesis of the neuroses no longer appear to be a valid
reason for this state of affairs. I am inclined to believe that
because of analysts' own blind spots concerning incest, because
of countertransference issues to their patients' transference,
and because instructors who supervised the training of today's
analysts did not recognize or even suspect incest, many incest
cases go unrecognized. I have noted antipathy to recognizing
and working with derivatives of incest to be especially great in
cases of maternal incest (children who had been masturbated
by their mothers from infancy, often until adolescence). Such
countertransference-based reluctance can often lead to either
a superficial treatment or to the patient's dropping out of the
treatment altogether. If patients leave treatment in which incest
is unrecognized and with continuing personality problems and
unresolved intrapsychic conflicts, they often seek treatment

with another therapist to relieve their continuing intrapsychic pain or to help them minimize their tendencies to act out. Of seven "incest" patients in treatment with me in recent years, four had been in prior treatment, with a total of seven prior therapists.

Continued experience in the conduct of psychoanalysis, greater comfort with the disclosure and working through of disquieting historical and conflictual elements in our patients' analytic material, and increased reliance on our countertransference, will make us better able to treat these cases. Despite such reminders, our own resistances in recognizing incest-related material persist. This was evident in the fact that when I presented material about maternal incest at psychoanalytic meetings, my audience often seemed perturbed and ill at ease. They accepted maternal incest only if it had occurred in families of low social and economic status. They were shocked and unbelieving when I described socially stable and economically well-off Caucasian families in which the fathers were middle-class professionals and the mothers had at least a high school education. In general, they seemed to attribute more serious pathology to mothers who molest their children of either sex than to fathers who sexually molest their daughters. I feel that further studies on incest may explain whether this is actually so. Are we inclined to let fathers "off the hook," as if to say "boys will be boys"? I suggest that the well-known sentiment that mothers should be pure and virginal, far removed from sexual interests in general and from sexual desires for their children in particular, could be the reason for this. Possibly, the average mother is more inhibited than is the father in acting out sexual fantasies with their children.

I hope that the contributions in this present volume will lead us to consider further questions. Are there patterns in the analyses of certain patients that might make us suspect that incest has occurred although the patient has not made any overt mention of it? Are there common pitfalls to which analysts should be alerted in analyses where incest has occurred? How should incest material be handled? The first pertains to the relative culpability of each parent (regardless of which parent had incestuous experiences with the child), and second, to whether incest can ever be an advantage to the child. My experience is that incest occurs only in a markedly dysfunctional family. Maternal incest, as I have reported it in young children, takes place in a family where pathology is rampant. The mother is possessive, but only intermittently gratifying; as she was over-involved with her own mother, so is she overinvolved with her child. The father, usually very passive, with a poor sense of self, is emotionally distant from both his wife and his child. Alcoholism and poverty were not significant familial factors in my "maternal incest" cases. In paternal incest, while the father is held responsible for the act, the mother is considered equally responsible and very culpable by some authors (Browning and Boatman, 1977; Finklehor, 1979; Bigras, 1990; Steele, 1990). In cases where the mother had conscious knowledge of the incest or where she encouraged her daughter to continue an incestuous relationship with the father in order to placate him or to extract money or gifts from him, the mother is both disturbed and responsible. However, where a mother is physically and emotionally ill and the father and child turn to each other, can it really be considered the mother's fault? Ruth Fischer (1991) has joined me in asking whether we hold mothers responsible for everything evil that happens.

Do analysts use sexist attitudes in suggesting that the mother is fully culpable in maternal incest and that she is also largely culpable where the perpetrator of incest is the father? If a mother is emotionally unavailable to the father, why is his alternative choice of his daughter as a sexual object so easily justified? Certainly, in the best of all worlds, both parents are mature, reliable people who are available to each other as partners and lovers and are available to their children as parents, fulfilling their parental functions of physical and emotional support and protection. We react with discomfort when either parent fails to honor the incest barrier, but we find the mother at fault in each instance! Clearly, more thinking is needed here.

Authors have reported the multigenerational aspects of incest and suggest that without interventions incest often repeats itself with the former victim as the perpetrator. Recent contributions to developmental literature by Sroufe (Sroufe and Ward, 1980; Sroufe and Fleeson, 1986) attest to this. He alludes to studies that revealed that "spousification" had occurred, that is, that parents who themselves had been exploited by a parent abuse their own sons and daughters. While the manner of the abuse of their children was not identical to what their parents had done to them, the meanings were the same. In some cases, fathers' abuse of their daughters may cause these daughters (even after treatment) to continue to interact with their fathers in an erotic secretive fashion, even though overt sexual activity has stopped between them.

There are so many who must be made aware that incest is inimical to normal, healthy development. Actually, psychoanalysts are not the first line of defense here. The first line consists of parents, who may need help in being honest about what they are doing with their children and to face the truth of their mate's behavior vis-à-vis their children. The next line of defense to protect children from incest is comprised of family physicians, pediatricians, school nurses, or others who as health professionals are in regular contact with the child. In our positions as experts in the field of emotional development who are called upon to diagnose and treat severe psychopathological processes, it behooves psychoanalysts to function in these very important areas of prevention and early intervention. By addressing the psychopathology of incest, we are making an important inroad into the prevention and amelioration of the profound psychological trauma—the trauma of transgression—caused by the use of a child's body for the sexual gratification of the parent.

REFERENCES

Bigras, J. (1990), Psychoanalysis as incestuous repetition. In: *Adult Analysis and Childhood Sexual Abuse*, ed. H. Levine. Hillsdale, NJ: Analytic Press, pp. 173–196.

Brenner, I. (1988), Multi sensory bridges in response to object loss during the Holocaust. *Psychoanal. Rev.*, 75:573–587.

Browning, D., & Boatman, B. (1977), Incest: Children at risk. *Amer. J. Psychiat.*, 134:69–72.

Dlin, B. (1985), Psychobiology and treatment of anniversary reactions. *Psychosomat.*, 26:505–520.

Erikson, E. H. (1959), Identity and the Life Cycle. *Psychological Issues*, Monograph 1. New York: International Universities Press.

Ferenczi, S. (1933), Confusion of tongues between the adult and the child. In: *Final Contributions to the Problems and Methods of Psychoanalysis*. London: Hogarth Press, 1955, pp. 156–167.

Finkelhor, D. (1979), *Sexually Victimized Children*. New York: Free Press.

Fischer, R. (1991), The unresolved rapprochement crisis: An important constituent of the incest experience. In: *The Trauma of Transgression. Psychotherapy of Incest Victims*, ed. S. Kramer & S. Akhtan. Northvale, NJ: Jason Aronson.

Frank, A. (1969), The unrememberable and the unforgettable. *The Psychoanalytic Study of the Child*, 24:48–77. New York: International Universities Press.

Freud, A. (1965), *Normality and Pathology in Childhood*. New York: International Universities Press.

Freud, S. (1918), From the History of an Infantile Neurosis. *Standard Edition*, 17. London: Hogarth Press, 1955.

Katan, A. (1973), Children who were raped. *The Psychoanalytic Study of the Child*, 28:208–225. New Haven, CT: Yale University Press.

Kernberg, O. (1976), *Object Relations Theory and Clinical Psychoanalysis*. New York: Jason Aronson.

Kramer, S. (1974), Episodes of severe ego regression in the course of adolescent analysis. In: *The Analyst and the Adolescent at Work*, ed. M. Harley. New York: Quadrangle Press, pp. 190–231.

——— (1980), Residues of split-object and split-self dichotomies in adolescence. In: *Rapprochement*, ed. R. Lax, S. Bach, & J. A. Burland. New York: Jason Aronson, pp. 417–438.

——— (1983), Object-coercive doubting: A pathological defense response to maternal incest. *J. Amer. Psychoanal. Assn.*, 31(suppl):325–351.

——— (1987), A contribution to the concept "the exception" as a developmental phenomenon. *Child Abuse & Neglect*, 11:367–370.

Laufer, M. (1968), The body image, the function of masturbation and adolescence: Problems of ownership of the body. *The Psychoanalytic Study of the Child*, 23:114–137. New York: International Universities Press.

Litin, E., Griffin, M., & Johnson, A. M. (1956), Parental influence in unusual sexual behavior in children. *Psychoanal. Quart.*, 25:37–55.

Mahler, M. S., & McDevitt, J. B. (1980), The separation-individuation process and identity formation. In: *The Course of Life*, Vol. 1, ed.

S. I. Greenspan & G. Pollock. Adlephi, MD: U.S. Government Printing Office, pp. 395–406.

Margolis, M. (1977), A preliminary study of a case of consummated mother-son incest. *The Annual of Psychoanalysis*, 5:267–293. New York: International Universities Press.

——— (1984), A case of mother–adolescent son incest. *Psychoanal. Quart.*, 53:355–385.

Parens, H. (1973), Aggression: A reconsideration. *J. Amer. Psychoanal. Assn.*, 21:34–60.

Sachs, O. (1967), Distinction between fantasy and reality elements in memory and reconstruction. *Internat. J. Psycho-Anal.*, 48:416–423.

Shengold, L. (1967), The effects of overstimulation: Rat people. *Internat. J. Psycho-Anal.*, 48:403–415.

——— (1974), The metaphor of the mirror. *J. Amer. Psychoanal. Assn.*, 22:97–115.

——— (1979), Child abuse and deprivation: Soul murder. *J. Amer. Psychoanal. Assn.*, 27:533–557.

——— (1980), Some reflections on a case of mother/adolescent son incest. *Internat. J. Psycho-Anal.*, 61:461–476.

Silber, A. (1979), Childhood seduction, parental pathology and hysterical symptoms. *Internat. J. Psycho-Anal.*, 60:109–116.

Sroufe, L. A., & Fleeson, J. (1986), Attachment and construction of relationships. In: *Relationship and Development*, ed. W. Hartup & Z. Rubin. Hillsdale, NJ: Lawrence Erlbaum, pp. 51–71.

——— & Ward, M. (1980), Seductive behavior of mothers of toddlers. *Child Development*, 517:1222–1229.

Steele, B. (1990), Some sequelae of the sexual maltreatment of children. In: *Adult Analysis and Childhood Sexual Abuse*, ed. H. Levine. Hillsdale, NJ: Analytic Press, pp. 21–34.

Williams, M. (1987), Reconstruction of an early seduction and its aftereffects. *J. Amer. Psychoanal. Assn.*, 35:145–165.

Woodbury, M. (1966), Altered body ego experiences. *J. Amer. Psychoanal. Assn.*, 14:273–303.

Chapter 5

Battered Spouse Syndrome: A Psychoanalytic Perspective

Nadine A. Levinson, D.D.S.

Battered Spouse Syndrome is an enigmatic problem that has become more prevalent in recent years. In 1992, there were 4 million homes devastated by intrafamily violence. Two to 4 million cases involved children suffering abuse at the hands of their parents and 1.8 million women were battered by their partners (*AMA News*, 1992). Abused or battered individuals undergo serious physical and psychological injury as a result of deliberate assaults by their partners. In addition to the physical damage, victims often suffer crippling dependence, psychosomatic problems, traumatic neurosis, depression, suicidal ideation, and an incapacitating assault to self-esteem, respect, and confidence (Hilberman, 1980). The victims are typically women who feel emotionally dependent, immobilized, and helpless with small children, and they are usually isolated socially from friends or extended family. Drug abuse and alcoholism are often facilitating factors (Hilberman, 1980; Goodstein and Page, 1981). The couples are besieged with loss of control of aggressive behavior. Frequently the assault is relatively unprovoked; however, the female victim usually rationalizes or justifies the abuse on the basis of her fantasied misbehavior. Self-blame combined with being blamed by others is typical. The assault sets up a cycle of placating or pleasing the assailant.

Then later, identification with the aggressor and further escalation of violence can occur. Suffering in silence may even perpetuate the violent pattern in the assailant with the victim's passivity seeming to stimulate further sadism. Regularly, the abuser, feeling transiently guilty for the violence, makes empty promises of change or reparation. These actions by the batterer only reinforce the cycle of abuse and reparation as they intertwine with the unconscious wishes of the victim for restitution. Frequently, regression and violence is induced with accompanying panic and anxiety by the threat of separation if the battered partner seeks treatment.

Often after repetitive abuses, many women painfully tear themselves away from their companion and use the services of a shelter. There, they can protect themselves, reconstitute, explore options, and it is hoped, take effective action in learning more about themselves and their own motivation. Guidance and group counseling are the usual treatment modalities.

Violence can occur against men, although such occurrences are less frequent. According to *Time* Magazine (1992), 95 percent of the abused partners are women. However, spousal violence can be viewed as occurring along a continuum where one extreme can be reflected by the husband as victim of the wife; in the middle, by both spouses in mutual combat with each other; and at the other extreme, the more traditional role of the wife as the victim of the husband.

I have had the atypical experience of treating three different women in psychoanalysis during a time when spousal abuse was occurring. In each of the three cases, the women were the perpetrators, although also the victims in two of the cases. This paper will discuss the distinctive dynamics of each of these cases.

CASE 1

Jan was a newly married, attractive 26-year-old woman with a borderline personality structure who sought psychoanalysis because of depression and jealous rages. She suffered intense disappointment when her husband challenged her sense of entitlement, often becoming depressed and enraged and thinking her husband preferred other women. For example, she would start arguments with him if she thought he even glanced at another woman. Jan also complained of long-standing problems with separation from her parents, conflicts over her anger, and low self-esteem. Her history involved child abuse by her older brothers who beat her up unmercifully, and later, teased and taunted her about her large "tits and ass." They would pinch her breasts or try to pull down her bathing suit. She reported one situation during adolescence when her brother dragged her into a closet and attempted intercourse with her. Afterward, he threatened to hurt her if she told their parents. She felt that her parents never protected her despite her complaints and pleading. Jan experienced her mother as weak, clingy, and controlling. She perceived her father as cold, critical, and preferring his sons to her. After her parents' frequent fights, her mother would become depressed and come to Jan's room to complain or lock herself in the guest bedroom and drink herself into a stupor.

After three months of preparatory psychotherapy, Jan felt she was ready to start analysis in order to get to "the depth of my problems." She had achieved a greater sense of separation and individuation from her family as well as more control over her angry rages at her husband. Since she seemed to make constructive use of the psychotherapy and to respond positively to the interventions that addressed her dependency conflicts, we decided jointly that a trial psychoanalysis might be helpful for her continuing pervasive jealousy and self-defeating behaviors, such as not being able to hold down a job or stay in school. I was concerned about her early history of abuse, but Jan seemed insightful, verbal, and had clearly benefited from the lifting of her repression surrounding the physical and sexual abuse by her brother. Nonetheless, I was not sure whether she could tolerate the affects of a more intense treatment. But I hoped that her identification with her aggressor brother and her need to exploit me or feel exploited by me in the transference could be talked about and interpreted. She had not provided a history to indicate a severe impulse disorder that might contraindicate psychoanalysis.

As the analysis got underway, there was an uncontrollable regression of ego functioning such that reality and fantasy were not well differentiated. She became convinced that if her husband looked at or even had a thought about other women, he would surely act on it. Initially, we worked repetitively on the difference between having a thought and acting on it. She could acknowledge her fear of some of her own sexual thoughts and feelings, but had difficulty accepting her projections and externalizations in relation to her husband and eventually, to me. I also interpreted that her memories about her brothers and their abuses colored her perception of her husband and her need to provoke a fight with him in order to reassure herself he was not like them. What became more disturbing to me was the emergence of material suggesting a lack of intrapsychic boundary between Jan and her mother. Jan recalled being told by her mother that her father had numerous affairs when she was a child. She was convinced that she, like her mother, had married a man who also was unfaithful. The genetic determinants for provocatively berating her husband for even looking at other women became more clear, stemming from a pathologic identification with her mother that most likely defended against early loss (Asch, 1988). At this time in the analysis, there was an intensification of an idealized maternal transference paralleling the devaluation of her husband, despite my interpretations of the defensive splitting. She viewed me as the good mother who would protect her from her parents, her husband, and eventually, as I chipped away at her projections, her own thoughts.

Jan admitted to being more provocative with her husband. She would relentlessly interrogate him on his minute-to-minute activities away from her, push him away, and end up feeling alone and deprived. She tried taking a job, but could not concentrate because she was so preoccupied with her fear that her husband was cheating on her. I interpreted her desperate need to feel in control and master her intense feelings about her early traumas where she had been the passive victim. If she could push her husband away with her accusations, she would not have to fear his spontaneously leaving her. Jan felt "terrible" and ashamed after these verbal fights with her husband. I tried to help her to understand how her masochistic behaviors in relation to feeling alone, separate, and worthless only gave her a false sense of control as she ended up feeling so bad. That is, I confronted her role in provoking actively what she feared the most—abandonment and rejection. In reaction to the weekend absences or my vacation, Jan would miss a session, not call to cancel, and then return to her next session expecting me to verbally attack her. I interpreted her need to reassure herself that I would not get angry and throw her out when it was really she who was angry at me for leaving. In this context, Jan recalled that at age 6, her mother had become depressed and left the family to return to her own mother in Europe. Jan remembered this period as a chaotic time.

Her provocativeness toward her husband remained at a verbal level for about a year. However, his loss of his job coinciding with one of my vacations triggered a regression in Jan. She acted out both sides of her conflicts over separation, dependency, and control by becoming pregnant and then having an abortion; both Jan and her husband started spending more money compulsively. Finally she physically hit her husband for the first time in the marriage, provoking him into beating her.

Jan came into the office on a Monday morning following their fight with a black eye, bruises on her body, and a hearing loss sustained from a blow to her ear. She began the session with a pleasurable dream, ignoring her dramatic appearance. Jan soon explained with embarrassment that she had provoked her husband by accusing him of not being at work because he was having an affair. Her feelings had crescendoed so quickly that she then threw a glass at him, hitting him in the face. Jan felt a sense of passive terror and yet, was enraged at his perceived infidelity; depression and self-denigration were intense. I felt like a bad mother who had not sufficiently protected her. My previous interpretations to strengthen her ego capacity to handle her strong affects, to assist her to stay in control of her feelings and not act, especially in relation to separations, and her capacity to better differentiate reality from fantasy, seemed not to have taken hold. I wondered if my recommendation for analysis had been in her best interests. I also felt unsure of her husband's impulse control, now knowing he had a "prior" severe cocaine addiction.

Feeling that I had fostered too severe an ego regression, I asked Jan if she would like to sit up in a chair so we could face one another. Jan stated she was relieved to be able to look at me as she felt so out of control with rage toward everyone, including herself and me. I said that we could try to understand more about her angry feelings and the purpose and meaning of her own role in initiating the fight with her husband. We began by exploring what she was doing to protect herself from the recurrence of more physical violence. She felt she could not be protected by her parents because she was fighting with them as well. I was deeply concerned for her safety as well as for that of her husband. Therefore, I emphasized the reality issues and referred her to a Battered Woman's Center for consultation and possible refuge, if necessary. Jan called there, but never went for help. She did not want to leave her husband and desperately clung to the fantasy that everything would be okay if he would just be more available and never look at other women. It was evident that she had little insight into her provocativeness. The transference was equally colored by projection and externalization. She was furious at me, feeling that I was not available for her and that I enjoyed her plight because it made me feel superior. At the same time, she felt hopelessly dependent on me. I interpreted that these dependent rageful feelings toward her husband and me recapitulated how she had felt toward her mother, who because of her own problems was not available for Jan. In retrospect, staying in the here and now rather than making genetic interpretations might have been more useful.

In response to the interpretation, Jan recalled feeling lonely on the weekend for her husband and me. She poignantly stated, "I feel like I wanted more of you. Five days a week are not enough!" After the fight, she yearned for me or her parents to step in and do something. However, she was ashamed and did not tell her parents about the incident, fearing their rejection and disappointment. I interpreted that she wanted me to do something and be more active to stop her rages and to protect her because she felt unable to control herself. These feelings became more intense when we did not meet because she felt bereft without my support. At those times, her husband seemed like her brother and I like her parents. Jan responded with rage, "My parents were never there for me; now you and my husband aren't there for me either." She recalled how she used to provoke her brother in order to get him in trouble and to get her parents' attention. However, she only got beaten up as a result of these provocations while her parents never took a stand. Later in the session, she began to rationalize her husband's violence as a part of his stress from losing his job. Jan felt that if she could just get rid of her jealousy and "learn how to be good and less angry," the violence would be controlled.

She remained with her husband but continued her accusations until he decided finally to leave her (only reinforcing her belief that he had been cheating). Jan then became critical of her analysis because I was no longer her idealized savior. She came late, would not call to cancel, and eventually, stopped paying for her treatment, while continuing provocatively to spend freely at the stores. In those analytic sessions which she did attend, she displayed a range of ambivalent feelings from compliance to angry defiance. I interpreted her acting out of her rage at me and her wish to provoke me to be the victimizer as a way to rid herself of her own rage at me; then, she could feel that I was out of control, not her. She was angry at me as she felt that I could not protect her from herself and her husband. Any attempts to analyze her self-defeating behavior and her victory in defeating me at her own expense as a way to control her fears of closeness were to no avail. Eventually, we decided jointly to interrupt the analysis, agreeing that a supportive psychotherapy was a better form of treatment for her at that time.

In retrospect the analysis seemed to have aroused dependent, needy feelings which Jan could not contain within the transference. She regressed to a preoedipal sadomasochistic transference and acted it out in her marriage. After destroying that relationship she played out both roles with me, by submitting or defying, or by being the victim or victimizer. Jan perceived closeness as equivalent to submitting to a sadistic object.

Sadomasochistic defenses protected her from her fears of closeness in addition to reenacting the traumatic fights with her
brothers and parents. Her profound need to punish herself
created a negative therapeutic reaction that was not penetrated
by the analysis of her behavior and its motivation. Obviously,
many questions remain unanswered about the genetic determinants of Jan's self-destructive behavior and the best choice of
therapy for her. Did the analysis foster too great a regression
for this previously traumatized patient? Was psychoanalysis the
treatment of choice or might psychotherapy have been better?

CASE 2

Leanne was a 37-year-old married woman with characterologi-
cal problems, masochism, and depression. She regarded her
marriage of ten years as unstable; yet she came for treatment
for herself, not just to fix the marriage. She suffered from low
self-esteem, separation anxiety, and conflicts over her aggression. During the first year of analytic treatment, Leanne flooded
the hours with material about her chaotic external and internal
worlds; marital strife with her husband was the major focus of
the hours. At times of my absences, she would get into calami-
tous fights with him, wishing he were dead, and having many
frightening and guilt-provoking dreams of this occurring. I
helped her to look at, rather than act on her angry feelings in
her dysfunctional marriage. Gradually we connected these
fights to arguments that she had witnessed between her parents
during her early childhood. Recognition of the precipitants of
her rage allowed Leanne to identify a cycle in the abuse: escalation, violence, and reparation. Usually both she and her husband were drinking and some separation or anticipated separation was evident. After they both became aware of these
antecedents, Leanne could leave the house and go to a hotel
until things cooled off. Her leaving allowed for a safe atmo-
sphere and gave us time to analyze further the intrapsychic
determinants.

     Leanne was a second-born child who had always feared
her own rage, preferring instead to be the victim or the "door-
mat." She would receive bloody noses and bruises from her

younger brother and older sister rather than fight. She recalled tearfully, how at 3 or 4 years old, her mother would put her in the tub or hold her down, relentlessly scrubbing her genitals and poking at all of her orifices in order to cleanse them. She wanted to fight back, but just had to lie there. Leanne was also exposed to numerous physical fights between both parents before they divorced when she was 4 years old. Her parents continued to argue over the children even after the divorce, just as the children fought among themselves. Leanne was forced to visit her alcoholic father every other weekend. During her latency and adolescence, she would remain in bed during these visits, inciting his wrath.

In the analysis, Leanne described how her husband would constantly threaten to hurt her or hit her; at times he actually shoved her. Her husband was like her father, alcoholic and easily provoked. One three-day weekend, she and her husband got drunk, fought, and he pushed her down while both of them were partying with friends. She took to her bed depressed and feeling like a worthless victim. In analyzing the traumatic evening, Leanne realized how she, herself, had contributed to the chaos by getting drunk, calling him names, and doubting his loyalty and fidelity to her. She later found out that it was she who had first punched him in the stomach and then threw dishes about in the kitchen. Her husband's response was also one of depression and despair. He felt great remorse after the incident, and frightened of his own potential for violence and loss of control. Consequently he entered three-times-a-week psychotherapy with a colleague.

In contrast to Jan, Leanne was able to explore her own role in provoking her husband. The weekend of the fight was her one-year anniversary in treatment; she then became aware of an unconscious goal to have been finished with her analysis by that time. Finishing in a year would have reassured her that nothing was really wrong with her and that she had been "fixed" by me. She felt terrified of her neediness, realizing that she needed much more from me than a year, and enraged that I had not met her expectations.

Leanne had the fantasy that she could be as strong as any man and feared that she could kill if she got angry enough!

She knew how to get her husband angry and realized that her own anger and abuse were ways to defend against her separation anxiety and fears of neediness. Her hostility allowed her to feel powerful and in control of her feelings about being left, although she was in fact, the one thinking of leaving. The fight had also replicated her parents' own sadomasochistic warfare, as well as her passive role with her siblings, and thus, was an attempt at active mastery of an earlier, passively experienced traumatic situation. As a child, she had been beaten by her father for calling his sister a name. Leanne's parents had a "blow-out fight" in the kitchen, when her mother found out about the beating. My patient and her siblings watched with horror as dishes were thrown and her mother stabbed her father in the hand with a fork.

Leanne also remembered feeling that she was especially loved and cared for by her mother when she was in crisis, not when things were going well. During her childhood, Leanne would make herself get nosebleeds in order to stay with her mother and avoid being "shipped off" to her father's for the weekend. Even earlier, at 2 years of age, she had felt "shipped off" to school at the same time that her brother was born. She began to see her need to be victimized not only as a way to punish herself for her destructive rage (at her mother, husband, and brother), but also as a way to obtain her mother's special nurturance. Similar issues were evident in the transference. The fight with her husband created a crisis and allowed her to justify returning to the analysis to stay and be taken care of by me and to undo the trauma of being "shipped off" by her mother. I was aware of my guilty feelings at being the bad mother while I struggled with how to interpret her rage without gratifying her need for punishment.

Interpretation of Leanne's projections, externalizations, and need to take action, rather than to be passively abandoned (interpreted in the transference, the present, and the past) was effective in modifying Leanne's preference for action over understanding. Accepting her own rage at both her mother and father displaced onto her brother and husband, allowed her to control her actions. But Leanne maintained a tendency to blame herself and to cover up her husband's dysfunction. This self-blame provided her with a sense of control. If there were something wrong with her she could change it as opposed to accepting her own sense of helplessness at the thought that his problems might remain outside her control.

CASE 3

I will mention only briefly the case of Jackie, a 30-year-old woman who was married for eight years. She began analysis a few months ago for low self-esteem, depression, frigidity, and fears of flying, large crowds, and insects. Dependency feelings were stirred up in the analysis in response to the uncovering of memories of childhood disappointments and maternal care deficits. On a long weekend, she became angry that her husband had not taken care of her 2-year-old daughter in the way that she would have liked. He had tapped their daughter lightly on the head with a newspaper and the daughter cried. Jackie was outraged, slugged her husband, and later that evening, became aware of her wish to provoke him to hit her back. She was amazed at her lack of self-control and felt quite ashamed. At that point in the analysis, she felt very childish and needy about missing her analysis on the weekend. She felt that I could listen to her and take care of her, whereas her husband could not.

Talking about her loss of control led to painful memories of being hit repeatedly by her older brother during childhood. Her mother seemed never to be around to protect her. For the first time she began questioning why her mother was so unavailable. Jackie linked these memories to her fear of being a bad mother. She began to express her wish that I protect her (be a good mother), but realized that the protection which she wanted from me was to control her own angry feelings. She realized that she was furious at her mother whom she had felt not to be there to take care of her. Her husband was confused with her brother and mother in her mind and she now understood her wish that I be her protecting mother. Her need to act diminished with interpretation of her feelings of deprivation and their antecedents in relation to her disappointment with her mother and me.

DYNAMICS OF THE CASES

With these three patients, there are significant maternal and paternal deficits in parenting with obligatory pseudoparenting by the older siblings. Each woman had a history of sexual frigidity (they were anorgasmic with their husbands), multiple abortions, and a premarital pregnancy suggesting enactments of unresolved sexual and dependency conflicts. All three patients were financially independent, yet still felt held in bondage and controlled by their spouses. They were openly provocative and precipitated their own abuse by physically abusing their husbands. Eruption of aggressive behavior occurred on weekends in the context of an idealized maternal transference to their analyst; each of them described feeling dependent, needy, and devalued. Two of the three husbands had difficulties with drugs and alcohol, severe depression, and a history of being physically abused. There was the typical cycle of escalation of affect with regression, attack, counterattack, and retribution. After the attacks husband and wife alike felt guilty, their self-esteem plummeted, they lost confidence in themselves and their spouse, and they were frightened about their own rage as well as that of their spouses. The three wives returned to their sessions, feeling guilty, fearing my disapproval, and wishing for my support.

Real childhood trauma occurred in each of these women's childhoods. These patients had felt unprotected by unavailable parents who fought between themselves. They observed their parents abusing each other as well as their siblings. My patients experienced extraordinary guilt from their perceived past culpability for aggressive actions or fantasied transgressions. Divorce between the parents was present in the second two cases, while Jan's parents remained locked in a continuing sadomasochistic relationship. These women enacted with their husbands their parents' repetitive fights from their past.

Each of their mothers was perceived as being either victims or victimizers. In the minds of my patients, their mothers were unavailable or severely depressed. All three mothers of my patients alternated between being inordinately submissive and outwardly sadistic with their own husbands. The mothers conveyed to their daughters a martyred and passive-dependent maternal attitude. In wishing not to be like their mothers, my patients' own dependent needs were ego dystonic, and fear of these needs triggered their violent aggression. Submission and dependence were confused as psychic equivalents. The fighting would end up in reparation and making up with their husbands, thus gratifying their wishes for reunion with their internalized preoedipal mother. All three women had an ego ideal based on an ambivalent identification with their mother. As Leanne said, "I would shoot myself in the foot if I thought I was like my mother." This identification influenced their choice of spouse, their marital relationship, and their maternal attitudes. Jan and Leanne chose abusive and alcoholic men like their father and siblings. Jackie chose a husband very different from her father and brothers, yet also distant and, at times, unavailable and unprotecting like her mother.

The sibling attacks were painfully discussed by all three women. They in turn identified with the aggressor sibling and actively did to their husbands what was done to them. Thus, the sequelae of sadistic attacks by siblings seemed to create a tendency toward sadomasochism and a proclivity to misperceive current object relationships. These identifications with the sadistic sibling, however, should be regarded as an attempt at adaptation, unfortunately gone awry. Curiously, the psychoanalytic literature lacks any clear statement about the identifications with sadistic siblings, but instead emphasizes identifications with the sadistic parent. Berliner (1947, 1958) views masochism as reflecting the wish to be loved by the sadistic love object, usually the depriving preoedipal caretaker. Sugarman (1991) emphasizes identification with the aggressor as part of a triad for masochism involving the defenses of reversal, and turning passive into active. In masochists, Asch (1988) emphasizes the preoedipal need to control and preserve a primitive attachment as well as the wish to engender guilt. Unfortunately, these needs to perpetuate an object tie to the early objects result in self-defeating behaviors.

TREATMENT ISSUES

Some common transference–countertransference themes can be outlined. These include identification with the analyst as aggressor, wishes for unconditional love, need to control the analyst–mother to undo narcissistic vulnerability from the past, need to make the analyst feel guilty, and need to defeat the analyst and themselves as an expression of aggressive wishes and punishment for them. Initially these conflicts are externalized and exacerbate long-standing marital discord. Their regression during analysis was triggered by dependency wishes and longings to feel at one with the maternal object/analyst in order to feel safe, lovable, and valued. However, such idealized transference often defended against a sadomasochistic one. Jan projected her own rage onto me by viewing me as angry and sadistic. My silence was perceived by Jan as taunting and punishing her. At other times, she felt that I saw her as so insignificant, that she was not worth a word. She went to great lengths to evoke my anger and to make me feel guilty, and as worthless and angry as she. No matter what I interpreted, she continued to spiral downwards with a negative therapeutic reaction. Using the feelings that she evoked in me, I interpreted her need to defeat me and make me feel as helpless as her as a way both to express and defend against her rage, unfortunately at her own expense. She was actively setting up a rejection so as not to be the passive victim and ended up feeling more frustrated and defeated. Interpretations based on these difficult sadomasochistic transference and countertransference interactions must be tactful and well timed in order to avoid a sadomasochistic reenactment.

The crises created on the weekend by both Leanne and Jackie allowed for a fantasied union with the perfect mother who would always be warmly accepting. Their idealizing transferences defended against their fear of abandonment at the hands of a cold and rejecting mother (for Leanne) or an unavailable mother (in Jackie's situation). In all three cases, I was made to feel guilty for being the inadequately providing or protecting mother. This countertransference paradigm corresponds to a complementary identification (Racker, 1968) with the projected object relationship. Racker also warns against a masochistic transference–countertransference collusion in which the analyst's own unconscious masochism leads to countertransference errors.

SADOMASOCHISTIC ISSUES

Are these women masochists or sadists? Does a masochistic character disorder explain the origin of the mistreatment, brutality, and need to stay in a painful relationship? Contemporary nonanalytic theories stress learning theory and societal stereotypes and sex-role socialization norms to account for why women stay in sadomasochistic relationships. Hilberman (1980) proposes that women stay in relationships because they are dependent upon the fulfillment of their identities through their husband. The perception of women as powerless or unfeminine if independent and assertive may also play into and enhance these intrapsychic dynamics. Concepts about learned helplessness (Seligman, 1975; Walker, 1977–1978) attempt to explain why women stay in dangerous situations despite other options. As a child the victim experiences trauma that he or she cannot control and thus, later, the motivation to respond to trauma is greatly impaired. As with the Stockholm Syndrome, where the captive shows terror, immobility, love, and infantile dependence on the captor, such behaviors tend to promote survival (Hilberman, 1980).

Psychoanalytic views are often misrepresented as proposing that female masochistic characters seek punishment, and thus stay in relationships where they are chronically mistreated. In fact, guilt-ridden individuals who may be gluttons for punishment and may derive gratification from being in painful and humiliating relationships, have other multidetermined intrapsychic and interpersonal reasons for staying. These other needs and functions include the alleviation of guilt, identification with the sadistic partner, need for self-definition, maintenance of object ties, need for control, and reality issues (Meyers, 1988). Sugarman (1991) has discussed in detail the multiple developmental antecedents of masochism. Ideally, these complex personality dynamics must be uncovered, differentiated, and ultimately interpreted in both partners. A psychoanalytic approach may best be characterized by Anna Freud: "It is the psychoanalyst's job to examine external events from the aspect of their impact on internal life and trace their past, present and possible future significance" (A. Freud, 1981, p. 33).

Some of the mistaken ideas about the psychodynamics of victims of spousal abuse are based on false assumptions and understanding about masochism. Masochism can be described narrowly as a tendency for physical or mental suffering in order to achieve sexual gratification (Freud, 1919, 1924). Even with this definition, Freud acknowledged that suffering was a condition serving an adaptive–defensive function, rather than reflecting a propensity for instinctual gratification. A broad view of masochism (Maleson, 1985; Grossman, 1986) reflects a complex relationship between "perversion, character pathology, and gender, along with contributions of such salient developmental factors as preoedipal influences, object relationships, feminine superego formation, aggression, and defensive, adaptive, and narcissistic needs" (Levinson, 1991, p. 471). The culture-bound hypothesis proposed by Helene Deutsch (1944) that women are inherently passive, submissive, and masochistic is no longer considered seriously. The abused child of the past can be either the abuser or the victim in adult life. Masochistic tendencies can occur in both men and women, and may result from violence, as opposed to being the cause of it (Blum, 1982). With any case of spousal abuse, the analyst never assigns guilt, but tries to understand.

What about the husband beating? Although women may tend to handle aggression by internalizing it and turning it against themselves (Freud, 1933), outwardly sadistic behavior is not sex- or gender-linked. Violent behavior is not limited just to men. All three women were aware of their wish to hurt their partner. Together, we understood this wish as a need to feel in control of painful affects arising from their disappointment at not receiving the care for which they wished. They also expressed the wish to regain all the power in their marriages. We were able to link these longings back to preoedipal issues including their mothers' perceived lack of care and absolute power that gets displaced to their husbands. As early as 1931, Freud astutely observed, "many women who have chosen their husband on the model of their father, or have put him in their father's place, nevertheless repeat towards him, in their married life, their bad relations with their mother. The husband of such a woman was meant to be the inheritor of her relation to her father, but in reality he became the inheritor of her relation to her mother" (Freud, 1931, pp. 230–231).

Spousal abuse is similar to child abuse where the child's fear of the parent is coupled with the natural dependency. A. Freud (1981) noted that abused children tend to blame themselves and do not hate or avoid abusing parents as they fear loss of love and dependency gratification. Their dependency often gives rise to a passive-submissive position, which ties the victim to his or her aggressor. This form of masochistic behavior can be aroused in response to violence. Such masochistic binding to the abusing spouse can be even stronger because of the actual oedipal meaning of the marital relationship. The after effects of abuse may lead to sexual inhibition as seen in all three of my cases.

Spousal abuse is best understood as reflecting the roles that both partners play in reenacting and repeating abuse from their own past. There are always two victims; the sadist and the masochist are one and the same. Each member of the couple suffers from intense self-blame and loss of self-respect, although each may have different types of defensive patterns to handle these painful affects. Men may tend to deny their narcissistic vulnerability and dependency needs by acting out with violence, while women tend to become more self-effacing and self-blaming. Early childhood experiences and identifications serve as models for these conflicts and their specific defenses.

Psychiatric labeling and attributing blame to the victim, much like rape, are antitherapeutic. The victim–victimizer role must be understood in the context of defensive–adaptive needs if future incidents are to be avoided. Masochism is not an explanation but a description of psychological sequelae. A psychoanalytic perspective is one which emphasizes psychological understanding, not guilt, blame, or punishment and thus, further abuse.

In summary, a contemporary psychoanalytic understanding of wife battering regards it as a complex and multidetermined phenomenon, that interweaves developmental, environmental, psychological, and biological factors. Regardless of the causative factors, continued abuse will contribute to both partners (victim or victimizer) suffering greatly in self-esteem, respect, confidence, fear at the partner's rage, and their own fury.

114   Victims of Abuse

It undermines personality organization and induces further regression. A therapeutic, nonjudgmental stance rather than a punitive position must be taken by the therapist. Although there is a reality as to the physical damage, psychological consequences ensue for both parties and optimally, both partners require treatment.

REFERENCES

AMA News (1992), Family violence and the physician. Special issue of vol. 35, no. 1, January 6, 1992, pp. 1–43.
Asch, S. (1988), The analytic concept of masochism: A reevaluation. In: *Masochism: Current Analytic Perspectives*, ed. R. Glick & D. Meyers. Hillsdale, NJ: Analytic Press, pp. 93–115.
Berliner, B. (1947), On some psychodynamics of masochism. *Psychoanal. Quart,* 16:459–471.
——— (1958), The role of object relations in moral masochism. *Psychoanal. Quart.,* 27:38–56.
Blum, H. (1982), Psychoanalytic reflections on the "beaten wife syndrome." In: *Women's Sexual Experience: Explorations of the Dark Continent,* ed. M. Kirkpatrick. New York: Plenum Press, pp. 263–267.
Deutsch, H. (1944), Feminine masochism. In: *The Psychology of Women: A Psychoanalytic Interpretation,* Vol. 1. New York: Grune & Stratton, pp. 239–278.
Freud, A. (1981), A psychoanalyst's view of sexual abuse by parents. In: *Sexually Abused Children and Their Families,* ed. P. B. Mrazek & C. Kempe. New York: Pergamon Press, pp. 33–34.
Freud, S. (1919), A child is being beaten. *Standard Edition,* 17:177–204. London: Hogarth Press, 1955.
——— (1924), The economic problem of masochism. *Standard Edition,* 19:157–172. London: Hogarth Press, 1961.
——— (1931), Female sexuality. *Standard Edition,* 21:223–243. London: Hogarth Press, 1961.
——— (1933), Femininity. *Standard Edition,* 22:112–135. London: Hogarth Press, 1964.
Goodstein, R., & Page, A. (1981), Battered wife syndrome: Overview of dynamics and treatment. *Amer. J. Psychiatry,* 138:1036–1044.
Grossman, W. (1986), Notes on masochism: A discussion of the history and development of a psychoanalytic concept. *Psychoanal. Quart.,* 55:379–413.

Hilberman, E. (1980), The "wife-beater's wife" reconsidered. *Amer. J. Psychiatry*, 137:1336–1347.
Levinson, N. (1991), Masochism. In: *Female Psychology: An Annotated Psychoanalytic Bibliography*, ed. E. Schuker & N. Levinson. Hillsdale, NJ: Analytic Press, pp. 471–493.
Maleson, F. (1985), The multiple meanings of masochism in psychoanalytic discourse. *J. Amer. Psychoanal. Assn.*, 32:325–326.
Meyers, H. (1988), A consideration of treatment techniques in relation to the functions of masochism. In: *Masochism: Current Analytic Perspectives*, ed. R. Glick & D. Meyers. Hillsdale, NJ: Analytic Press, pp. 175–188.
Racker, H. (1968), *Transference and Countertransference*. New York: International Universities Press.
Seligman, M. (1975), *Helplessness: On Depression, Development, and Death*. San Francisco: W. H. Freeman.
Sugarman, A. (1991), Developmental antecedents of masochism: vignettes from the analysis of a 3-year-old girl. *Internat. J. Psycho-Anal.*, 72:107–116.
Time Magazine (1992), Rx for domestic violence: What the doctor should do. June 29, 1992, p. 38.
Walker, L. (1977–1978), Battered women and helplessness. *Victimology: An. Internat. J.*, 2:525–534.

Chapter 6

Posttraumatic Stress Disorder and the Legal System

Don Houts, M.D.

Posttraumatic stress disorder (PTSD) was a term created by the American Psychiatric Association in the 1980 DSM-III. But, by then, the concept of psychological trauma was already several hundred years old. Samuel Pepys, one of the two most important diarists of literature, experienced the burning of London in 1666 (as described in Mendelson, 1987). His writings reveal that he suffered from a full spectrum of PTSD symptoms. Charles Dickens was involved in a train wreck on June 9, 1865, when several coaches fell off a bridge. Ten were killed and 49 were injured. Dickens was not hurt, but he wrote, "I am curiously weak, weak as if I were recovering from a long illness. I begin to feel it more in my hand. I sleep well and eat well; but I write a half a dozen words, and turn faint and sick" (quoted in Mendelson, 1987, p. 48). It was some time before he was willing to ride by train again, and then he preferred slow trains.

In the middle to late 1800s, psychiatry was emerging as a separate specialty from neurology. As a part of that movement, Breuer and Freud (as discussed by Peebles, 1989) discovered a psychological means of treating neurological-like symptoms. They first organized their theory in 1893 around a notion of psychological reaction to trauma. This was also the period of the industrial revolution, and society was moving from a rural-agricultural society, to an urban-industrial one. Previously, when serious accidents occurred on the farm, extended families managed the consequences. Accidents began to happen more often away from home with the changes brought about by an industrial society, and there needed to be a way for the legal system to evaluate workers' responses to injuries, as well as people's responses to injuries outside the industrial arena. So, at the same time that psychiatry was developing as a discipline, civil courts became the venue for dealing with work-related injuries that happened away from home. Workers' compensation law was being created in Germany in the 1880s, and by the 1920s, nearly every state in the United States had adopted such legislation.

The development of psychiatry's influence in the courts lagged behind the development of the law for dealing with such injuries, however. In the early years, awards in civil cases or workers' compensation cases were tied to physical injury. The notion of a broken bone was comprehensible, while the notion of a "broken mind" was usually not. An 1882 English case was an early one in the literature (Mendelson, 1987) involving an emotional injury. A man was working in a telegraph office when a locomotive derailed as the result of a wrong switch being thrown. The locomotive smashed down one of the walls. Although the telegraph operator was not physically injured, he was granted temporary disability due to fright. But only six years later a woman, who had a similar case and who had won an award in a lower court, lost her case on appeal. She had been frightened when her buggy was briefly trapped on a railroad with the train approaching. Although no one doubted that she was emotionally harmed, the case was reversed because she was not physically injured or disabled, and specifically to discourage such claims. The language of the appeals court stated that to leave the lower court's ruling intact would be to leave "a wide field opened for imaginary claims."

It was through reactions to combat stress rather than through reactions to the stress of civil events that more sophisticated stress-response conceptualizations evolved. In the American Civil War, before the development of psychiatry, combat stress reactions were viewed as cowardice. By World War I workers compensation laws had been enacted in many states, and *shell shock* was a diagnostic term with clear-cut biological ties. The notion was that reactions such as tremors and paralysis resulted from neurocortical changes caused by the concussions of exploding artillery shells. But this theory did not last because people also developed the disorder without being near artillery; and once the war ended, many patients recovered, which disputed the theory of neurocortical changes. In 1920, the War Office officially recommended not using the term *shell shock* anymore.

By the time of World War I, Freud believed neurosis to be based on internalized conflicts, and he doubted that objective danger alone could give rise to a neurosis. After World War I, Ferenczi, Abraham, Simmel, and Jones applied combat stress reactions to unconscious conflict, and talked of "war neuroses" (Peebles, 1989). These analytic pioneers thought that conflict arose between a soldier's unconscious wishes to save his life by escaping and the conscious motives prohibiting the enactment of such wishes. In World War II, the term *combat exhaustion* was used, which still maintained a tie to Freud's idea of the wish to flee combat being at the root of most stress reactions.

Since then, the terminology and dynamic understandings have continued to evolve. In 1952, DSM-I (as quoted by Peebles, 1989) used the diagnosis "gross stress reactions," which referred to rather transient phenomena. In 1968, DSM-II used the diagnosis "transient situational disturbances" to refer to "fear associated with military combat and manifested by trembling, running and hiding" (p. 49). As reported above, it was not until 1980 that the term *posttraumatic stress disorder* finally appeared in DSM-III. Acute and delayed or chronic subtypes were described. But, in 1987, DSM-III-R dropped the acute versus chronic or delayed subtypes. While following the basic schema of the 1980 version, a few minor changes were made in the criteria for the diagnosis. In ICD-9, in 1991, the diagnoses used are "acute reaction to stress," and "prolonged posttraumatic emotional disturbance."

With these newer terms, one can see the growing interest in theories of trauma arising from information-processing models of the mind, and a movement away from a classical psychoanalytic focus. Horowitz (1974, 1976), who has written a number of articles since 1974 on this topic, suggested, reminiscent of Breuer and Freud's earlier affect-trauma model (as reviewed by Peebles, 1989), that a stress reaction was the mind's way of trying to grasp, organize, and integrate overwhelming stimuli. He pointed to the reexperiencing and avoidance or withdrawal from those stimuli (Horowitz, Winer, Kaltreider, and Alvarez, 1980). At present, it is generally accepted that PTSD can develop in people with no significant preexisting psychopathology. For example, a 1985 study (Mendelson, 1987) reported that 40 percent of survivors who had ejected from military aircraft experienced prolonged emotional symptoms, this being a group of young men who had been "highly selected" and trained, and had been presumably very emotionally stable. The need to eject from an aircraft, which would occur under only the most dire of circumstances, could easily overwhelm one's defenses.

Perhaps it is a refinement of the proposed neurocortical changes inferred in the discarded term *shell shock*, that we now know a number of neurological changes associated with combat trauma, including sympathetic arousal—increased baseline heart rate, increased systolic blood pressure; alterations in the neuroendocrine system—higher urinary norepinephrine/cortisol ratios; and alterations in the sleep-dream cycle—increased REM latency, less REM sleep, diminished stage 4 sleep, and reduced sleep efficiency (Kolb, 1987). Coming closer to the old term *shell shock* is the fact that some combat veterans never get used to sounds reminiscent of their original traumas, which suggests that some changes may be permanent. For example, being exposed to sounds of war results in increased heart rate while controls have no changes in such physiological measures (Kolb, 1987).

But the diagnosis of PTSD remains a controversial one from a number of perspectives. Some of these controversies involve questions of whether DSM-III and now DSM-III-R actually define a distinct clinical entity, because there is a clear overlap of anxiety, depressive, and dissociative features with other DSM-III-R diagnoses. However, as it now stands, PTSD is made up of four groups of diagnostic criteria, A, B, C, and D.

Category A requires "an event that is outside the range of usual human experience and that would be markedly distressing to almost anyone." In the text of DSM-III-R, but not formally a part of the criteria, is the phrase, "and is usually experienced with intense fear, terror and helplessness." Usually, the trauma is a significant one, such as a threat to one's life or physical integrity, or harm to a family member, or seeing another person suffer a major trauma.

Category B is for symptoms which suggest a reexperiencing of the traumatic event, and of the four symptoms, at least one must be applicable: recurrent and intrusive distressing recollections of the event; recurrent distressing dreams of the event; sudden acting or feeling as if the traumatic event were recurring (flashbacks); and intense psychological distress at exposure to events that symbolize or resemble an aspect of the traumatic event, including anniversaries of the trauma.

Category C is for an avoidance of stimuli associated with the trauma, or numbing of general responsiveness (not present before the event), needing at least three of seven symptoms: efforts to avoid thoughts or feelings associated with the trauma; efforts to avoid activities or situations that arouse recollections of the trauma; inability to recall an important aspect of the trauma; markedly diminished interest in significant activities; feelings of detachment or estrangement from others; restricted range of affect; and sense of a foreshortened future.

Category D has to do with increased arousal, and two symptoms out of six must apply: difficulty falling or staying asleep; irritability or outbursts of anger; difficulty concentrating; hypervigilance; exaggerated startle response; and physiological reactivity upon exposure to events that symbolize or resemble an aspect of the traumatic event.

A final criteria is that the minimum number of symptoms must last for a month, which infers that such symptoms constitute a "normal period of distress."

Category A is called the "stressor criteria," and the inclusion of the "stressor criteria" is the most controversial aspect of the diagnosis. Interestingly, this is an etiological factor and not an outcome or symptom, as are the other PTSD criteria. Furthermore, DSM-III-R is mostly a descriptive nosology. (Other exceptions to a strict disciplinary etiology are the diagnoses of organic mental disorder and substance abuse.) Regarding this etiological factor, there is ambiguity about what would be unusual and distressing to anyone; that is, a New Yorker observing a mugging in New York (far too common) versus a Midwestern tourist in New York seeing the same thing. In DSM-III-R, peculiarly, a car accident that results in physical injury is included, while a car accident that does not result in injury is excluded. The inclusion of this stressor criterion is also controversial in that some people develop the remaining symptoms in categories B, C, and D as a result of less significant traumas, but are not given the diagnosis because their initial event did not meet the criterion of category A. Less significant events, which can cause qualifying symptoms in B, C, and D, and which last more than a month, that are excluded from a PTSD diagnosis, are such things as a noninjury auto accident, money problems, family illness, burglary, bereavement, separation, legal troubles, breakup with a best friend, or involuntarily taking someone into one's house.

One study that casts doubt on this stressor criterion demonstrated that the experience of having been through a major disaster did not predict the level of PTSD symptoms, while such things as concurrent money difficulties, household illnesses, and so on did increase PTSD symptomatology significantly (Solomon and Canino, 1990). Of course, going through a disaster increases the likelihood of having one of these "secondary disasters." Nonetheless, it may be that such secondary disasters are even more important in predicting individual outcomes than the disaster itself. At any rate, one argument with which most psychoanalysts would concur merely suggests that rather than limiting the diagnosis PTSD to a major trauma, we should recognize a continuum with some people being more vulnerable to less extreme events leading to a full PTSD.

Another controversy about the diagnostic concept suggests that PTSD be removed from its link to anxiety disorders in DSM-III-R. For example, ICD-10 (as discussed by Davidson and Foa, 1991) has a separate category for disorders related to stress and trauma, of which PTSD is one, along with adjustment disorders and enduring personality change after a catastrophic stress. Yet PTSD shares common features with panic disorder, phobic anxiety, generalized anxiety disorder, and obsessive–compulsive disorder. Another suggestion is that the separate diagnosis of PTSD is not needed, since it is only the etiologic stressor criterion which makes the diagnosis different from one or more of the other anxiety disorders. This perspective suggests that PTSD symptoms are fully explained within these other diagnoses. The intrusive symptoms of PTSD can be understood as panic attacks brought on by a particular stimulus. The autonomic arousal in PTSD is similar to panic disorder.

Fear-avoidance is similar to that seen in simple phobia, special phobia, and agoraphobia. There is an overlap of PTSD symptoms with those of generalized anxiety disorder in terms of arousal, hypervigilance, exaggerated startle response, poor concentration, irritability, and sleep disturbance. Links to obsessive-compulsive disorder are the persistent, recurrent, intrusive, and unwelcome images, as well as the connection to symptomatic improvement from identical antidepressant medications. (Although PTSD responds to a variety of antidepressants, obsessive-compulsive disorder responds only to serotonergic drugs such as Clomipramine and fluoxetine). Extra support for subsuming PTSD under the rubric of anxiety disorders comes from data from family studies which show that first-degree relatives of veterans with PTSD have an elevated morbidity for anxiety, but not depression (Davidson, Smith, and Kudler, 1989).

Other features of PTSD invite a connection to dissociative disorders. In the hours or days after a trauma, some dissociative symptoms or gross behavioral disorganization are common. Flashbacks and psychogenic amnesia may also be a part of the picture, especially in younger victims. It seems that PTSD is closer phenomenologically than the other anxiety disorders to the dissociative disorders. But dissociation is not found in all patients with PTSD, and if present, it is probably of less clinical significance than the anxiety.

Other controversies about the PTSD diagnosis concern whether there should be more or fewer categories, whether all symptoms as now described belong in the category where they now reside, and the number of symptoms which should be required in each category to justify the diagnosis. For example, some studies show that symptoms in B are much more prevalent after actual natural disasters than symptoms in C and D. Thus, perhaps the criteria for a diagnosable response to a traumatic event have been improperly written, or perhaps the measures for assessing responses have been inadequate.

Complicating this diagnostic quandary is the fact that PTSD is a disorder which may coexist with other disorders in the same individual. Such diagnoses as somatization disorder, schizophrenia, schizophreniform disorder, panic disorder, social phobia, obsessive-compulsive disorder, generalized anxiety disorder, alcohol abuse, and depression are all frequent in PTSD (Davidson and Foa, 1991).

One prospective study of forty-eight people with similar leg fractures failed to find differences between the poor outcome group with PTSD at six months postinjury and the good outcome group (without PTSD at six months) with respect to demographics, number of preceding life events, the presence of personality traits or disorders, and whether or not compensation was being sought (Feinstein and Dolan, 1991). Also, an excess of physical morbidity at six months was not present in the poor outcomes. Two variables were found to predict the poor outcome, an initial Impact of Events (IES) scale, developed by Horowitz et al. (1980—IES—15-item self-report of intrusiveness and avoidance symptoms) and weekly alcohol use above their respective medians; but the former was the more powerful measure. Thus, the way an individual initially assimilates and deals with a traumatic event ultimately has the greatest influence in determining the outcome. Levels of distress postaccident, suggestive of early failure to cognitively master a stressful situation, predict poor prognosis. This study clearly supports the need for good psychological response teams for major disasters.

Nearly all of the eighty-two cases which I have evaluated since 1981 have been within a medicolegal setting. Most are pretty straightforward examples of traumatic events that can happen anywhere, most of which just happened to occur at work. Although it is peripheral to the topic of PTSD, in thinking about such cases it is important to keep in mind that causation is crucial from a medicolegal perspective. But causation in the legal arena is not the same as in the psychiatric arena. The issue, legally, is one of proximate cause, which can more simply be explained as the "but for" rule. Someone may have been in a fragile emotional state ("eggshell"), but would not have become depressed/anxious/disabled "but for" the given event.

The 82 cases have occurred from the following traumas:

Motor vehicle accidents	19	(rarely the driver)
Miscellaneous industrial accidents	9	(explosion, burns)
Attacks and/or rapes	12	
Robberies	7	
Falls	3	
Dog attacks	4	(one quite minor)
Shootings (victim; observer; shooter)	4	
McDonalds massacre	2	(plus head paramedic, without PTSD)
Electrocution	2	

Other miscellaneous:

Actual Vietnam PTSD ($\times 4$) who had attorneys who tried to use that diagnosis in an attempt to defend later crimes (two murders) and bogus industrial claims
Bulldozer accidents $\times 2$
Korean POW
Holocaust survivor, delayed until later physical injury
Death of husband due to malpractice
Police abuse
Ice skating injury to daughter
Airplane propeller
Paramedic, cumulative trauma
Buried alive
Ran over another fisherman in speedboat
Las Vegas hotel fires
Knocked over by a crane
Best friend decapitated in fishing accident
Subacute sexual harassment

Ages of patients:
```
<20 ( 3)
20–29 (29)
30–39 (24)
40–49 (16)
50–59 ( 6)
>60 ( 4)
```

A few other facts were discerned from examining these cases. More than one Axis I diagnosis was present in forty-nine of the cases, major depression and psychological factors affecting physical illness being the most common. Personality disorders were present in twenty-six of the cases. It is important to note that if a patient has an antisocial personality disorder it does not mean the diagnosis of PTSD is necessarily false. Examples where there has been a clear PTSD in the face of a prior antisocial personality include the airplane propeller case, one electrocution, and one attack. However, in the latter case, it was antisocial behavior which provoked the brutal physical attack that led to the PTSD. There were Axis III diagnoses in sixty-three of these cases. Examples of patients without an Axis III diagnosis were the fireman in the hotel fires, a speed boat operator who ran over his friend; a cop who witnessed the shooting of a hostage; a man who was buried alive in a ditch; two uninjured employees who were present at the McDonalds San Ysidro massacre; a robbery victim; the mother of a small girl who was injured in an ice skating accident; a victim of police verbal harassment; a wife whose husband died as the result of medical malpractice; and a fisherman who lost his best friend in a gruesome accident at sea.

The term *PTSD* has often been used loosely by psychiatric "expert witnesses," who have not attended to the necessary DSM-III-R criteria because the diagnosis has a certain "legitimacy" in the court system. The concept of stress caused by a trauma is easily understood by a juror or a compensation board. The notion of external causation is easier to justify than the inferred "personal weakness" associated by many people with depression, anxiety, or adjustment disorder. Luckily, accuracy of diagnosis in the legal system is not as important as it is in psychiatric academic settings because financial awards are not given for a particular diagnosis, but for the degree of injury or disability.

The major task of psychotherapy with a patient who has PTSD is to help them deal with loss in some form. The loss may be of physical function, the loss of a job, the loss of a loved one, or perhaps just the loss of an overall sense of safety in the world at large. Sometimes a patient's decision to pursue legal recourse for their trauma actually serves the therapy in terms of bringing to the patient a sense of mastery where none had been. But another way that people can be victimized is through the very process of litigating the event in which they were traumatized.

Filing a claim of psychiatric injury gives the defense the right to investigate all aspects of someone's life, including their past history. All psychiatric records can eventually be subpoenaed. I routinely warn patients about the enormous emotional strain of pursing a "stress claim" since the legal process can serve as a further anchor to the time of the traumatic event and deter rather than facilitate emotional progress.

A final word needs to be said about the outcome in the litigation of such cases. The term *greenback poultice* was used by Scrignar (1988) who wrote:

> Many physicians and jurists are of the opinion that traumatized patients with significant psychiatric illness will recover following successful litigation. However, Daniel Sprehe (1984) in a follow-up of 108 patients over a ten-year period has reported that 78 percent of his patients with significant psychiatric illnesses were "no better" and 58 percent were not working following successful adjudication of their cases. The "greenback poultice" is more fantasy than fact. As Valliant (1981) has pointed out, continuing psychiatric therapy following settlement of the legal issues is required if traumatized patients are ever to return to the work place [p. 95].

Leonore Terr (1988) has reported several studies since 1983 about the children involved in the Chowchilla school bus kidnapping of 1976. All twenty-five of the children, who had

128   Victims of Abuse

ranged between five and teenage years, still had some manifestations of PTSD, and there was considerable similarity of syndromes over the ages. None were "toughened" by the experience. Thus, one should not be surprised when patients continue
to report PTSD symptoms long after the event, even when
litigation was quite successful.

REFERENCES

American Psychiatric Association (1968), *Diagnostic and Statistical Man-
    ual of Mental Disorders*, 2nd ed. (DSM-II). Washington, DC:
    American Psychiatric Press.
——— (1980), *Diagnostic and Statistical Manual of Mental Disorders*, 3rd
    ed. (DSM-III). Washington, DC: American Psychiatric Press.
——— (1987), *Diagnostic and Statistical Manual of Mental Disorders*, 3rd
    ed. rev. (DSM-III-R). Washington, DC: American Psychiatric
    Press.
Davidson, J. R. T., Smith, R. D., & Kudler, H. S. (1989), Familial
    psychiatric illness in chronic posttraumatic stress disorder. *Com-
    preh. Psychiatry*, 30:339–345.
Davidson, R. T. D., & Foa, E. B. (1991), Diagnostic issues in posttrau-
    matic stress disorder: Considerations for the DSM-IV. *J. Abnorm.
    Psychol.*, 100:346–355.
Feinstein, A., & Dolan, R. (1991), Predictions of posttraumatic stress
    disorder following physical trauma: An examination of the stres-
    sor criterion. *Psycholog. Med.*, 21:850–891.
Horowitz, M. (1974), Stress response syndrome, character style, and
    dynamic psychotherapy. *Arch. Psychiatry*, 31:768–781.
——— (1976), *Stress Response Syndromes*. New York: Jason Aronson.
——— Wilner, N., Kaltreider, N., & Alvarez, W. (1980), Signs and
    symptoms of posttraumatic stress disorder. *Arch. Gen. Psychiatry*,
    37:85–92.
ICD-9 (1991), *International Classification of Diseases: Clinical Modifica-
    tion*, 9th rev. ed. Salt Lake City: Med-Index Publications.
Kolb, L. (1987), A neuropsychological hypothesis explaining posttrau-
    matic stress disorder. *Amer. J. Psychiatry*, 144:989–995.
Mendelson, G. (1987), The concept of posttraumatic stress disorder:
    A review. *Internat. J. Law & Psychiatry*, 10:45–62.
Peebles, M. J. (1989), Posttraumatic stress disorder: A historical per-
    spective on diagnosis and treatment. *Bull. Menninger Clinic*,
    53:274–286.

Scrignar, C. B. (1988), *Posttraumatic Stress Disorder: Diagnosis, Treatment, and Legal Issues*, 2nd ed. New Orleans, LA: Bruno Press.

Solomon, S. D., & Canino, G. J. (1990), Appropriateness of DSM-III-R criteria for posttraumatic stress disorder. *Compreh. Psychiatry*, 31:227–237.

Sprehe, D. J. (1984), Workers' compensation: A psychiatric follow-up study. *Internat. J. Law & Psychiatry*, 7:165–178.

Terr, L. C. (1988), What happens to early memories of trauma? A study of twenty children under age five at the time of documented traumatic events. *J. Amer. Acad. Child & Adol. Psychiatry*, 27:96–104.

Valliant, G. E. (1981), Natural history of male psychological health: Work as a predictor of positive mental health. *Amer. J. Psychiatry*, 125:1435–1439.

Chapter 7

Somatization as a Response to Trauma

Ada M. Burris, M.D.

THE IMPORTANCE OF THE BODY

From the earliest days of infancy the body is used to communicate. Infants have intense emotional experiences intimately connected with a growing awareness of their bodies. Hunger, cold, and pain are recorded mentally as bodily distress. Warmth, holding, and satiation are recorded as contentment. Therefore it is not surprising that in times of great distress the mind will bypass the mental symbolic chain of thought and word expression and send warning signals through the body, its earliest carrier of messages. The dual development of body image and expression of affect must be investigated if we are to understand somatic response to trauma.

We know more about the development of body image than we know about affect differentiation. The primary caretaker, usually the mother, acts as stimulator and container for the infant, helping him or her to define body boundaries. She tries to answer signals from the body to keep the child as comfortable and free from pain as possible. The child comes to trust the caretaker to attend to its needs and it begins to understand its own body's needs and boundaries. Very young infants can be seen exploring their bodies through sight and touch and they

131

also mimic facial expressions and gestures of the caretaker. As the perceptual apparatus matures, a clearer picture emerges through sight, touch, and proprioception. The development of language, the increased motility and fine muscle coordination, and the acquisition of capacity for symbolization, further the development of an internal picture of the body.

Between 18 and 36 months, children develop a sense of themselves as a whole, separated person with a body that works. There is an awareness of gender identity, body boundaries, and a mental representation of body image. This *core* body image remains essentially intact, despite the vicissitudes of normal growth, unless there is severe trauma, illness, or loss of the primary caretakers. Severe attacks on the integrity of the body are major insults to the child's sense of an intact, valued, and loved body image. There is instead an undefined, unstable, and damaged self-image with little chance for developing or increasing self-awareness and self-esteem.

THE DEVELOPMENT OF AFFECTS

Information about the development of affects is not as clear. Henry Krystal in 1974 proposed a developmental line for affect. He suggested that the earliest affect precursors were the bodily states of contentment and distress, out of which developed pleasurable and painful affects. These things distinguish this early affect. First, it is experienced as a bodily sensation; second, it is not put into words; and third, it is not differentiated but remains a general sensation of pain and pleasure. The task of the growing child then, is to differentiate the general sensation of pain or pleasure into specific affects, to verbalize the experience, and to desomatize the feelings.

Just as we develop a core body image, so also, according to Emde (1984), do we develop an affective core. This provides us with "a core of continuity for our self-experience, an affective self throughout development. It helps us to get in touch with our own consistent feelings, so we know we are the same in spite of the many ways we change; and, it helps us to get in touch with others and be empathetic" (Emde, 1984, p. 38). The development of the affective core proceeds as follows. Out of the general distress affect there is a gradual differentiation of anger, shame, guilt, envy, anxiety, and depression. The feeling of depression can further be differentiated into feelings of despair, grief, sadness, anger turned inward, and so on. The general feeling of contentment can also be differentiated into security, pride, joy, love, and tenderness.

Gradually, as feelings are recognized and identified, they are put into words. This is the development of verbalization. Words become containers for affects. With the growing tolerance for affects and the naming of affects, understanding and mastery develop and there is greater self-awareness. The process of self-care develops including healthy attention to the body's needs, self-soothing, forgiving, appreciating, and making right the internal world.

The third part of the maturational process is desomatization. There is a gradual recognition of what is psychological and what is somatic. Krystal (1982) says, "Affective responses that are primarily somatic are felt as dangerous and overwhelming and call attention to themselves rather than to the emotional states that they signal" (p. 365). Increasing recognition of the emotional state decreases the need for somatic response, and increases the ability to use the affects as signals.

SOMATIC COMMUNICATION OF TRAUMA

We can now explore the consequences of major trauma as it relates to children and adults, especially as it relates to expressions of somatization. Krystal believes that in the face of massive trauma, the development of affect is arrested in young children. In adults, there is a regression to previous levels of functioning. The response then in both children and adults is dedifferentiation, deverbalization and resomatization. We may see the development of alexithymia, which means the inability to recognize, name, or verbalize emotions; anhedonia, which is the inability to experience pleasure; or somatization, which is the bypassing of mental processes and language and direct expression of danger in the body. As Joyce McDougall (1980) says, "Mental conflict is disavowed and thrown out of the psyche to be discharged through the body and its somatic functioning instead" (p. 419). She believes that this shift from mental functioning to bodily discharge is particularly likely to happen when there has been a catastrophic narcissistic wound or an unexpected object loss. The following examples are meant to illustrate this more primitive means of communication, and how some conflicts and affects are expressed through the body.

Somatization may be seen when there is a fear of being overwhelmed by affect. A young woman experienced severe and incapacitating leg pain several years into her therapy. There was even evidence of progressive muscle weakness, but no medical cause could be found. In the therapy sessions, she could talk of nothing else than her leg pain and her fear of incapacitation. I began to feel very anxious and helpless, and my wish was to send her from specialist to specialist to find the cause of the mysterious malady. After much work on the part of both of us, she was able to uncover memories of being exposed to highly charged sexual activity as a young child. The sexual encounters to which she was witness, but not participant, were not only sexually charged but full of aggression and danger. As a very young child she had been exposed to highly stimulating and fearful affects which threatened to overwhelm her. When in therapy she was threatened with the return of the memories as well as reliving the affects, she bypassed them by developing a very serious and disabling physical illness. In the transference, she was terrified that I had become her careless, sadistic caretaker, and at times I could begin to feel the helplessness she must have felt as a young child. Working through the experience enabled her to gradually identify and put into words the fears that the overwhelming erotic feelings combined with the danger would lead to her fragmentation, loss of identity, inability to function, and finally to her death. The ability to identify those threads of affect enabled her to master her anxiety, to tolerate the feelings without fear of falling apart, and to use the therapy and her own resources to soothe and care for the damaged and frightened little girl part of herself. Almost imperceptibly, the focus of attention shifted away from the somatic complaints and back to the intrapsychic conflict.

Somatic illness may represent confusion of the body boundaries and issues of separation-individuation. McDougall (1989) in her book *Theaters of the Body* describes a woman who suffered from a serious neurodermatitis. The skin swelled, itched, and became red and infected. There was real concern for her welfare. As she became able to express in words what her body was trying to communicate, a very dependent, unfulfilling, unpredictable connection to her mother emerged. She became aware of enormous rage and said, "As long as my skin screamed, I knew I was alive. And so were the others! I hadn't killed them. My rage only hurt me." In this case, the skin represented the painful connection to her mother which she hated but felt unable to break. She repeated this ambivalent relationship with her therapist. She feared merging with the therapist and losing her identity. Yet, separation meant being alone, and uncared for, which to her infant self meant death. If her skin no longer swelled or itched, she would be uncertain if she was separate. Her painful skin reassured her of her boundaries, and that she was held together and would not fall apart. In this case, the illness was preserved to prove that she was alive and separate from her mother, but also in a paradoxical way was serious enough to lead to her death as payment for her guilt about her rageful wish to be separate.

Somatization may be an identification with an ambivalently held internal object. A woman in analysis had always been her alcoholic mother's caretaker. She had grown up in a chaotic home with frequent moves, a seductive stepfather, and an unreliable mother. It was an unpredictable, uncertain environment. She became "superdaughter" and took care of everyone. Mother was always physically ill and anxious, so that in addition to caring for her own family as an adult, she continued to care for her mother until she died. In the year following mother's death, she alternately raged at her for the injustices she felt and mourned her loss with tears and great sadness. I thought the work was going along well when she developed severe gastrointestinal problems. The pain, nausea, and inability to eat became a serious medical problem and my competent, take-charge patient became a whining, complaining, very sick child. I found myself irritated with her, and scared that the therapy had precipitated a regression which could be very damaging to her. Finally, I became aware that she had become her mother. I was feeling the anxiety she had felt as a child. During the time I thought she had been doing the work of mourning, she was probably in fact "taking care of me." She was being the good patient, and I was happy indeed to have such smooth sailing. We discovered that her somatic disorder was an identification with the sick mother and a way to hang onto her. As McDougall (1980) says, "An internal object that cannot be relinquished cannot be mourned" (p. 4). It was a long, hard process to free herself from this destructive identification with the mother, to finish the mourning process and to discover her own separate identity.

TREATMENT CONSIDERATIONS

In all of these examples it is important to remember that there are serious and sometimes life-threatening illnesses. Medical evaluation and treatment must be a part of the therapy. McDougall has on occasion even discontinued psychotherapy for periods of time until the somatic situation stabilizes. In psychosomatic illnesses, it is important to remember that the somatization is a form of communication that must be understood and interpreted. Some have called it a form of acting out; that is, doing to avoid remembering. In order to understand this communication we must pay close attention to everything that is said in describing the symptoms. This will give us clues to the conflicts, the internal objects involved, and the affects. It is also important to pay attention to our own responses. What we feel may be a clue to what the patient is feeling and projecting into us. The task is to translate these feelings into words and give them back to the patient in a helpful way. There will be some difficult times because there is often a paucity of dreams, a decrease in free association, a lack of memories, and all the things we use to advance our understanding of patients. Often all we have to work with are monotonous recitations of the somatic symptom. It takes great patience to listen and try to hear something new and useful. We are often put into the place in transference of a mother with a preverbal child whose messages to us are cries and sounds which we must interpret as best we can, or we are put into the role of helpless victim of an abusive caretaker.

In the regressed place of somatization, the fears of return of trauma, or the recognition of the primitive, unconscious dangers, present untold anxiety to these patients. There are primitive fears of loss of body integrity, loss of identity, fears of fragmentation, of going crazy and of dying. It is our task as therapists to help our somatic patients to gain a confidence in the integrity of their bodies and to help them name, express, and tolerate feelings so that they can ultimately use the feelings as signals which can be utilized for growth, and a confidence in the integrity of their minds.

REFERENCES

Emde, R. (1984), The affective self. In: *Frontiers of Infant Psychiatry*, Vol. 2, ed. J. Call & R. Tyson. New York: Basic Books.

Krystal, H. (1974), The genetic development of affects and affect regression. *Annual of Psychoanalysis*, 2:98–126. New York: International Universities Press.

——— (1982), Alexithymia and the effectiveness of psychoanalytic treatment. *Internat. J. Psychoanal. Psychother.*, 9:353–378.

Levine, H. (1990), *Adult Analysis and Childhood Sexual Abuse*. Hillsdale, NJ: Analytic Press.

McDougall, J. (1980), Psychosomatic states, anxiety, neuroses and hysteria. *Contemp. Psychoanal.*, 16:417–459.

——— (1989), *Theaters of the Body*. New York: W. W. Norton.

PART II

Treatment Challenges with the
Traumatized Patient

Chapter 8

Repetition, Reenactment, and Trauma: Clinical Issues in the Analytic Therapy of Adults Who Were Sexually Abused as Children

Howard B. Levine, M.D.

HISTORICAL

In 1896, Freud proposed that the *universal* etiological agent in neurosis was a sexual seduction in childhood. While he no doubt did so under the influence of actual reports of childhood seductions by *some* of his patients, there is much to imply that in many of the cases treated in this early phase of his work, the evidence that Freud used for the reconstruction and interpretation of childhood sexual trauma was highly speculative. In a recent article reviewing the evolution and evidentiary basis of Freud's "seduction theory," Schimek (1987) concluded that Freud did not turn his back on firm evidence of actual childhood trauma, as Masson (1984) has claimed. Rather, Schimek noted that at this point in his career, Freud was an overzealous interpreter of childhood sexual injuries and would take this or

Portions of this chapter were adapted from *Adult Analysis and Childhood Sexual Abuse*, ed. H. B. Levine. Hillsdale, NJ: The Analytic Press, 1990.

141

that current symptom and find a way to forcefully insist to his patients that it must be the symbolic equivalent or consequence of a memory of a childhood sexual trauma.

Freud, himself, came to recognize the limitations of this early theory, when his self-analysis and broadening clinical experience led him to implicate as seducers of children men whom he knew to be of impeccable integrity, including his own father! The resulting crisis in his thinking ultimately led Freud to appreciate the central importance of unconscious fantasy in human mental life and gave birth to psychoanalysis as we know it today. Years later, in his "Autobiographical Study," Freud (1925) described this momentous change in his views as follows:

> I was at last obliged to recognize that these scenes of seduction had never taken place, and that they were only phantasies which many patients had made up or which I myself had perhaps forced on them. . . . When I had pulled myself together, I was able to draw the right conclusions from my discovery: . . . I had in fact stumbled for the first time upon the *Oedipus complex.* . . . Moreover, seduction during childhood retained a certain share, though a humbler one, in the aetiology of neuroses [pp. 34–35].

Freud's subsequent exploration of the influence of innate sexual and aggressive drives on mental functioning and development, and the corresponding turn from historical to psychic reality that followed upon the revision of the seduction theory, led to a relative deemphasis of external factors in the elaboration of psychoanalytic theory. However, while Freud no longer believed that childhood sexual seduction was a *universal* factor in the etiology of neurosis, his continued references to actual childhood trauma in his writings and clinical work indicate that he never lost sight of the potential significance that real childhood events, including actual sexual trauma, had for the development of neurosis (see Levine [1990, pp. 5–10]; Baranger, Baranger, and Mom [1988] for more detailed discussions of these issues). Indeed, as a clinical therapy, psychoanalysis would be inconceivable without consideration of the impact of actual childhood experience on emotional development.

Where Freud's revised theories, and those of later psychoanalytic contributors, departed from the early seduction hypothesis was in their recognition that the experience and sequelae of actual trauma occur in relation to a far more complex view of mental functioning and development than was originally postulated. In contrast to the seduction hypothesis, current analytic theories take into account intrinsic factors that relate to constitutional givens (e.g., strength of drives or innate capacities for the development of ego functions), and study the ways in which they influence processes of perception, memory, and the construction of experience. Thus, the ultimate meanings that a childhood traumatic experience, sexual or otherwise, will come to have for an adult will be complex and multidetermined (Kris, 1956). They will go beyond the details of the actual trauma itself to reflect: (1) how that trauma is experienced by the child in line with pretraumatic and ongoing developmental issues and conflicts; (2) elements of the various ways in which 'the trauma was responded to by the child and the child's network of supportive objects and caretakers (i.e., how the trauma was elaborated in fantasy and play, connected with character and symptom formation including the regressive reversal of previously attained levels of development, whether or not the child was believed by others or helped to deal with the trauma); (3) contributions of the trauma to subsequent developmental disturbances; and (4) how the affects and memory traces connected to the trauma underwent repression, distortion, and symbolic elaboration (for an illustration and discussion of these complex developmental issues, see Levine [1990], esp. pp. 11–17). In the words of one colleague, "We cannot know whether, in what ways, or to what extent a given incident is traumatic until the future happens!"

In fairness to many critics of psychoanalysis, the new emphasis on internal factors did lead to a relative neglect in recognizing the extent and consequences of actual childhood sexual trauma and incest. This relative neglect mirrored and was part of the more general denial of childhood sexual injury and incest that still exists in our society today. However, with the increasing awareness in recent years that childhood sexual abuse is a major problem in our culture from which no class or segment of our society is immune, analysts have more actively joined in the vigorous pursuit and investigation of the problems presented by the treatment of patients who were sexually abused as children.

The hypotheses and formulations that follow are drawn from the combined clinical experience of one such group, colleagues at the Boston Psychoanalytic Society and Institute, with whom I have been meeting for the past three years to study the analytic treatment process in adults who were sexually abused as children. Most of the cases reviewed were in analysis or intensive psychotherapy (two to four times a week). As a result, our sample may be skewed by being drawn from the higher end of the spectrum. However, from what I have been able to gather in talking with colleagues in various places around the country, there is much that we have learned that is relevant to less intensive treatments and to therapeutic work with all such patients, no matter how severe their degree of illness.

DEFINITION AND SYMPTOMS

Following the work of Steele (1990), we define childhood sexual abuse as:

> [T]he involvement of dependent, developmentally immature children in sexual activity that they do not fully comprehend, without consideration for the child's stage of psychosocial sexual development. [This can occur in many forms and] at any age from infancy through adolescence with various family members, relatives or strangers. It can be a single, isolated incident or repeated frequently over many years. It may be homosexual or heterosexual with either girls or boys, and involve anything from fondling to full genital intercourse or variations of oral and anal contact. It may be done with some degree of love and gentleness or involve verbal threats and physical violence.

All of these variables have a bearing on what the sexual experience means to the child and how it is woven into the child's psychic development and affects later behavior. . . . [T]he sexual events themselves are not the simple, direct cause of subsequent difficulties. . . . The trouble comes when the sexual activities are instigated by a person older than the child and are beyond the child's ability to truly understand or emotionally manage the affects and conflicts that are generated. The activity is not a consensual one between peers but is exploitative, more for the satisfaction of the perpetrator than the child victim. . . . [T]he degree of trauma is related to the discrepancy between the intensity of the noxious stimulae and the ability of the child's ego to cope [pp. 21–22].

The broad range of possible variables involved in childhood sexual trauma means that adults who were sexually abused as children are members of a heterogeneous group that defies simple categorization. Although recent studies have indicated that a very high percentage of hospitalized borderline patients have an underlying history of childhood sexual abuse, a positive history of a childhood sexual trauma will not be correlated with any one particular type of character structure. It may be associated with neurotic, borderline, or psychotic character formations.

Similarly, there have been a wide variety of adult symptomatic consequences of childhood sexual trauma reported in the literature (e.g., Goodwin, Simms, and Bergman, 1979; Steele and Alexander, 1981; Lindberg and Distad, 1985; Bryer, Nelson, Miler, and Krol, 1987; Shengold, 1989; Deblinger, McLeer, Atkins, Ralphe, and Foa, 1989; Bernstein, 1990; Burland and Raskin, 1990; Levine, 1990). These include depression, low self-esteem, phobias and anxiety states, impulsive or self-punitive behaviors, eating disorders, learning disabilities, cognitive dysfunctions, self-doubting and confusional states, promiscuity, seductive behavior, sexual inhibitions and dysfunctions, distrust of others, depersonalization, dissociative phenomena, psychosomatic, self-destructive or self-mutilating reactions.

Many of the symptoms encountered are related to the patients' reliance upon a repertoire of dissociative defense mechanisms, such as ego splitting, denial, and dissociation. These follow from the injured child's attempts to control or eliminate the overwhelming affects of the traumatic situation by averting their attention, both at the time of the injury, and subsequently, at such moments when the trauma might be recalled. The long-term effect of these defenses may range from a true forgetting (repression) of some or all of the trauma to a failure to take its emotional consequences into account (disavowal, denial, or splitting). Thus, in therapy, patients may repress or knowingly withhold the fact of a childhood trauma in the course of an evaluation or even a lengthy treatment or they may report details of the trauma without feelings, emotional engagement, or a sense of its relevance for or impact upon their lives.

When neglected or forgotten memories "return" in dissociated or symbolic forms, they may contribute to such phenomena as psychosomatic symptoms, sexual dysfunctions, nightmares, panic attacks, impulsive behaviors, or the "flashback" experiences described in the literature on posttraumatic stress disorders (PTSD), all of which, incidentally, may bear a striking resemblance to the hysterical attacks described by Breuer and Freud (1895) in *Studies on Hysteria*. The effects of repressed or dissociated memories of childhood sexual trauma on adult sexual functioning can be particularly troublesome. Foreplay, intromission, or coitus may associatively trigger memories related to past traumatic experience resulting in intrusive affects or images or disturbed bodily sensations. The latter may range from displeasure, aversion, or physical pain to muted feelings, frigidity, and anorgasmia. Often, patients will report seemingly incomprehensible feelings, such as rage during the sexual act, even when they had initiated or consented to lovemaking. Kramer (1990) called these physical sensations, which can persist throughout adulthood and which she believes often follow from childhood incestuous contact with either father or mother, "*somatic memories*."

Given the wide range of possible adult consequences of childhood sexual abuse, it is particularly important not to pre-judge the meaning or impact of a given traumatic experience on an individual patient. Rather, one must try to understand each patient's uniquely subjective response to their own life experiences.

TRANSFERENCE AND TRAUMA

Despite the extraordinary degree of symptomatic variation noted among adults who were sexually abused in childhood, there is a broad area of common dynamic issues that unites these patients, determines the kinds of clinical challenges that they may present to their psychotherapists, and warrants their being studied as a group. The most significant feature shared by these patients is the way in which the memory of the trauma and its associated events tends to unconsciously organize and inform their experience of virtually every relationship of any import. This is particularly true of the transference relationship, where patients who were sexually traumatized in childhood can experience an enormous pressure to reexperience and relive aspects of the sexual abuse in ways that range from the symbolic (e.g., fantasies that a therapist is being manipulative and dishonest for his or her own purposes) to the literal and concrete (e.g., attempts to seduce the therapist or engage him or her in corrupt or shady dealings, or fears that the therapist is being sexually seductive). Often, elements of symbolic repetition can occur around boundary issues that may arise either within the therapy (e.g., in the handling of insurance payments, clinic fees, or negotiations around hours) or in the patient's outside life (e.g., a special sensitivity to ferreting out or accusing others of perverse, corrupt, or abusive behavior).

Careful study of clinical material suggests a model in which significant childhood trauma produces an unconscious preoccupation with certain possible relational outcomes or a tendency to anticipate or construe situations in a particular way. This preoccupation reflects an unconscious organizational schema within the mind to which current experience is continually being assimilated. Thus, each new event is experienced in line with the ways in which previous significant traumas have imposed their outline on the patient's tendencies to organize new experience. And, simultaneously, each subsequent trauma can serve as a starting point for a new or modified organizational schema that will influence the experience of still later occurrences.

Clinically speaking, this means that an important feature of the transference in these patients—perhaps for all patients—is apt to be the (often unconscious) fear, anticipation, or conviction that something traumatic is likely or about to recur or is in fact actually occurring in the present moment. This view is consistent with Freud's (1920, 1926) concepts of traumatic fixation and the operation of the repetition compulsion in the service of attempted mastery of infantile trauma.

Appeals to complex theoretical constructs, such as "traumatic fixation" or "the repetition compulsion," however, do not really explain why childhood sexual traumas exert this almost magnetlike effect on the unconscious minds of some patients and not on the minds of others. I have observed similar phenomena in situations of significant, nonsexual, early childhood trauma, such as early parent loss, and to a lesser extent, in the analysis of children of survivors of the Holocaust (Levine, 1982). Perhaps the determining factor is a matter of the balance struck between the extent, frequency, and severity of the trauma and the child's potential for an adaptive response. As noted earlier, the latter will not only be determined by the child's pretraumatic level of ego development, but by the quality and availability of the child's protective and supportive network in the posttraumatic period and the additive weight imparted by subsequent life events (i.e., the extent, frequency, and severity of subsequent traumatic events, including nonsexual traumas, and the capacity of the child and his or her protectors and caretakers to respond to and ameliorate the impact of *those* occurrences).

The strong pressure mobilized by the treatment situation to repeat elements connected with the trauma, coupled with the tendency to reenact what cannot be comfortably remembered (Freud, 1914), may leave these patients particularly vulnerable to becoming sexually involved with their therapists (Smith, 1984) or to becoming masochistically enthralled to a charismatic therapist, who may use the patient in a narcissistically appropriating, self-gratifying manner. (Recall that narcissistic appropriation of the child for the purposes and needs of the adult is, by definition, an important component of a childhood sexual trauma.) While this latter kind of exploitation may not go so far as to include actual physical or sexual relations between therapist and patient, the elements of transgression of boundaries and symbolic reenactment of the trauma are evident.

At times, the compulsion to repeat the trauma may be so powerful, and the line between reality and fantasy so tenuously drawn, that the "as if," illusory quality of the transference may disappear (Levine, 1982). Then, for the patient, *the experience of the therapy situation may feel like or even become the trauma.* Patients may, either consciously or unconsciously, fail to distinguish between the therapist's attempts to help them talk about their past and the seduction itself. Thus, they may believe that the therapist is hurting them, intruding on their privacy, becoming voyeuristically invested in the gruesome or exciting details of their childhood sexual experiences, using them for his or her own pleasure, and failing to protect them from the pain of remembering. In this regard, the quality of the transferences that develop in these cases can, at times, be more akin to transference psychoses than to the usual neurotic transferences.

A brief summary of two hours from the treatment of a woman in her mid-thirties, who had been incestuously involved with both parents, may further illustrate these phenomena:

The patient began the hour concerned about a relative's behavior at a family party. Elements of this behavior led associatively to memories of how, when the patient was between 3 and 5 years old, mother would use the patient's body to masturbate herself. Further thoughts led to pleasant memories of childhood visits to the rodeo with her family and her pleasure and excitement at watching the calf roping. Next, she thought of how "tied" she still was to her parents and her traumatic past. How both parents had tied her to them, greedily appropriating her childhood for their own sexual and narcissistic pleasure. The image of the calves with their legs tied up then gave way to father holding her hands and arms down as he molested her. As she talked, she became quite anxious and upset, and

unconsciously assumed on the couch the posture she was describing, writhing, while holding her hands behind her over
her head.

In the next hour she was afraid to go further. She reported
that following the previous hour, she had been terribly anxious
and depressed all day. The memories of the incest had disorga-
nized her thinking. She feared seducing the analyst or being
seduced or taken advantage of by him. She worried that the
material of the last hour, or this dialogue itself, might be the
prelude to a seduction.

For each belief about the therapist's motivations that the
patient develops as part of the transference, the therapist is
susceptible to parallel feelings (countertransference). Thus, it
is not unusual for therapists to find themselves at various times
feeling stimulated, tempted, repelled, judgmental, identified
with or protective toward these patients. While these are feelings that are best recognized and attended to by the therapist
in the privacy of his or her own personal treatment, self-reflection, or supervision, the fact of their being engendered and
felt, often as an impulse to reciprocal action, is an expectable,
almost inevitable part of the treatment process (see Sandler's
[1976] discussion of the therapist's "role responsiveness").

In one dramatic example, while listening to a patient talk
about seemingly unrelated matters, a colleague experienced a
sudden, inexplicable fantasy of engaging with his patient in a
crude and impulsive sexual act. As he silently mused over the
possible meanings of this fantasy, the patient confessed that she
had been avoiding telling him that as a young girl, she had been
similarly approached by her father. The surprising frequency
with which such experiences in the therapist precede the discussion or confirm the details of a childhood sexual trauma in
the patient leads to the conjecture that information about the
trauma is being unconsciously communicated in nonverbal
forms by the patient and may be potentially available to the
therapist via the countertransference. The expectation that
such countertransference feelings will be a normative part of
the therapy experience can alert the therapist to the likelihood
of their appearance and allow him or her to judiciously use
their presence as further data about the quality and meaning

of the patient's transference relatedness and the traumatic past around which that transference is organized.

In another case, a patient's adamant suppression of memories, thoughts, and feelings relating to sexual and masturbatory fantasies and experiences reflected more than the usual resistance based upon anxiety, guilt, and fear of a humiliating exposure. In addition to these motivations for refusing to talk, this patient was constantly and unconsciously enacting her need to prove that she could successfully provoke and repel the exploratory "advances" of the therapist. For the therapist, access to this dimension of the transference first became available in the form of a series of fantasies that reflected the patient's slyly encouraging him to become more and more intrusive and aggressive in his mode of questioning.

It is important to recognize that no matter how great the pressure that a patient may feel internally or attempt to mobilize in the therapist to literally or symbolically reenact the transgression of a childhood sexual trauma, *under no circumstances is it appropriate for the therapist to offer direct gratification of the patient's wishes for a symbolically or literally corrupt or physically gratifying relationship*. To do so not only would repeat the traumatic past in the therapy, but would constitute a violation of the patient's rights in the present and a breach of therapeutic ethics and responsibility.

DISTRUST AND THE LOSS OF PARENTAL PROTECTION

Inherent in situations of severe childhood trauma is a sudden and unexpected loss of the child's sense of an omnipotent, protective parent (Levine, 1990). In normal development, this unconscious belief in the omnipotence of one's parents is gradually relinquished in innumerable encounters with the reality of parental limitations throughout latency and during adolescence. In contrast, the phase inappropriate loss of a feeling of parental protection that can result from a child's experience of a childhood sexual trauma disturbs the background of "basic trust" (Erikson, 1954) on which so much of development depends, and deprives the patient of an important component of

the "background of safety" (Sandler, 1960), which is essential
to the formation of a therapeutic alliance and the unfolding of
the psychotherapeutic process. As might be expected, problems
in trust and loss of safety are particularly striking in the treatments of those adults who were either violently abused in childhood or were betrayed by those on whom they most depended,
as in cases of parental incest.

These feelings of lost protection often become connected
in the patient's inner world with intense conflicts over abandonment and separation. In such instances, patients may be so
vulnerable to feeling abandoned, that they may cling desperately and masochistically to an intrusive, cruel, seductive, or
neglectful relationship (Valenstein, 1973). As noted by Steele
(1990), many victims of paternal incest suffer pretraumatic deprivation in their mother–child relationship, making the overtly
incestuous object tie with the father their best or only source of
comfort or warmth. The fact that so many of these patients
seem particularly vulnerable to feeling abandoned around
times of separation and loss emphasizes the need for careful
working through of these issues in the transference.

In instances of parental incest, the roots of the trust issue
are further complicated by the central role that the parents play
in the development and maintenance of the child's morality
and reality sense (Ferenczi, 1933). It is important for therapists
to bear in mind that, although it has been reported with a lesser
frequency, mothers may also be the perpetrators of childhood
sexual abuse (see Kramer [1983, 1990]; Margolis [1991] for
further discussions of maternal incest). When they are, maternal overstimulation (Shengold, 1989) and narcissistic appropriation of the child for the mother's gratification, even in the
absence of cruelty and neglect, may simultaneously be experienced by the child as a sexual trauma, an abandonment, and a
loss of parental protection.

Many times, paternal incest occurs in the setting of a preexisting state of relative maternal deprivation. That is, a mater-
nally deprived child may turn to a father as a compensatory
substitute for warmth, gratification, and protection. The father
may also feel deprived either in his relationship to his wife or
in his own childhood relation to his mother (or both). The

result is a father–child pair in which the prospect of closeness can readily stimulate intense, frustrated, archaic needs for closeness. In such a pair, if these needs become erotized and the adult's controls are weakened by psychosis, alcoholism, psychopathy, impulsiveness, or the like, the danger of incestuous action becomes heightened. Should the incestuous breach then occur, it may carry with it for the child the important intrapsychic meanings of the repetition of the loss of the protecting, nurturing mother and the loss or destruction of the father as a life-giving object and a substitute source of nurturance, protection, and attachment.

This possibility of a preexisting maternal deprivation makes it difficult to separate the extent to which such findings as mistrust, fear of closeness, and difficulties in reality testing or in establishing a conviction about what one knows to be true, are functions of a childhood sexual trauma per se or are related to nonsexual traumas occurring within a disordered mother–infant relationship. The importance of this issue in the treatment of adults who were involved in parental incestuous relationships as children is, however, attested to by the fact that the exploration and affective reliving of the incest trauma often becomes engaged around an actual separation from the therapist in the context of the patient's experiencing a sense of safety in the therapeutic relationship. Even in those instances in which a consciously recalled memory of incest is part of the patient's presentation in therapy, the issue may not be affectively engaged until the patient experiences a bond of security, safety, or trust in the therapeutic relationship and that bond is threatened by an interruption, such as a vacation or other extended absence. It is then, on the brink of feeling "abandoned" during the period of impending separation, that the patient may begin to painfully and affectfully recall aspects of the childhood trauma or even initiate a precipitous action related to that trauma, such as the decision to confront one's parents about its occurrence. The consequence of either course of action may be to inadvertently and unconsciously create a situation in which the patient feels overwrought and unprotected by the therapist, much as they must have felt during the original traumatic episode.

The mode of organizing one's psyche around conflicts and derivatives of the childhood sexual trauma has enormous implications not only for the nature of the transference that unfolds, but for the difficulties encountered in the development of a therapeutic alliance, as well. As Raphling (1990) has described, these patients are liable to demonstrate a fierce resistance to the formation of a therapeutic alliance. This resistance is partly based on the intense pressure to repeat or reexperience the trauma that arises whenever a close relationship is at hand. Patients cannot trust themselves or their therapists not to engage in illicit, symbolic, or actual traumatic repetitions of the childhood trauma. The patient's distinctions between fantasy and reality, past and present, remembering and reliving may be either threatened or lost. Adult, cooperative parts of the patient's ego, including the capacities for self-observation and the formation of a therapeutic split, are often overwhelmed by the intrusion of powerful negative or erotic transferences.

THE ROLE OF VICTIM

The formation of a therapeutic alliance not only necessitates the patient's emotional investment in and recognition of the presence of another object, with all of the dangers of injury, seduction, and betrayal entailed by that. It also ultimately requires an acknowledgment of previously unacceptable sexual and angry feelings in oneself, and the relinquishing of characteristic defensive stances against these, such as entitlement, projection, blaming the abusers, and clinging to a self-definition as victim.

It is not unusual for patients who were sexually abused as children to hold to a relationship to the therapist that is marked by a defensive counterdependency and self-sufficiency for very long periods of time, or to defensively rely upon a self-defined and socially supported role as "victim." The exploration of this position must be handled with particular sensitivity. The sexually traumatized child *was* victimized by the adult. And in today's society, there is enormous cultural support for viewing adults who were sexually abused as children only as "victims" (note the commonly used term *survivors* of incest). In attempting to explore the defensive uses to which a patient may be trying to put the childhood sexual abuse in the current treatment, a therapist must be sensitive to these cultural forces and take care not to fall into the stereotyped role of blaming the victim.

From a *moral* point of view, in the adult–child relationship, the burden of restraint clearly lies with the adult, who has a direct responsibility to care for and protect the child. In this sense, these patients were the victims of their seducers. At the same time, from an *analytic* point of view, we must not lose sight of either the defensive uses to which a patient may put the victim status or the wishful components that may have been unconscious motivational factors in the childhood sexual encounter (Greenacre, 1950).

Alternatively, some patients may attempt to protect their emotional attachment to an abusing parent by denying the extent of the damage done by inappropriate sexual behavior. Such denial may be easier to maintain where the sexual aspects of the approach were attenuated (e.g., overstimulation without penetration or invasive fondling), and were made in a "warm" and "loving" manner. In such instances, realizing one's "victimhood" (i.e., recognizing that a traumatic or developmentally disturbing situation had indeed taken place) may be an important first step in a therapeutic process that will attenuate the protective denial and lead to a more balanced view of one's past and present psychic realities.

I recall one patient, whom I would more properly describe as overstimulated rather than sexually abused. Beginning in childhood and long into her teenage years, her father would cuddle with her in bed each morning in a way that she found consciously pleasurable, although unconsciously disturbing. When she presented for treatment as a university student who could not complete her courses, her symptoms included many dependent and infantile character traits that interfered with and denied her potential role as an effective, adult woman. She rapidly developed an intense erotic transference, the manifestations of which included angry seductive demands for physical contact and feelings of being teased, hurt, and played with by her therapist. Exploration of these feelings eventually led to her realizing the part that father's persistently overstimulating behavior played in driving her to masochistically submit to precocious sexual activity with her first boyfriend. In particular, she recalled a moment at 13 or 14 years of age, in which she recognized that the way that she and her boyfriend lay in bed together after intercourse, with his leg swung over her body, was exactly how father lay with her each morning. At that time, she dealt with this realization by quickly avoiding any awareness of the sexual implications and possibilities of her father's behavior. The full range of the latter knowledge remained repressed until she was confronted with it by her therapist in the course of treatment. ("That kind of thing should have stopped long ago!"). In the course of exploring her feelings about what had taken place, she came to realize that what tormented her most about what had happened was her guilt at the thought that she desired and found pleasure in father's sexually stimulating behavior.

A patient who defensively clings to the victim role may do so in the service of limiting the scope of what is available for self-observation and therefore for exploration within the treatment. In many instances, early childhood seductions become the basis, by way of identification with the aggressor, for later seductive behavior in early adolescence or adulthood (Bigras, 1990). For example, one patient who had been sexually abused by both parents in early childhood and latency reported that during adolescence she actively sought out her father for sexual contact and attempted to seduce other older male acquaintances. While the reconstruction and understanding of these events was leavened by the recognition of the role played by the earlier seductions and her identification with her aggressors, it would have been a serious omission not to address the guilt that followed from her subsequent active, sexual provocations or to view her only as a "victim" or "survivor" of incest.

The definition of self as victim can also have important consequences for a patient's attitude toward his or her activity, assertiveness, adult responsibility, and desire. Ehrenberg (1987) noted that incestuous and sexually abusive relationships in childhood can have a:

[P]rofound impact on the nature of the [adult] individual's patterns of relation to desire [in both a sexual and a more general sense.] . . . To the degree that arousal of the victim's own desire is experienced as the basis for the vulnerability [to the trauma], the relation to desire becomes quite problematic. This is particularly so when the relationships in question endured over considerable periods of time. In such instances, it is clear that unless the child had been a cooperative participant, and derived some gratification from the involvement, the relationship could not have been possible. The individual's coming to terms with his or her own participation in these early relationships, . . . constitutes one of the pivotal issues in treatment [pp. 593–594].

Needless to say, these are issues that can be taken up only with the greatest tact and care, after the basis for the protective security of the therapeutic relationship has been carefully established.

DOUBTING

When patients who suffered childhood sexual abuse do relate memories of the abuse experience, it is often with a great deal of doubt and uncertainty about what actually happened. This may be as true for those patients who enter therapy aware that a sexual trauma took place in childhood, as it is for those whose memories of the abuse emerge from repression or are reconstructed during the course of treatment. The intensity of the doubting may surprise an unsuspecting therapist, especially when the patient is dealing with memories rather than attempts at reconstruction, and the memories relate to a time in childhood when a patient would ordinarily be expected to have a clear sense of what was real or fantasy. Kramer (1983) described one aspect of this problem as "object-coercive doubting" and related it to maternal incest. Doubting, however, may occur in any case of parental incest, regardless of the sex of the parent involved, and many instances of nonparental childhood sexual trauma, as well (Levine, 1990). The doubting and confusion, coupled with a reliance upon dissociative defenses, may even evolve into a global cognitive style that leads to generalized difficulties in learning (Bernstein, 1990; Kramer, 1990).

At some point in the treatment, the doubting and uncertainty about what really happened, was it real or fantasy, may assume center stage for the patient and produce difficult technical challenges for the therapist. Patients may beseech the therapist to offer them help, certainty, or confirmation in knowing what took place or demand that the therapist express belief in their doubt ridden accounts. At one level, this phenomenon may represent a transference repetition. That is, the patient is asking, "Will you recognize and identify for/with me what is really going on as I wished my parents or other significant adults to do? Or will you turn away and pretend not to notice or even covertly foster the continuation of the incest as my parents did?"

Simultaneously, the doubting may unconsciously repeat the trauma. That is, the patient, in the unconscious role of the incestuous parent, may be angrily or seductively attempting to make the therapist "do something" to relieve the patient's distress. Or, the angry doubting and cranky demands may reenact feelings of undischarged sexual tension, which were an important part of the abuse experience (Shengold, 1989).

In relation to the therapist's proper role in the treatment, the elements of narcissistic use of the object and the demand for transgression of boundaries inherent in this transaction are readily apparent to the observer. These meanings, however, are apt to be much less apparent to the patient. The result is often some of the most complex and difficult moments in the therapy. Regression, a weakened alliance, hypersensitivity, and confusion on the part of the patient can run headlong into the therapist's countertransference strain. The latter arises because the therapist is under attack and being forced by the patient to take sides, to know omnisciently what was or was not real or to otherwise abandon a position of abstinence, neutrality, and an optimum analytic stance.

In trying to find one's way through this complex and demanding set of problems, a therapist must assess the extent to which some active support for the patient's reality testing is necessary or possible. In childhood, many of these patients did not have relationships with adequately protective or reality supporting figures who would affirm that the seduction of children was wrong and not the fault of the child, or to whom they could "report" their abusers. For many patients, the limitations of the adults in their world were compounded by their own childhood feelings of guilt or by threats made or enticements not to tell. For example, one patient reported that her father, with whom she had an incestuous sexual relationship for many years, would always say, "A person is always free to choose what they want." The contribution to later doubting and confusion about what is real in such pronouncements is apparent.

Clearly, then, some patients in this most difficult moment in treatment seek to enact the wish that the analyst function in a longed for, but never provided, protective parental role. But what are the consequences of the therapist's attempting to satisfy this desire? Will doing so prove helpful or will it unconsciously reenact some component of the sexual trauma? Will it foster regression by attempting to fulfill a universal childhood longing for an omniscient object? Will it encourage a sense of entitlement as compensation for the sexual trauma or reinforce a patient's view of him- or herself as victim and thereby contribute to a suppression of either fears or perceptions of assertive or seductive behavior?

These are difficult questions, the answers to which must be determined in each individual instance. Therapeutic technique at such moments of strain must be guided by the therapist's assessment of the extent to which the patient is able to bear the existential burden of not knowing and can accept the necessary uncertainty that surrounds almost any "truth" that derives from the subjective realm of psychic reality. To what extent can a therapist ever really know what happened? As Freud (1899) said in his paper on screen memories, we may not have memories from childhood, but only memories about childhood. That is, the best that we may be able to do is reconstruct what is "likely" rather than what was "true" (Sherkow, 1990).

From this perspective, and that of technique, the therapist may not have to decide whether something was actually real or not. Instead, one only has to recognize and acknowledge the tremendous importance that the wish for certainty holds for the patient. One has to explore the fact and consequences of the patient's uncertainty and doubting, examine the ways in which doubting the experience may have been reinforced by the child's own guilt and by the action of the parents. One must explore the meanings that the doubting assumes and the uses to which it is put in the transference, and try to follow the evolution of the material within the therapeutic process. As several colleagues have noted, a shift in their own orientation toward the process of treatment and away from the need to know for certain what happened when and with whom has freed them, and, ultimately, their patients for a more effective engagement within the therapy.

SUMMARY

Given the protean manifestations of the adult consequences of childhood sexual abuse, patients with a history of childhood sexual trauma may present within any conceivable diagnostic category. Commonly, they may manifest some combination of depression and low self-esteem, problems in intimate relationships, impulsiveness or extreme constriction, phobias and anxiety phenomena, sexual dysfunctions, or psychosomatic disturbances. The important diagnostic question, "How do I know when my patient has had a childhood sexual trauma?" is best settled by studying the patient's response to the treatment setting and relationship, including the patient's reactions to the therapist's tentative and judicious attempts to reconstruct the existence and consequences of presumed childhood trauma. In particular, the presence of a transference and countertransference in which the form and content of the therapeutic relationship revolves around fears of repetition and pressures to repeat elements of the childhood sexual trauma and its consequences, is a strong presumptive sign of a positive history of childhood sexual abuse.

The traumatic aspects of the original events will not only include components of the actual trauma (e.g., overstimulation, fear, invasion, pain, guilt), but may also include feelings of being abandoned, narcissistically appropriated for the gratification of the other, and the loss of the omnipotent, protecting parent. The ways in which these elements of the original trauma are remembered and repeated in the treatment will be influenced by the levels of development that the child had attained prior to the onset of the trauma and by subsequent, posttraumatic events, including the elaborations in fantasy to which the child resorted in attempts to deal with the original trauma.

For each position that the patient experiences in the transference, the therapist is susceptible to experiencing pressure toward adopting a similar or a complementary role in the countertransference. The therapist's tendency toward countertransference enactment (role responsiveness) can offer important clues as to what is being unconsciously mobilized in the therapeutic relationship. However, no matter how great or how well rationalized these impulses toward the patient may be, it is essential that the therapist not act upon them. Rather, the therapist should attempt to use awareness of these impulses as further data about the patient that is being communicated via the countertransference (Heimann, 1950). In order to effectively do so, a therapist must have considerable familiarity with and objectivity toward his or her own personal conflicts, as well as the capacity to bear them without acting upon them. The attainment of these capacities may require personal therapy, clinical supervision, or consultation and a commitment to continued self-inquiry. Such endeavors require time and effort, but the therapeutic advantages that they can convey are well worth it.

It is through the analytic exploration of the patient's dreams, symptoms, and history and developments within the transference and countertransference, that both patient and therapist may come to move toward a sense of conviction about what may or may not have happened in the patient's past. When present in the therapist, this conviction may then be offered to the patient in the form of tentative reconstructions. As with any other interpretive intervention, the therapist must then follow

and explore the patient's response to these proposed reconstructions in the continued elaboration and working through
of the therapeutic process. Although the patient may be
wracked with doubts and confusion and may demand certainty
from the therapist, what may prove most important to the patient in the treatment process is the therapist's unflinching focus
on trying to understand all that is going on between them in
the therapy, rather than focusing exclusively on trying to find
out what happened, when, and with whom. To the extent that
the need to know the answers to these questions is mobilized in the
treatment, this need is and should properly remain within the prov-
ince of the patient.

In the end, there is far more to the treatment of adults
who were sexually abused as children than we now know. While
this means that each therapy begun must remain in part an
experiment and an exploration, we can take heart from our
clinical experience, which indicates that significant therapeutic
results are possible through psychoanalysis and analytic therapy. The treatments are long and hard, but as one patient,
wracked by discouragement, fears, and crippling inhibitions in
her sexual life has repeatedly said to me, "As hard as it is, this
therapy is my only hope. What other options are there?"

REFERENCES

Baranger, M., Baranger, W., & Mom, J. M. (1988), The infantile
    psychic trauma from us to Freud: Pure trauma, retroactivity and
    reconstruction. *Internat. J. Psycho-Anal.*, 69:113–128.
Bernstein, A. E. (1990), The impact of incest trauma on ego develop-
    ment. In: *Adult Analysis and Childhood Sexual Abuse*, ed. H. B.
    Levine. Hillsdale, NJ: Analytic Press, pp. 65–91.
Bigras, J. (1990), Psychoanalysis as incestuous repetition. Some techni-
    cal considerations. In: *Adult Analysis and Childhood Sexual Abuse*,
    ed. H. B. Levine. Hillsdale, NJ: Analytic Press, pp. 173–196.
Breuer, J., & Freud, S. (1895), Studies on Hysteria. *Standard Edition*,
    2. London: Hogarth Press, 1955.
Bryer, J. B., Nelson, B. A., Miler, J. B., & Krol, P. (1987), Childhood
    sexual and physical abuse as factors in adult psychiatric illness.
    Amer. J. Psychiat., 144:1426–1430.

Burland, J. A., & Raskin, J. A. (1990), The psychoanalysis of adults who were sexually abused in childhood: A preliminary report from the discussion group of the American Psychoanalytic Association. In: *Adult Analysis and Childhood Sexual Abuse*, ed. H. B. Levine. Hillsdale, NJ: Analytic Press, pp. 35–41.

Deblinger, E., McLeer, S., Atkins, M., Ralphe, D., & Foa, E. (1989), Post-traumatic stress in sexually abused, physically abused and non-abused children. *Child Abuse & Neglect*, 13:403–408.

Ehrenberg, D. B. (1987), Abuse and desire: A case of father–daughter incest. *Contemp. Psychoanal.*, 23:593–604.

Erikson, E. (1954), *Childhood and Society*. New York: W. W. Norton.

Ferenczi, S. (1933), The confusion of tongues between the adult and the child. *Internat. J. Psycho-Anal.*, 30:225–230.

Freud, S. (1896), The aetiology of hysteria. *Standard Edition*, 3:191–221. London: Hogarth Press, 1958.

———— (1899), Screen memories. *Standard Edition*, 3:301–322. London: Hogarth Press, 1962.

———— (1914), Remembering, repeating and working through. *Standard Edition*, 12:145–156. London: Hogarth Press, 1958.

———— (1920), Beyond the Pleasure Principle. *Standard Edition*, 18:3–64. London: Hogarth Press, 1955.

———— (1925), An autobiographical study. *Standard Edition*, 20:3–70. London: Hogarth Press, 1959.

———— (1926), Inhibitions, symptoms and anxiety. *Standard Edition*, 20:77–172. London: Hogarth Press, 1959.

Goodwin, J., Simms, M., & Bergman, R. (1979), Hysterical seizures: A sequel to incest. *Amer. J. Orthopsychiat.*, 49:698–703.

Greenacre, P. (1950), The prepuberty trauma in girls. *Psychoanal. Quart.*, 19:298–317.

Heimann, P. (1950), On countertransference. *Internat. J. Psycho-Anal.*, 31:81–84.

Kramer, S. (1983), Object-coercive doubting: A pathological defensive response to maternal incest. *J. Amer. Psychoanal. Assn.*, 31(suppl.):325–351.

———— (1990), Residues of incest. In: *Adult Analysis and Childhood Sexual Abuse*, ed. H. B. Levine. Hillsdale, NJ: Analytic Press, pp. 149–170.

Kris, E. (1956), The recovery of childhood memories. *The Psychoanalytic Study of the Child*, 11:54–88. New York: International Universities Press.

Levine, H. B. (1982), Toward a psychoanalytic understanding of children of survivors of the Holocaust. *Psychoanal. Quart.*, 51:70–92.

────── (1990), *Adult Analysis and Childhood Sexual Abuse*. Hillsdale, NJ: Analytic Press.

Lindberg, F., & Distad, L. (1985), Post-traumatic stress disorders in women who experienced childhood incest. *Child Abuse & Neglect*, 9:329–334.

Margolis, M. (1991), Parent-child incest: Analytic treatment experiences with follow-up data. In: *The Trauma of Transgression. Psychotherapy of Incest Victims*, ed. S. Kramer & S. Akhtar. Northvale, NJ: Jason Aronson, pp. 93–114.

Masson, J. M. (1984), *The Assault on Truth*. New York: Farrar, Straus, Giroux.

Raphling, D. (1990), Technical issues of the opening phase. In: *Adult Analysis and Childhood Sexual Abuse*, ed. H. B. Levine. Hillsdale, NJ: Analytic Press, pp. 45–64.

Sandler, J. (1960), The background of safety. *Internat. J. Psycho-Anal.*, 41:352–356.

────── (1976), Countertransference and role responsiveness. *Internat. Rev. Psycho-Anal.*, 3:43–48.

Schimek, J. G. (1987), Fact and fantasy in the seduction theory: A historical review. *J. Amer. Psychoanal. Assn.*, 35:937–966.

Shengold, L. (1989), *Soul Murder. The Effects of Childhood Abuse and Deprivation*. New Haven, CT: Yale University Press.

Sherkow, S. (1990), Consequences of childhood sexual abuse on the development of ego structure. A comparison of child and adult cases. In: *Adult Analysis and Childhood Sexual Abuse*, ed. H. B. Levine. Hillsdale, NJ: Analytic Press, pp. 93–115.

Smith, S. (1984), The sexually abused patient and the abusing therapist: A study in sadomasochistic relationships. *Psychoanal. Psychol.*, 1:89–98.

Steele, B. (1990), Some sequelae of the sexual maltreatment of children. In: *Adult Analysis and Childhood Sexual Abuse*, ed. H. B. Levine. Hillsdale, NJ: Analytic Press, pp. 121–134.

Steele, B. F., & Alexander, H. (1981), Long term effects of sexual abuse in childhood. In: *Sexually Abused Children and Their Families*, ed. P. B. Mrazek & C. H. Kempe. New York: Pergamon, pp. 233–234.

Valenstein, A. (1973), On attachment to painful feelings and the negative therapeutic reaction. *The Psychoanalytic Study of the Child*, 28:305–392. New Haven, CT: Yale University Press.

Chapter 9

Boundary Violations in Psychotherapy: Sexual and Nonsexual

Maria T. Lymberis, M.D.

Since the 1970s ethical issues have been at the forefront of public concern and debate. This stems from the sobering realization of the true dimensions of abuse, misuse, and outright harm to individuals, groups, and to the environment by individuals in leadership positions, not only in government but in the professions, indeed in all groups starting with and including the family.

As the spectrum of abuse of power, ranging from Watergate to child abuse, began to emerge in the media, the societal demand for accountability took on a new urgency and gathered momentum.

In medicine, this has been expressed through legislative mandates, government regulation, and the utilization of business and management techniques in the delivery of health care. Organized medicine, including psychiatry, has responded to this societal change with a renewed commitment to medical ethics as the foundation of medical practice.

Medicine, as the oldest profession, has, from its inception, based its authority on the ethics of responsibility as first codified in the Hippocratic oath almost 3000 years ago. In the United

165

States, the Amerian Medical Association (AMA) first revised and adopted its own version of the Hippocratic oath in 1847. Since then there have been several revisions—in 1903, 1912, and 1957. In all of these revisions the fundamental tenets of the Hippocratic tradition have been maintained.

In the 1980 AMA revision of medical ethics (AMA proceedings, 1980), several aspects of the Hippocratic tradition were, for the first time, significantly modified in keeping with contemporary realities (Dryer, 1988). These changes involved the following:

1. Medical knowledge is no longer regarded as absolute or certain; medical decisions are now based on a risk/benefit analysis.
2. The physician is no longer an absolute authority; the paternalistic attitude of the Hippocratic tradition has given way to the concept of the patient as a full partner in medical treatment. The basis of the doctor–patient relationship is informed consent, a process that runs throughout the entire treatment.
3. The hallmark of the Hippocratic tradition, the exclusivity of the doctor–patient relationship, is still affirmed. However, confidentiality is no longer absolute but "within the constraints of the law." Physicians are no longer exclusively dedicated to individual patients nor do they function exclusively as that patient's agent, but they increasingly "recognize a responsibility to participate in activities contributing to an improved community" and are urged to accept their "responsibility to seek changes in those [legal] requirements which are contrary to the best interests of the patient."

Among the medical specialties, the American Psychiatric Association (APA) was the first to focus attention on the ethical basis of practice. In 1973 the APA first adapted the AMA Medical Ethics to address the specific needs of psychiatric practice. Since then, the APA's *The Principles of Medical Ethics with Annotations Especially Applicable to Psychiatry* (1989a) has undergone numerous revisions as various ethical issues in clinical practice arose. These revisions resulted in the 1973, 1978, 1981, 1984, 1985, 1986, 1989, 1992 editions of *The APA Principles*. Beginning with the 1978 edition *The APA Principles* have included specific procedures for ethics complaints. The procedures, like the annotations, are also being revised and refined. They are nationally applied by all of the district branches of the APA and are designed to safeguard the integrity of the profession and accord due process to member defendants and complainants alike. The APA's commitment to professional responsibility through accountability has led to a major educational effort to sensitize members to the realities of ethical dilemmas in clinical practice.

From 1985 through 1991, the APA Work Group, later named the APA Ethics Subcommittee on the Education of Psychiatrists on Ethical Issues, worked with the APA Ethics Committee to develop two educational videotapes on the problem of sexual involvement with patients (1986, 1990). Since then, the APA Ethics Committee has been actively involved in addressing the ethical dimensions of the economics of clinical practice and currently the ethical issues in managed care. In this presentation I will discuss and give examples from clinical practice involving sexual, financial, and other potentially harmful interactions with patients. I conceptualize these as instances of boundary violations in clinical practice.

THE CONCEPT OF BOUNDARIES IN PSYCHOTHERAPY

Psychiatric practice, like all medical practice, is defined by the ethical principles developed by the profession and by legal principles and customs. Medical practice is a joint venture enterprise between patients and physicians. This is in the spirit of the tradition of individualism, freedom of choice, and independence which is part of the American heritage. The doctor–patient relationship is based on informed consent and is defined by the ethical principles and the legal fiduciary duty.

Section 1, Annotation 1 to *The Principles of Medical Ethics* (1989a) states: "The patient may place his/her trust in his/her psychiatrist knowing that the psychiatrist's ethics and professional responsibilities preclude him/her gratifying his/her own needs by exploiting the patient" (p. 3).

Section 2, Annotation 2 to *The Principles of Medical Ethics* states: "The psychiatrist should diligently guard against exploiting information furnished by the patient and should not use the unique position of power afforded him/her by the psychotherapeutic situation to influence the patient in any way not directly relevant to the treatment goals" (p. 4).

The fiduciary duty that a physician has toward his or her patient requires that the physician act for the benefit of the patient once the physician accepts the trust and confidence that the patient places in him or her. The courts routinely scrutinize transactions between individuals in fiduciary relationships. The doctor–patient relationship is one example of such a relationship.

Persons acting as fiduciaries for others are not permitted to use the relationship for their personal benefit at the expense of the individual toward whom they have a fiduciary duty. Examples of such relationships involve, among others: parent-child, teacher-student, supervisor-supervisee, parishoner-priest, attorney-client, to mention just a few. Trust, confidentiality, loyalty, and neutrality are all part of the fiduciary duty in such relationships.

Ethical and fiduciary principles provide the foundations of clinical practice, regardless of theoretical orientation, technical therapeutic principles, or type of practice. Both the ethical and legal principles serve as boundaries for the doctor–patient relationship and warn clinicians of the potential for abuse of their power over their patients by defining the ethical and legal responsibilities toward their patients.

In practice, boundary violations can result whenever the doctor–patient relationship is altered by the initiation of any other type of relationship with the patient or by the assumption of any other role vis-à-vis the patient. This is the problem of "double agentry."

Problems of double agentry were first identified in institutional settings. In 1978, the Hastings Center, an ethics think tank, issued a special supplement: *In the Service of the State: The*

Psychiatrist as Double Agent. Double agentry was found to occur in a variety of situations such as in cases of conflicting responsibilities, confused legalities, undefined purposes, contradictory roles, conflicting loyalties, and multiple agentry. Current pressures for access to care and for cost containment are restructuring the health care delivery system by driving practitioners out of solo practice and into large group or institutional practice settings where problems of double agentry abound. Any practitioner whose primary allegiance to the needs and interests of the patient is in conflict due to the demands of the institutional setting in which he or she is practicing, is in a situation of double agentry.

The classic example is the situation where psychiatrists working for the government are to confirm the statement of a person that he or she is a homosexual, knowing that such an admission would be used by the Immigration and Naturalization Service (INS) as the basis for excluding an immigrant from entry into the United States. The APA Ethics Committee has defined participation by a psychiatrist in such a role as unethical and has urged psychiatrists to refuse to so act and to protest such practices.

Double agentry is currently of major concern because of the emergence of new practice models and settings. For example, employee assistance programs often require that practitioners notify the program of the patient's progress and for program personnel to participate in treatment planning. In such situations it is essential that the patient be fully and explicitly informed and able to give *uncoerced* consent. However, the therapist has to be aware that even if consent for release of information is obtained, only focused, narrow information should be given and confidentiality of the details of the treatment should be preserved.

Corporate practice settings such as HMOs or other prepaid, managed care organizations are fertile ground for double agentry problems for practitioners. Double agentry can result when corporate policy dictates are contrary to the individual patient's needs and interests. Conflicts may arise with respect to need for admission or for treatment when the plan dictates only limited treatment, which may be substandard, given the specific clinical needs of the patient. Conflicts also may arise when a patient needs a specific treatment not available within the plan, or when the plan requires full disclosure of treatment as part of internal quality assurance requirements with the result that there are compromises in patient confidentiality.

As a general rule, practitioners in such plans should insist on maintaining responsibility for decision making in patient care without interference for management. This is not easily achieved. Individual psychiatrists need to remember that they can receive assistance and consultation from their professional society in addressing these issues.

In fact, membership in one's professional organization can strengthen one's professional identity and offer the individual the strength to stand up for ethical principles in situations of confused responsibilities, roles, or loyalties.

Clinical practice is replete with possible conflicts of interest. Consider custody evaluations where parents fight for child custody or conflicts around patient care and research or clinical case publications. In fact, all aspects of the therapeutic relationship from hours, fees, billing practices, records, and confidentiality can be involved in conflicts of interest with resultant boundary violations.

In 1989 the AMA Council on Ethical and Judicial Affairs released its report on "Conflicts of Interest" (APA, 1989b). The report addresses the impact of financial arrangements on professional practice. The guiding principle in all cases of conflict between the physician's financial interest and the physician's responsibilities to the patient is that "the conflict has to be resolved to the patient's benefit" (p. 7).

Other areas involve billing practices where psychiatrists misrepresent their relationship with other practitioners by billing as the attending physician at their rate, while the actual treatment is rendered by another practitioner who is less qualified, and the specific type of service is not disclosed. Such cases have resulted in lawsuits and findings of fraud against the psychiatrist and the institution in which the psychiatrist was working.

The Institute of Medicine acknowledged that "All compensation systems—from fee-for-service to capitation or salary—present some undesirable incentives for providing too many or too few services" (1989b, p. 2). The aim is to seek arrangements that encourage the physician to function as a professional. In a climate dominated by the "entrepreneurial health care market," the physician still has to place the needs of the patient first.

The report (APA, 1989b, pp. 3–6) listed specific situations that present conflicts of interest. These are situations where physicians:

1. Dispense drugs or devices to patients for profit.
2. Refer patients to facilities or services centers owned by the referring physician wholly or in part (in California there is currently a legislative proposal making such practices illegal).
3. Pay or are paid by third parties for the referral of patients (fee splitting).
4. Enter into joint ventures for profit where the physician's income is directly or indirectly tied to the number of referrals or amount of revenue generated by the physician.

The operating principle is that fee splitting is unethical and that referrals should be made upon evaluation of competence and ability of the practitioner or health care facility to meet the needs of the specific patient. It is unethical to intentionally limit utilization of needed medical services contrary to standards of care. Physicians should inform patients of this and protest such limitations.

In the remainder of this paper I shall focus on the clinical aspects of boundary violations and present some cases illustrating various boundary violations.

SEXUAL BOUNDARY VIOLATIONS

Despite the explicit 2500-year-old prohibition set out in the Hippocratic Oath against sexual involvement with patients, and in every revision of medical ethics since then, the issue has remained one of the most disturbing and controversial ones in the entire health care field. Even today, after specific legislation has been enacted by several states making sexual involvement with a current patient, and in some states, an expatient, a violation of law, the debate continues over the issue of posttermination sexual relations and on whether or not the "strict" ethical and legal principles that were articulated for psychotherapy should apply to the entire health care field. The debate is symptomatic of the widespread use of sexualization as a defense against the individual and societal awareness of psychological pain and trauma. Denial, repression, and dissociation are powerful defenses protecting us from confronting what Judith Herman so aptly has called "the Unspeakable" (1992, p. 1). No one wants to remember or bear witness to the existence of "man's inhumanity to man" otherwise known as "domestic violence," "child abuse," "soul murder," and the myriad of other varieties of individual and collective atrocities. Yet as therapists we are daily confronted with the effects of psychological trauma as we struggle with our patients to make sense of complex symptoms, reenactments, and work through transference and countertransference constellations.

In a recent book, *Incest-related Syndromes of Adult Psychopathology*, Richard Kluft has identified "The Sitting Duck Syndrome" to describe a group of patients whose sexual involvement with a previous therapist was based on a susceptibility to revictimization due to repressed childhood traumatization, not exclusively incest trauma (1990, p. 263).

Progress in the professional acknowledgment of the reality of sexual abuse of patients by health care providers was made when in December 1989 the AMA formulated its policy statement on sexual misconduct in the practice of medicine.

The AMA (1991) has unequivocally stated that "sexual contact or a romantic relationship with a patient concurrent with the physician–patient relationship is unethical" (p. 2741); that "sexual or romantic relationships with former patients are unethical if the physician uses or exploits trust, knowledge, emotions or influence derived from the previous professional relationship" (p. 2743). However, we still don't have official adoption by the AMA or APA of the principle "Once a patient, always a patient."[1] The debate continues as current surveys (Gartrell, Milliken, Goodson, Thiemann, and Lo, 1992) document the extent of the sexual misconduct problem in general medical and surgical practice.

The issue of sexual abuse of patients by health care providers exposes the humanity, vulnerability, and psychopathology of providers and is thus threatening to the profession, the individual professional, as well as patients and society at large. Studies are now in progress on therapists who have sexually abused patients. Glen Gabbard (1991) has described the lovesick therapist whose narcissistic needs are a major factor (p. 652). Robert Simon (1987) and other forensic experts (Simon, 1992) have called attention to the observation that also has been made by numerous people who have studied such cases, namely that, when one analyzes cases of therapist–patient sexual misconduct, the sex is but the most "sensational" boundary violation (p. 338). Characteristically, sex is the last step on a slippery slope of multiple, less dramatic boundary violations such as these:

1. Assuming the role of "real friend" in the patient's life by participating in the life of the patient outside the treatment; such as dinners or other social engagements, or lending a patient money, or employing a patient in one's business or home, or revealing to the patient one's feelings about the patient, especially sexual feelings and personal sexual arousal.
2. Failure to identify countertransference reactions because of the therapist's compromised functioning, perhaps due to a life crisis, resulting in excessive narcissistic need for love, activation of omnipotent rescue fantasies, or heightened grandiosity.
3. Failure to seek consultation or refer a patient who presents with an intractable, negative therapeutic reaction or stalemate. The therapist instead acts out with the patient, offering special hours or extensions of payments to placate the

---

[1]In July, 1993, the APA revised Section 2, Annotation 1 of *The APA Principles*, stating: "Sexual activity with a current or former patient is unethical." This change will be part of the 1993 revision.

patient, rather than exploring the meaning of the situation, guarding the treatment contract, and maintaining the therapeutic alliance.

Studies by Robert A. Nemiroff (1992) have drawn attention to therapists' vulnerability at different developmental phases and crises in their lives. In particular, the middle-aged, male therapist is vulnerable at times of personal illness or loss to the transference of a young female patient. Studies from Wisconsin, a state that has mandatory reporting by the subsequent therapist of the name of the previous, allegedly abusive therapist, indicate that therapists who sexually abuse multiple patients have severe character psychopathology with antisocial features. In California, repeat offenders may get a prison sentence and lose their license. However, the statute is only a few years old and there are no data as yet.

Psychiatrists have ethical and legal responsibilities as directors, supervisors, employers or when practicing in association with nonmedical professionals. Psychiatrists can play a key role in preventing sexual misconduct through education on the handling of the erotic transference and by calling attention to the ethical and legal requirements with respect to sexual misconduct in the health care field. Various states have specific laws (criminal and/or civil) that deal with sexual misconduct. Few states have mandatory reporting laws. California has a mandatory information law. The California law requires that therapists inform every patient, who alleges sexual involvement with a prior therapist, of their options by giving the patient the California Consumer Affairs brochure, "Professional Therapy *Never* Includes Sex" (1990). Consultations with one's own professional ethics committee as well as legal consultation from one's malpractice insurance can often be very helpful because such patients present complex problems for subsequent therapists. Proper attention to the ethical and legal requirements is the best protection against psychiatrists being held vicariously liable for the actions of their supervisees, associates or trainees.

CLINICAL EXAMPLES

Case 1

This is a malpractice case illustrating a number of boundary violations. Specific authorization to release the data anonymously has been obtained from the consulting attorney and client–patient.

The patient was a nonmedical mental health trainee who entered treatment for depression in her mid-thirties following her husband's death. The patient's history included severe multiple childhood traumas including: repeated moves; witnessing death and mutilated bodies; discovering her father's dead body just after his suicide, followed by years of depression; traumatic separations from her mother following her father's violent death; corporal punishment at the hands of caretakers for crying during placement in adolescence after father's death; at least three episodes of molestation by nonfamily adult males in childhood; and a recent experience with a prior therapist who made overt sexual advances toward her.

The patient had made an extensive search to find a reliable therapist in order to avoid a repetition of the experience with the previous therapist. She started treatment with someone she felt she could trust. After two years of essentially uneventful psychotherapy, the patient expressed to her therapist her desire "to be a nonintrusive member of your family." The therapist gratified the patient's wish in the following ways: he referred his own private patients to her for diagnostic evaluation; invited her to his home for dinner with his family; exchanged gifts with her at holidays; invited her to social functions at his home; gave her his own professional writings to read and help edit; wrote recommendation letters for her application for professional employment; gratified her request to become her supervisor; disclosed his own and his family's illnesses to her and shared with her his feelings about these.

The therapist's involvement with the patient intensified in the following ways: (1) he visited her at her office on her birthday, bringing her flowers and a heart-shaped piece of jewelry for a present; (2) he invited her to participate in his business dealings with clear expectations of her being employed by him, and urged her to encourage the participation of her peers in the business. Finally there were multiple episodes of close embraces, kisses, and several instances of touching of her buttocks. This patient developed a full-blown, posttraumatic stress syndrome which was ushered in by atypical headaches and somatization disorder. The patient was given a variety of diagnoses and treatments until she was finally able to confront her past traumas and revictimization. The subsequent psychotherapy helped her integrate past and present. She empowered herself through the malpractice action.

This case illustrates the variety of boundary violations and the technical, ethical, and legal aspects of such violations. Not every violation is unethical or illegal or even a deviation of "proper" psychotherapeutic technique. This case illustrates the slippery slope of boundary violations. From the perspective of clinical practice, one would need a full, detailed analysis to trace the transference and countertransference derailment. Several of these boundary violations may be psychotherapeutically valid, technical interventions backed by theoretical concepts. Others are clearly unethical practice, illegal, and constitute substandard or negligent care. Thus the range of the slippery slope often ends in tragic situations.

Case 2

The second case is also from a malpractice case, which also involves a woman. She was in her late twenties when she sought treatment, a few years after the death of her father. She is the oldest of three sisters and was married in her late teens to her adolescent, first love and had a daughter at age 19. Her husband, two years her senior, was clearly neither ready nor interested in dealing with the realities of marriage and parenthood. When he insisted that he bring into their home his newborn baby by his girl friend, the patient divorced him. However, her disappointment and bitter disillusionment led to a reactive depression that lasted several years.

The patient sought treatment for her depression and anxiety about establishing her own manufacturing business. She selected a male therapist because of his radio programs and his "self-confidence and self-assurance." He told her he was highly experienced and had a great success rate. She was convinced of her inferiority and felt intimidated by bankers who told her she would never get any financial loans to start a business without a prior record of experience in her field. The therapist had a personal interest in business, having been involved in various ventures. He agreed to accompany the patient to various banks and help her deal with the bankers. The patient was in great financial need and was unable to pay for her treatment. The therapist proposed to treat her on loan. When the patient needed money for her business, the therapist proposed that they consider her fees for her treatment as his investment in her business and that he get a percentage of her business in exchange for her treatment. The percentage of ownership was raised over the sixteen years of treatment to approximately 25 percent.

Over the sixteen years the patient was able to establish an international company that became very profitable. The patient maintained weekly contact with the therapist for psychotherapy and sent to her therapist for evaluation and treatment: her lovers, her employees, her daughter, her friends. The therapist agreed to see everyone she referred to him and rarely declined to treat whomever she asked him to. He routinely discussed his views of their problems with her, violating their confidentiality.

The therapist disclosed to the patient details of his personal history including his past marriage and betrayal by his exwife. He told his family and his friends that he was a part owner of the patient's business. He invited the patient to his home and to his family functions. The patient was embarrassed that they all knew her and surprised that they thought her business belonged to her therapist. She was disturbed when she found out the therapist wanted out of her business, wished to recover his investment, and retire. She felt abandoned and threatened because, by then, she felt totally dependent on him.

The patient had great difficulties with her mother and sisters. One of the sisters became very ill and died from a chronic debilitating illness over a six-year period. The other sister was chronically envious and competitive with her. Her mother was ill and dependent on her. Her therapist was consulted by her about everything she did and she believed in his superior knowledge despite the fact that his advice was repeatedly wrong. Though he had agreed to do so, he never really provided any review of her actual business or offered any direct consultation or supervision of it, even when she specifically requested him to do so, such as when she was away on trips.

The realization that "he was a false mental support for me" came after the therapist asked her to buy him out because he needed the money. When she offered to pay him a modest amount, the therapist exploded, accused her of making him sick and devastating him "after all I have done for you." He accused her of loving one of her employees more than him "after I made you what you are." He accused her of being incredibly greedy and foolish in not agreeing to buy him off, and threatened to sue her in order to collect what he considered his share of his patient's business.

This patient developed a reactive depression. At the time of the initial consultation, which her attorney had requested, the patient was blaming herself for the "breakup" of their relationship. She slowly and painfully recognized the meaning of her intense dependency on him. She stated, "What made him special to me was that he was always very interested in me from the very beginning." This patient cried over her realization: "I had a father who didn't even notice me and who died and left me. My mother always needed to see me as great. I was very hurt by my daughter's father. I can't even call him my exhusband—that was the great disappointment. I ended up having to be in charge and take care of everyone and now he wants me to take care of him too."

In this case, the therapist had "lost" his daughter through the divorce and his hunger for her was acted out with this patient. The patient told me that she felt she had a lot in common with his daughter. The therapist's hunger for his daughter mirrored the patient's hunger for her lost father. They found each other and proceeded to act out the respective roles, obtaining and receiving actual gratification in the transference–countertransference of the treatment relationship. The therapist assumed multiple roles vis-à-vis this patient which involved him in direct conflict of interest and violated his ethical and legal responsibilities toward her. The patient was aware that every time the therapist asked for a percentage of her business, she felt "strange" but felt she had no choice. At the beginning, she was desperate, later she was in mourning and exhausted after her sister's six-year battle with illness and her eventual death. Still later she continued to feel unable to separate from her therapist, viewing herself as totally dependent on him. This patient's problems with individuation, sexual identity, and a defective sense of self were never addressed but, even worse, she became trapped in the transference–countertransference with a therapist whose narcissistic and selfobject needs led to her abuse.

This patient has yet to deal with the full impact of the abusive, negligent psychotherapy in which she was involved. She was retraumatized by the therapist through the repetition of the disappointment in her father and first husband and the reliving (with the therapist) of the needy, dependent selfobject relationship with her mother. Despite a great business success, she lives a withdrawn, constricted personal life and suffers from depression.

Case 3

This case is from a consultation with a colleague who told me of his friend, the patient, and who gave me permission to release the data anonymously.

The patient had been in psychoanalysis for four years for neurotic difficulties. During the treatment the patient had greatly improved and had become extremely wealthy. During the last year of treatment, the psychiatrist disclosed to his patient that he was involved in a business project and solicited investment in this project by the patient. The patient felt very grateful and loyal to his analyst and willingly invested in the deal. The psychiatrist and the patient became socially involved around this business deal and their involvement continued after termination of the treatment.

A psychiatrist, a close friend of the patient, witnessed the extensive business dealings between his friend and his colleague and informed his friend that this was improper. The patient defended his analyst and denied there was any impropriety. It was at that time that I was consulted about this. I informed the colleague that, without the patient's consent, *no* ethics complaint could be made.

Some years later, the colleague called and gave me this follow-up. Some years later, the patient sought treatment with a different analyst. During his second analysis, he realized that his previous analyst was unethical and that he had been exploited. He sought and found his exanalyst. He had an extensive meeting with him during which he confronted him with his rage about the past exploitation. The exanalyst acknowledged his wrong-doing and apologized to the patient.

No malpractice suit or ethics complaint was ever filed. The patient specifically refused to take any further action.

This is the norm for the vast majority of cases of boundary violations, whether they be sexual or nonsexual. This conforms to much of what we are learning about other varieties of abuse throughout the human life cycle. I elected to include this case, even though it is essentially hearsay (I never personally interviewed the patient) because it illustrates other issues besides the obvious boundary violation.

I want to focus attention on the witnessing of abuse. The colleague/friend was disturbed. Calling me was part of his having to work through his own indignation, alarm, and helplessness. It isn't only in psychotherapy that we have to *endure*, contain, and metabolize, it is in life too.

It takes courage and hope to know and endure without giving in to one's righteous indignation or distorting one's vision of the truth. The colleague did his friend a great service by telling him what he saw. The friend had to work it through and get to it on his own.

In a real sense, my presentation here is my attempt to deal with my witnessings. In 1977, when I started working in this area, I reconnected with my past and my roots. I had a renewed appreciation of the need of the ancient Athenians for their theater. I came to understand why they used the tragic dramas as a religious experience. They had to metabolize their own awareness of the true dimensions of the horrors of everyday life lest they became victims of their psychic defenses, oscillating between the axes of psychic numbness and victim–abuser.

Case 4

This case comes from the ethics files. Details have been omitted to maintain confidentiality.

A female patient, a divorced woman with a preteenage son, had been in psychotherapy for many years for depression with psychotic features. The psychiatrist had recently established a private business and convinced his patient to invest her money from the sale of her home in his newly established corporation. The psychiatrist had encouraged the patient's identification with him and supported her decision to sell her home in order to begin medical studies in Europe at the age of 34, accompanied by her 11-year-old child for whom she was the sole parent. While in Europe, the patient had expected that the psychiatrist would support her emotionally and financially through her investment in his company. When the unrealistic situation led to her eventual deterioration, she returned home and filed an ethics complaint against her psychiatrist.

The psychiatrist was found guilty of exploitation of the patient. He was sanctioned for his ethical misconduct with expulsion from his district branch of the American Psychiatric Association.

Case 5

This case also comes from the ethics files and details are also omitted to preserve confidentiality.

A female patient was in treatment for adjustment problems centered around her divorce. She improved and began to look for work. The psychiatrist offered her employment in his office and continued the treatment. The patient realized that the psychiatrist was often intoxicated during work hours and was acting inappropriately with female patients who were calling and complaining. She filed an ethics complaint against her employer–psychiatrist and a malpractice suit. Several other patients also filed ethics complaints.

The psychiatrist was found guilty of numerous ethics violations and was expelled from his district branch and the American Psychiatric Association.

These cases both involved boundary violations that resulted in the expulsion of a member from the professional
society. These ethics sanctions occurred prior to the establishment of the National Data Bank. Since the fall of 1990 there is
mandatory reporting of both disciplinary actions and malpractice awards or settlements on physicians and dentists to the
National Data Bank. Eventually the practice of all licensed
health care professionals will be monitored by the National Data
Bank. This imposes a very high standard of accountability for
the entire health care field. This has implications for the training of professionals. The practice of psychotherapy always required that practitioners have an intimate understanding of
their own psychological function, traumas, vulnerabilities, and
dysfunctions. This is no longer required for "training purposes" by the analytic institutes for the few clinicians who want
such training. It is a requirement for *survival* as a psychotherapist. Both personal treatment and supervision are a must and,
as Freud said, "interminable," with reentry on an as-needed
basis.

My experience in this field has taught me that the usual
measures of training, experience, title, rank, institutional affiliation, age, and gender cannot offer protection from committing such violations. The only protection is awareness and alertness to the potential for such outcomes, never forgetting that
"the road to hell is paved with good intentions."

Case 6

This case came from consultation and I have permission to give
the data but not the names.

A child psychiatrist was treating a child patient whose parents were divorcing. The father died in an auto accident and the mother became depressed. The psychiatrist was childless and became interested in adopting the patient. His wife insisted that he obtain consultation prior to making this offer to the mother of the patient. The consultant recommended that the psychiatrist seek treatment for his own depression and explore adoption in conjoint sessions with his wife. He advised against any mention of adoption to the mother of his patient and recommended supervision of his treatment of this patient.

The treating psychiatrist agreed with the recommendations. No ethics violation actually occurred.

Case 7

This case came from the national press.

On June 29, 1990, the *Los Angeles Times* reported that a psychiatrist practicing in New York pleaded guilty to two counts of securities fraud before the U.S. District Court. He had been treating the wife of a financier. When his patient disclosed her husband's plans to assume the chairmanship of a major bank, he notified his broker of that fact and bought $171,130 worth of bank stock. When the announcement of the financier's attempt to become the CEO of the bank was made public, he sold the stock, making a $27,475 profit.

The psychiatrist was investigated by the Securities and Exchange Commission and was charged with insider trading. The psychiatrist neither admitted nor denied the charges but surrendered the profits and paid a fine of $26,933.74.

DISCUSSION

Traditionally, ethical issues have been taught as part of the technique of treatment. Since Freud's recommendations on technique, psychotherapists have been warned they must maintain a position of neutrality and abstinence. In recent years extensive discussion has taken place about these technical recommendations. These attitudes have been found to be specifically contraindicated in the treatment of certain patients. Clinicians of varied orientations and theoretical views often have different technical recommendations, different styles and approaches to patients. However, the ethical and legal considerations are basic to clinical practice regardless of specific orientation, type of treatment, or psychotherapeutic approach.

The ethical requirement to put the care and needs of patients ahead of one's own requires considerable restraint, self-discipline, and a capacity for self-reflection in order to process and metabolize the myriad of pressures and influences stemming from the intensity of the clinical work. Practitioners with unresolved conflicts over ambition, desire for power, and opportunism, are at risk under the diverse circumstances that clinical practice presents (Rangell, 1980). Clinicians can be vulnerable to getting involved in boundary violations for a variety of reasons. Even the most experienced clinician can become vulnerable under conditions of a personal life crisis because of narcissistic vulnerabilities and deeply repressed omnipotent needs.

The consequences for patients of such violations vary, depending on the type of transgression. Ethical and legal violations may be involved. When the transgression fulfills the narcissistic needs of the patient or are part of revictimization, the recognition by the patient of the reality of the violation may take years. Denial, idealization of the therapist, and identification with him or her, as well as various transference configurations and defenses, tend to make recognition of the transgression by the patient very difficult. However, the damage to the patient can be extensive. Such experiences may be relivings or reenactments of past traumas with severe consequences in terms of life decisions and choices.

It is not unusual for patients to take years before they can recognize the fact of the transgression. The dynamics seen in patients who have been involved in nonsexual boundary violations with their therapists are similar to those seen in patients who have been involved in sexual boundary violations. Experience with cases of sexual misconduct has revealed that nonsexual boundary violations characteristically preceded the sexual by months or years in a significant number of cases. Patients involved with their therapists in nonsexual or sexual boundary violations are characteristically very reluctant to lodge complaints or file suits. However, the situation is changing as a result of increased patient education and public awareness.

In summary, patients who are abused by their therapists often exhibit:

1. Denial, repression, and dissociation;
2. Delay in recognition of abuse;
3. Self-recrimination and fear of personal exposure;
4. The need to report the abuse as part of healing and empowerment.

I close by quoting Judith Herman, who in discussing Kluft's 1990 book *Incest-Related Syndromes of Adult Psychopathology*, wrote "to speak publicly about one's knowledge of atrocities is to invite the stigma that attaches to victims. Those who attempt to describe atrocities that they have witnessed also risk their credibility" (p. 290).

REFERENCES

American Medical Association (1980), Proceedings of AMA House of Delegates: July 20–24, 1980. Chicago, IL: American Medical Association, pp. 204–208.

American Medical Association, Council on Ethical and Judicial Affairs (1989), *Current Opinions of the Council on Ethical and Judicial Affairs*, Opinion 8.14, Sexual Misconduct. Chicago, IL: American Medical Association.

———— (1991), Sexual misconduct in the practice of medicine. *J. Amer. Med. Assn.*, 266:2741–2745.

American Psychiatric Association (1973), *The Principles of Medical Ethics with Annotations Especially Applicable to Psychiatry*. Washington, DC: American Psychiatric Association.

———— (1986 videotape), *Ethical Concerns about Sexual Involvement Between Psychiatrists and Patients*. Washington, DC: American Psychiatric Press.

———— (1989a), *The Principles of Medical Ethics with Annotations Especially Applicable to Psychiatry*. Washington, DC: American Psychiatric Press.

——— (1989b), Conflicts of interest. Ethics Committee, *Ethics Newsletter*, Volume 5, #2.

——— (1990 videotape), *Reporting Ethical Concerns*. Washington, DC: American Psychiatric Press.

California Department of Consumer Affairs (1990), *Professional Therapy Never Includes Sex*. Sacramento, CA: Medical Board of California.

Dryer, A. R. (1988), *Ethics and Psychiatry*. Washington, DC: American Psychiatric Press, pp. 15–28.

Gabbard, G. O. (1991), Psychodynamics of sexual boundary violations. *Psychiatric Annals*, 21:651–655.

Gartrell, N. K., Milliken, N., Goodson, W. H., Thiemann, S., Lo, B. (1992), Physician-patient sexual contact: Prevalence and problems. *West. J. Med.*, 157:139–143.

Hastings Center (1978), *In the Service of the State: The Psychiatrist as Double Agent*. Special Supplement. Hastings-on-Hudson, NY: Hastings Center.

Herman, J. L. (1992), *Trauma and Recovery*. New York: Basic Books.

Kluft, R. P. (1990), *Incest-Related Syndromes of Adult Psychopathology*. Washington, DC: American Psychiatric Press.

Nemiroff, R. A. (1992), Adult trauma and its consequences. Presented at the Victims of Abuse conference of the San Diego Psychoanalytic Society and Institute, February 15, 1992, unpublished.

Rangell, L. (1980), *The Mind of Watergate: An Exploration of the Compromise of Integrity*. New York: W. W. Norton.

Simon, R. I. (1987), *Clinical Psychiatry and the Law*. Washington, DC: American Psychiatric Press, pp. 276–304.

——— ed. (1992), *Review of Clinical Psychiatry and the Law*. Washington, DC: American Psychiatric Press.

Chapter 10

Countertransference Issues in the Treatment of Victims of Abuse

Edward L. Fields, M.D.

In the psychoanalytic and psychotherapeutic treatment of victims of abuse, it is common for therapists to experience strong and sometimes uncomfortable feelings, thoughts, and fantasies about their patients, themselves, and the therapy (Burland and Raskin, 1990; Levine, 1990; Lisman-Pieczanski, 1990; Raphling, 1990). Such responses may be considered countertransference reactions, which may occur as "general" reactions, as in any other psychoanalysis or psychotherapy, but also may include specific types of reactions which seem to occur commonly in the treatment of patients who have been victims of abuse.

The ability to recognize our countertransference reactions can be a crucial step in understanding and analyzing our patients' transferences. This step is often more difficult in the treatment of victims of abuse because the kinds of countertransference reactions that such patients and such treatments engender are often less acceptable, more uncomfortable, and sometimes frankly objectionable for us than many other countertransference reactions. As a result, such reactions may go unnoticed and unanalyzed by therapists unless extra effort is made to become aware of them.

187

TRANSFERENCE AND COUNTERTRANSFERENCE

One of the unique contributions of psychoanalytic thinking is the focus on understanding the unconscious factors in motivation (e.g., wishes and fears), in developing "meaning," in behavior, and in the functioning of relationships. A special area of interest is how these factors are expressed in the treatment itself, in the clinical phenomenon we call transference. Transference may be defined as the unconscious repetition and displacement of patterns of feelings, attitudes, and behavior experienced originally with important people in the past, but now reexperienced in the present and directed toward the therapist.

The analogue of transference is countertransference, defined originally by Freud (1910, 1915) as the analyst's reactions to the patient's transference. This definition has since evolved to include the analyst's own transference to the patient, especially when such reactions become an impediment to the treatment. Many analysts now include in the definition all of the analyst's reactions to the patient, both conscious and unconscious[1] (Tyson, 1986). I will use the term in this way in this chapter.

The "counter" in countertransference refers not to the idea of an opposing part, as in attack and counterattack, but rather to a complementary or parallel part to the transference (Greenson, 1967). It was thought at one time that countertransference was an unwanted occurrence and an obstacle to treatment, and it had a pejorative meaning (transference had been similarly regarded). But today it is recognized that the emotional reactions of the therapist can be an important aid in understanding the patient's transference; that is, countertransference can help us understand the hidden meanings (Sandler, Dale, and Holder, 1973) of certain verbal and behavioral expressions of our patients; at times the countertransference reactions are the first clue to this understanding (Heimann, 1950). Sometimes we are aware of a vague feeling, or a passing thought or fantasy, which does not seem to "fit"; that kind of

---

[1] Some analysts prefer to use the term *counterreactions* in this context (Moore and Fine, 1990).

experience may be an indicator of something that is happening in the treatment that we are not consciously aware of, and therefore, may constitute important information about the patient, ourselves, and the process.

What I have described so far refers in general to transference and countertransference. But what are the special issues that occur in the treatment of victims of abuse in this regard? The primary issue for such patients is the violation of boundaries—of the body (literally), of autonomy, and of the sense of self—and how these violations have led to patients' problems with trust, and to confusion over the difference between thoughts and actions.

These patients often fear that their therapists will literally abuse them again; and if not literally, then "abuse" them again by denying, not understanding, not accepting what has happened to them, or by judging or shaming them. In particular, the refusal by others to believe them, or to accept what has happened to them, is another kind of abuse that many of these patients have experienced.

In regard to the boundary between thoughts and actions, it seems that after the basic trust that patients had placed in important figures during childhood was shattered (especially if they were abused by their parents during childhood), the result is that the normal but forbidden wishes of childhood (e.g., certain sexual wishes), which usually are only fantasies, have become actual realities, so that the distinction between fantasy and reality has become blurred. It is often difficult from that point on for such patients to recognize that whatever they might think or feel will not necessarily take place just because they thought it or felt it. A corollary to this idea is that these patients often feel a sense of exaggerated responsibility, power, and control. In therapy, they may believe that if they think or feel a certain way, or especially if they *act* a certain way, they will cause the therapist to act, and the original trauma will be repeated. Because of these sensitivities they are exquisitely attuned to their therapists' behavior—appearance, tone of voice, and movements, as well as words. This sensitivity itself can put tremendous pressure on their therapists, since these patients will scrutinize us in ways that other patients may not.

From the countertransference view then, we need to be aware of these pressures on ourselves, and then to consistently recognize just how frightened, cautious, and vigilant these patients are, and why they feel they need to be so careful. We often have to repeatedly hear their accounts of the abuse, empathize with them, and to some degree feel their pain. That means experiencing their sorrow and rage, and the helplessness that they have felt in the past, and feel now, and it also means indicating our understanding and acceptance of their abuse, so that they can trust us, and go on in the treatment. But all of this can be extremely hard to do, especially when the therapist's natural inclination would be to try to get away from such uncomfortable feelings as quickly as possible.

As a result of going beyond these initial stages, we often become aware of other feelings that are less expected, such as wishes to deny the abuse or minimize it in order to get away from the pain. When that does not work, there are sometimes feelings of despair, hopelessness, disgust, outrage at the abuser, detachment, boredom, and emotional deadness. These feelings can be unexpected, not only in their quality, but also in their intensity, and this can cause great discomfort.

As we go still further in the therapy[2] (particularly in analyzing the frequent presence of emotional deprivation and internal conflicts that preceded, accompanied, or, especially, followed the abuse), we often have to face even more uncomfortable feelings within ourselves, those that are both less "expectable" and also less acceptable: a strange curiosity and voyeuristic fascination with the details of the sexual and aggressive or violent acts; and sometimes sexual arousal, anger, or hostility toward the victims themselves. Such feelings are often accompanied by a sense of shame and guilt, and therefore may be the most likely reactions to go unnoticed, and therefore, unanalyzed.

Often therapists will question their reactions, wondering whether they are normal. They will ask themselves whether

---

[2]I am not suggesting an actual temporal sequence in which countertransference reactions occur throughout the therapy, but I am suggesting a continuum of feelings in regard to how expected such reactions might be, especially when therapists are working for the first time with victims of abuse.

they are bad people, are unfeeling or overinvolved as therapists. Do their sexual feelings make them perverts or potential
child molesters? We think of ourselves as nice people. We try
to help, yet we are told by our abused patients that we are not
helping; that we are cold, don't really care, or that the patients
feel we are trying to take advantage of them, or we actually
enjoy hurting them. Sometimes we are told that we are being
abusive, and sometimes we feel we *are* being abusive. Yet at
other times we feel that we are the ones who are being abused.

How can we understand these feelings and reactions? I will
mention only two countertransference issues here. The first is
the general countertransference problem of the therapist's
blind spots, those unanalyzed transferences of the therapist to
the patient; the second involves the responses of the therapist
to the patient's transference, and it is this aspect of countertransference that I will highlight first.

The fact that the kinds of countertransference reactions I
described above occur regularly in the treatment of victims of
abuse suggests that there is some effect that such patients may
have on their therapists, presumably through the transference.
For example, when the issues of abuse are activated in the
therapy and specifically in the transference, the patient will
often experience the therapist as the "abuser." But the patient
may not only experience the therapist as abuser, but may act
and behave in ways that convey the experience of "victim" to
the therapist, and attempt (unconsciously) to elicit a complementary behavior from the therapist, as "abuser."

In this formulation I am utilizing Sandler's (1976) concept
of the "role-responsiveness" of the analyst, in which he proposed a model to explain how patients' intrapsychic "role-rela-
tionships" are played out in therapy. He described a process:

[In which the] role-relationship of the patient in analysis
at any particular time consists of a role in which he casts
himself, and a *complementary role* in which he casts the analyst at that particular time. The patient's transference
would thus represent an attempt by him to impose an
interaction, an interrelationship (in the broadest sense of
the word) between himself and the analyst [p. 44].

He then illustrated how, through subtle behaviors (unconscious to the patient, and often to the analyst at first) the patient
"attempts to prod the analyst into behaving in a particular way"
(p. 44).

I believe that the therapist's responses to such "prodding"
will depend on a number of factors, such as the patient's methods and effectiveness in this respect, or the therapist's blind
spots. But ideally the therapist's responses would be limited to
experiences (feelings, thoughts, and fantasies), and would not
be carried over into actions. Although minor enactments may
be unavoidable, and sometimes may even be instructive (Jacobs,
1986), our goal is not to reenact the trauma with the patient,
but to understand it, and then to utilize the patient's reexperiencing of the abuse in a constructive way, so that it can now be
consciously understood and resolved as well as possible. Patients
often will be able to see for themselves, after they have had
such transference patterns interpreted, how they have acted in
these same ways in relationships outside of the current treatment, and even before they were in treatment.

Although we must allow patients to experience us in a
variety of ways, including that of abuser (or of victim), we also
must be careful in our interventions. For example, if we rush
in quickly to "defend" ourselves, or to "rescue" our patient, who
is now feeling like the victim of our "abuse," we may deprive our
patient of the opportunity to explore and discover just what
had triggered his or her reactions at that moment, and of the
opportunity to understand the patient's own possible contribution in setting up these roles. We must also not deny, and therefore must be able to recognize, any contributions we have made
to the reactions our patients may have; for example, our usual
verbal interventions. We must also be vigilant about not contributing to further trauma through an enactment on our part;
for example, by actually becoming verbally abusive or sexually
seductive.

Our stance as therapists can be a real balancing act, which
requires that we monitor our own feelings throughout the therapy. This monitoring can help us get our bearings and keep us
on course. In addition, we must be comfortable enough with

our own feelings, thoughts, and fantasies, including those that are sexual, aggressive, and even violent in nature, to see the difference ourselves between thoughts and deeds. This distinction is important in order to allow therapists to feel, think, and fantasize, so that we can make use of all of these types of associative material in understanding ourselves and what is being generated in us in the interaction with our patient. In addition, we must be able to be appropriately supportive, as well as appropriately assertive in exploring and analyzing the material in the therapy. On the one hand, we must be supportive enough with victims of abuse so that they know that they can reveal to us, at their own pace, the horrors that they have experienced; our being too assertive in probing for details could be experienced as a repetition of the original trauma. On the other hand, our being overly or excessively supportive and not assertive enough in exploring the unconscious meanings, fears, and wishes of the patient may mean depriving the patient of the opportunity for a better resolution of the internal conflicts (particularly in regard to unconscious shame and guilt) which may perpetuate the clinical symptoms.

CLINICAL EXAMPLES

I am now going to describe three clinical vignettes of patients who were victims of abuse to illustrate certain kinds of transference and countertransference reactions that I have observed with such patients.

The first case exemplifies certain typical emotional responses that I had in the treatment of a victim of abuse, as well as how the absence of an expected reaction constituted a countertransference clue to the patient's transference. The second case demonstrates my countertransference reactions, based on both my transference to the patient and a transference reaction of the patient's in which he behaved in ways that elicited such a "role responsive" reaction from me, and one which I believe is common in certain victims of abuse. The third case illustrates what I believe is another common transference reaction in victims of abuse, and one which also was accompanied by a behavioral pattern which was unconsciously "designed" to elicit reactions from others, as well as from me.

This first case also illustrates certain typical features of some victims of abuse: first, the attempts to repress and deny the abuse, and to disavow certain kinds of knowledge and impulses; and second, the excessive sense of responsibility, as well as guilt and shame, which led to the patient's feeling that, "It's all my fault."

Case 1

The patient was a highly successful and now wealthy businesswoman in her early forties, married with several children, who entered treatment because of feelings of low self-esteem, which she, herself, had connected with her past history of severe poverty and deprivation during childhood. She was so ashamed of her family and her history that she felt that anyone who knew of her past would be disgusted by it and would shun and reject her, as had happened to her during her childhood. These themes were present early on in the treatment as fears that I, too, would judge her, reproach her, be disgusted with her, and reject her. Despite her fears, I did not have those kinds of emotional reactions at all. Instead (although I never discussed my reactions with her), I felt great sorrow and despair for her experiences of deprivation and poverty. But what I could not understand was why she still felt so responsible, ashamed, and guilty for these early circumstances, which I will now describe.

Her history was one of enormous deprivation: she grew up as the fifth of eight children, destitute, in the Mid-West dust bowl of the 1930s, in the middle of the Depression. She lived in the worst area of a small town. Her father was "the town drunk," her mother had epileptic seizures, and other kids would tease the patient that her mother was a "witch." The patient was embarrassed and ashamed of both her parents. When she was in elementary school her mother was sent to a state hospital for epileptics, and because her father was often drunk or in jail, she and the other children were sent to live with various relatives. The family was then sometimes together, but frequently apart, and because of the continued difficulties, the entire family was eventually split up, and the patient and her siblings became wards of the state, and were sent to live in foster homes. She was occasionally reunited for some periods with her family, however, and always believed her father's promises that he would get the family back together again, but he never did.

As she told me this history, she often cried, and I felt extremely sad too. It was a painful story to hear. As with other victims of abuse, she needed to tell me her story with all of its pain, and what she needed from me was that I listen and bear with her through the terrible sense of sorrow and despair. She had never actually told these details to anyone in her life, and so the telling and retelling served important functions for her. Among these memories was a most poignant one about how, as kids, she and her brothers and sisters would go to the park in the summer. They were constantly hungry, because there was never enough to eat. They would wait until other people who were having a picnic in the park would leave, and then they would go through the trash cans to pick out the scraps of food the picnickers had left behind. She felt so ashamed and humiliated in telling me of this behavior that she could barely get out the words.

As I sat there listening to this woman, the contrast was striking to me: here was an articulate, intelligent, well-dressed, successful woman who sat in my office telling me about these terrible events that she had experienced, and I was aware that part of my reaction was not only that I found it painful to hear, and difficult to believe, as I looked at her now, but also that I did not *want* to believe it either, just as she did not want to believe that these things had really been a part of her life.

Throughout the early part of the treatment she always felt relief after telling me one of these stories about the deprivation, but still was always expecting that the next story would be the one that would finally cause me to say, "I've had it!" and that the treatment was at an end. When I asked why she expected that kind of reaction she would associate to such reactions from other people, such as girls who wouldn't be her friend, boys who teased her about her family, and finally, the crowning blow of being placed in a foster home, with her sense of herself after that as "bad." She had the accompanying conviction after that time that everything bad that happened to her was of her own making, because she herself was bad.

But why was she bad? It wasn't only the emotional deprivation, or the poverty, but something that I have not yet mentioned, and that she did not mention for a long time: the sexual abuse. There were multiple instances with a number of people, but she could not tell me about the sexual abuse until she first "remembered" it herself; that is, until she felt trusting enough to tell me what she consciously knew, and until the therapeutic alliance was well enough established that she felt safe, and could allow some lifting of repression, and enough regression that the deeper transference feelings could develop. Up until this time, in the transference, I had been an idealized parent, mostly the father that she never had, to whom she could "confess" the terrible experiences of her life, but toward whom she felt only a sense of friendship and gratitude. Although she could not at first remember the episodes of sexual abuse, she would become anxious at certain moments during the sessions, for reasons which at first were not clear; but as we later learned, these were times when these memories were beginning to come closer to the surface. In particular, as the transference intensified, she started to feel even closer to me and began to recognize her affectionate feelings, which were soon followed by what she described as "pure, romantic feelings," and finally, by "those bad sexual feelings." Although the sexual feelings were the most disturbing to her, it was in the context of this developing erotic transference that she began to recall, literally in flashes of memory, the various sexual abuses. These had been perpetrated by several male relatives, as well as men in the various foster homes, throughout her childhood years, but had culminated at about age 11 in her father's sexual advances, when he attempted while drunk to actually have intercourse with her, until she managed to push him away. When she ran, crying and horrified, and told her mother, her mother said, "Oh, no dear, it must be your imagination."

Unfortunately, it had not been just her imagination. But for years after that she had tried to repress and deny the sexual abuse, much as her mother had done. But the intensifying transference now allowed these memories to emerge with a strong emotional reaction. It later became clear that much of the shame and guilt that she felt about the deprivation and poverty, and about her father's alcoholism and her mother's epilepsy, involved a displacement from the shame and guilt over the sexual abuse. Later in the treatment she acknowledged that she always *knew* that realistically she was not responsible for the poverty, or for her mother's and father's neglect, but she did feel responsible for the sexual abuse.

What also became clear through the transference was how she had disavowed her *own* sexual wishes and desires. She had felt so guilty over any sexual feelings and wishes in the past that she preferred to believe she did not have them. Instead, she would pride herself on being seen as a prude, and felt that sex was for men and for "loose women," because "nice girls just don't feel that way."

But as her sexual feelings toward me increased, her guilt now was over not only what had happened in the past, but over what she now feared, and, as she eventually recognized, wished would happen: that she have a sexual relationship with me. It was a great step forward in the treatment when she was actually able to verbalize this wish. We were then able to explore the meaning of such a wish to her, and the fantasies that surrounded it. Her fantasy of sex with me was that it would mean that she was both a desirable woman, and, in a more general sense, a worthwhile and lovable person. It was as if the sex would be a reparation for her sense of being defective, as well as the gratification of a forbidden wish.

In regard to my countertransference, I had begun to observe a change in my feelings when she first told me of her sexual desire for me. I became particularly curious when I noticed that I felt very little emotional response to what she said, and that seemed strange! At first I was puzzled by my lack of response and wondered if I was denying my own sexual response to her. I knew that when she had spoken in the past of all kinds of emotional experiences and feelings, I had always been able to empathize with and react to her emotions. Then,

in analyzing why I wasn't having at least *some* response, I realized that there was very little to respond to—she was not really
telling me her feelings, but was telling me *about* her feelings. In
order to be sure that this was not just my own perception of
what was happening, I asked her, as she was telling me about
her strong sexual feelings for me, what she was actually experiencing emotionally. She paused, then giggled nervously, and
said, "Not much. Actually, even though I was telling you what
I was thinking, it was as if side by side with that, somehow, I
was also going through the things on my shopping list that I
have to pick up on my way home!" I was then able to interpret
to her that she was holding back on her feelings because she
did not want to actually feel these strong sexual feelings; that
is, that she did not want to feel stimulated and aroused in my
presence. She agreed, became more anxious, and said that she
was afraid of "what could happen," then blurted out that she
was afraid that if she told me what she was feeling that "it would
lead to sex." I asked why, and as she started to cry she said,
"How can I tell you that I love you and want to have sex with
you, without it sounding like an invitation to actually *have* sex?"

This woman believed that she had to inhibit and then isolate her sexual feelings to keep herself from being aroused, and
to keep me from being aroused too, because just having such
feelings meant that they would be enacted, as she felt had happened with her father. These fears are similar to what I had
mentioned earlier about how, especially with many victims of
abuse, the thought equals the deed; in other words, to this
woman, just *wanting* to have sex was the same as *doing* it, and
as "wrong" as doing it. In addition, just because *she* wanted to,
in her mind, meant that I would comply. She felt that if she
did not control herself and her feelings, sex with me would be
inevitable, and then, as she said, "It will be all *my* fault," as she
had felt it was with her father.

In review then, my countertransference reactions included
my initial sadness and sorrow, as part of the pain that I felt in
enduring with her the reliving of each of her traumatic experiences, as well as the relatively pleasant reactions to her idealizing father transference; then, as she revealed the sexual abuse

with even more pain, I felt despair, anger, outrage, and help-lessness, plus an awareness of not wanting to hear more about it, and, like the patient and her mother, wished it had been "just her imagination." Next was my awareness of my—and then her—lack of feelings as she described her sexual wishes toward me, and this was a most important clue in understand-ing the struggle she had had with these desires, and how her attempts to deny the earlier abuse had led to her disavowal of all sexual wishes.

This case also illustrates the need to explore, in addition to the abuse, and in order to relieve the guilt and shame, the patient's unconsciously disavowed forbidden wishes. The themes presented here appear to be common and typical pat-terns of transference and countertransference reactions that occur in the treatment of victims of abuse.

Case 2

This vignette illustrates, in a sense, the opposite of the first case: not denial of abuse, but the use of it for secondary gain. Whereas the first patient blamed herself for the abuse, this man almost flaunted his abuse in his identification of himself as a victim, and only a victim, helpless to change, with the expecta-tion that others would, and should, do what he wanted for him.

The patient was a single professional man about 30 years of age, an only child who still lived with his mother. He came for treatment because he could not make a commitment to his girl friend, whom he loved. He said that he wanted treatment to help him understand and change that, so that he could get married.

The early phases of treatment were characterized by re-peated descriptions and reliving of the abuse suffered by the patient, and also by his mother, at the hands of a father who was physically and verbally abusive to both of them. The part that I am going to describe came later in the treatment after we had worked successfully on issues of trust and the pain of the abuse, among other issues. As with the first case, I had felt a variety of emotions regarding this man, and they were generally positive. But now, I was noticing that I had begun to feel vaguely and subtly aware of a feeling of disappointing him, as if I were not doing enough for him; it seemed that he had suffered so much, and "deserved" more, but that now I was letting him down by not doing enough to help him; that is, I felt guilty. But then I started to feel something that seemed to feel worse than the guilt: I was becoming irritated and annoyed in listening to his tale of woe—how he just could not break away from his mother, how he wanted to but was "unable," but if he did not, he would lose his girl friend for sure. Yet when I would ask him to analyze why he felt that he could not break away from his mother, he would answer helplessly that he was "unable" to do that either (although he had previously analyzed other issues), that he did not know why, and he wondered why *I* was asking *him*. Then he went on with questions as to why I was not coming up with answers; after all, he would say, he had done everything *he* could, and had been in treatment for over a year, and although he understood more about himself, and how he had been abused, it just did not help! He would ask, "So why aren't *you* telling me what to do? Haven't I suffered *enough* already? Isn't *anyone* going to help me?" He complained of feeling hurt and short-changed, and as he spoke to me he became sarcastic and demanding: "Why did you recommend this treatment if it wasn't going to help? Why am I paying you if the treatment isn't helping? Haven't I gone through *enough* already?" And then, in a small and whiny voice he said, "I came here because I wanted someone to comfort me, to take care of me, and to support me, and to tell me what was wrong and to fix it for me, or to tell me what to do to fix it—and instead . . . I got you!"

It was clear that he had begun to feel in the treatment itself that he was a victim, as if he had been forced to submit to treatment, and now to stay in treatment, and had no choice but to complain to me about how I was letting him down. As a result, I began not to look forward to seeing him, and I felt defensive and guilty, then began to feel resentful, and finally, because of the resentment I began to feel toward this helpless victim, even more guilty. "After all," I would say even to myself, "he *has* been abused, he can't help how he feels, and why am I feeling so angry anyway?"

This is an example of one of those unexpected and "unacceptable" feelings: anger toward a victim. Why was I angry? Did I have a right to be? Or should I feel guilty as I felt in the first place, or both? What was happening?

It seemed that things had been going well until about a month earlier. He had been feeling better, was even beginning to consider moving out from his mother's house, and he and his girl friend were talking about getting engaged. Then slowly, gradually, he stopped associating freely in the sessions, and would even say that he wasn't able to talk—not that nothing was coming to mind, but that he somehow "can't say it." He began to feel and act passively and helplessly, and would berate himself for it, yet continue to do it. Then he shifted his criticism onto me, as he started complaining (or rather, whining) about how not enough was happening in the treatment. Although his complaints were not directly about me at first, they did contain an indirect and subtle reproach, and that was when I had started to feel guilty, as if I were not doing enough for him. It had continued to escalate from there.

Then I recalled an incident he had described in which he felt guilty over being angry at his mother, because she had not been accepting her share of responsibility for a matter upon which both of them had agreed. Our analysis of that incident helped him to understand his feelings of guilt and anger, and to behave more appropriately with his mother; it also helped me at that time to see a new aspect of his relationship with his mother. It helped even more at this particular time for me to reflect upon this incident because I was able to see a parallel in the relationship he had with his mother and the one he had with me in the treatment. What had started out in the treatment as a shared enterprise had been shifted, unilaterally and unconsciously by him, and now unconsciously by me too, so that it now was all up to me: (1) he was now incapable and helpless; (2) he had been abused, and (3) he was entitled to *remain* helpless and be "totally" taken care of because he had been abused. I could see that in his identification with his mother he was playing out the same role with me that she had taken with him—that of the martyr, the helpless victim, who had been abused and suffered so much that she deserved, indeed was entitled to, special treatment, especially to be relieved of even normal, reasonable, and previously agreed upon responsibilities.

Some patients come to therapy with a sense of entitlement that therapy without effort will be their reward for suffering (Kramer, 1987; Raphling, 1990). When, as with this man, this theme of entitlement develops in the transference, the countertransference may take the form mine had taken. In other words I *agreed* with him that he deserved and was entitled not only to therapy, but therapy without pain, without expectations that he would at least try to change, in fact, that he would even have to talk! He had conveyed to me in the treatment, and I had "bought" the idea, that it was my job, all my job, not his, not even "ours," to change him.[3]

But analysis of my countertransference reaction helped me to understand and use the countertransference productively. When I analyzed my reactions, I realized that my guilt stemmed in part from his unrealistic expectation, which I now shared with him, that I could and should do it all for him. This was a role that he had come to expect his mother to play. When I now saw his expectation as unrealistic, I was able to disengage from this "role relationship" as his mother, the "responsible party" for him. Then, rather than reacting to his transference, as I had been doing, I was able to interpret to him that his claims of helplessness were exaggerated (he later said that he had begun to recognize this himself), and that he was using the realistic history of abuse and suffering as a rationale for being relieved of all of his responsibility. I made it clear to him that I was not denying or dismissing his history of abuse or suffering; rather, what I was challenging was the linkage that he was making between the abuse and his current perception of himself as helpless. There was no question that he had been helpless

---

[3]This is a point where treatment can go astray: when the countertransference is not analyzed and the therapist colludes with the patient's expectations and grants special favors. This is also the point where the boundaries can get crossed, and, to use the current phraseology, we may start down that "slippery slope" of boundary violations.

and unable to stop the abuse as a child, but he was now no longer incapable or helpless, especially in the treatment (and, in addition, he was not being abused). But he was now attempting to use his history of abuse unconsciously as a justification for having others do things for him that he was capable of doing for himself.

That is what *he* was doing. What about me? Why did I get caught up in it? Why did it make me feel guilty and angry? As I reflected on this question, I realized quickly that I had had experiences with family members of my own who had behaved in similar ways, and therefore, I had participated in this type of relationship before, and had gotten involved in it again. It represented a transference of mine to him, one of my "blind spots." But at least I was able to catch my reactions in time, and then to use my understanding of them in a way that was helpful in the therapy.

When I interpreted to him what he had been doing, and to some extent why, he understood and even felt relieved. He said, "I know I've been acting weird lately, and it's not the real me." Then he became curious as to why he was acting so passively at this particular time, and spontaneously associated to the fact it had started soon after he realized that he was making progress. I then suggested that the progress had made him anxious, and he laughed, and then began to laugh even harder and said, "You know, I remember now that about a month ago I started feeling good about myself, *really* good; in fact, so good that I started imagining getting married, but then I felt guilty for even *thinking* of leaving my mother." Now he became tearful, and as he sobbed, he said, "Just the thought of leaving her felt like I'd be hurting her . . . just like my father did!" In other words, to him, any attempt at separation was seen as a hostile action. I was then able to understand and further interpret that his passivity and handing over of responsibility to me, along with his sense of anger and entitlement, constituted a regressive defense against his ability to be active, which he had started to feel about a month earlier in the therapy, because such activity felt to him to be the equivalent of abusing his mother.

This man was not incapable of change; he was too afraid and guilty to change. Simply put, he had confused normal healthy strivings for independence and autonomy with hurtful abuse. Therefore, to him, becoming independent also meant feeling guilty.

From the countertransference standpoint, I think that this case illustrates how my brief countertransference enactment with him, once analyzed by me, was still able to be utilized productively in understanding this patient, and in helping him to understand himself. In addition, from my own experience in treating victims of abuse, as well as those of others (Krieger, Rosenfeld, Gordon, and Bennett, 1980; Cohen, 1988), it seems that the patient's perception of being "only" a victim is a common one, perhaps because these patients' experiences have been so powerful that they may act as "organizers" around which other aspects of their personalities may coalesce, so that they may then at certain times experience themselves as only, or totally, victims. In such cases the danger is that therapists may extend empathy beyond the appropriate bounds, and may want to rescue and protect patients from even the normal and necessary responsibilities of life. This tendency to see patients "only" or "totally" as victims can lead to the kind of impasse that I have described above.

In therapy then, the patient's experiences of abuse and victimization certainly must be acknowledged and worked through, but they must also be placed in the context of the individual's entire personality. Some victims will indeed be unable to be autonomous and independent, and supportive therapy would be most suitable for them. But for those with greater potential, a deeper analysis of the ways in which the abuse has been woven into the fabric of their personality can be most valuable.

Case 3

This patient, like the previous man, saw himself as repeatedly victimized and abused in relationships, and even by me in the treatment. Yet at times I felt that I was being abused by him!

He had a history as a child of severe physical abuse from an alcoholic father who often beat the patient and threw things during violent rages, especially while drunk. The patient, now in his twenties, came for treatment with a complaint of difficulties in relationships. There were many aspects to this treatment, and it was long and tedious. There was an extended period at the beginning of treatment in which the patient was detached and not very involved emotionally, and therefore it took some time before the therapeutic alliance could be developed. But gradually the work proceeded, and I will now describe events in the middle of the treatment when the patient was doing better in relationships, was feeling better about himself, but was still feeling abused by people, as he described in the following session.

I will preface the account of this session by noting a pattern which I had observed in previous sessions, regarding his descriptions of his interactions with other people in which he would present himself to someone as having a problem, which he then would tell the person about, but then would end up feeling that he was being abused by the very person that he had turned to for help. In this particular Monday session, he described his disappointment and anger over events of the previous weekend, when he had been treated abusively by a woman who stood him up for a Saturday night date. He complained that he did not understand "why I can't get rid of this anger." Although he said he was angry, I pointed out that he sounded disappointed and defeated, but not necessarily angry. He did not respond to my comment, but went on to associate to three separate conversations he had had on Sunday with male friends, in which he told each of them about being stood up by the woman; each man had reacted with anger at the woman, and then suggested that the patient call her and confront her, but he felt that he could not do that. He said that as he described the incident to each of them, each man gradually became more insistent, but the patient felt more passive. As each man became more frustrated and implored him to act, he became more helpless, and said that he now felt "doubly abused, first by her, and now even by them! And somehow I feel even more abused by them than I did by her."

He paused for a few seconds, and then went on in his associations to describe a phone call that he had received from his mother, also on Sunday. She was upset with the patient's sister, and as she described to the patient her problems with his sister, and how she was angry at his sister, he began to feel that his mother should speak to his sister. He said, "I told my Mom she should talk to her and let her know how she feels." But his mother said that she did not feel that she could do that, and the more the patient began to urge his mother to take an active position, the more she began to resist and back away from any such action. He then found himself becoming more and more frustrated with her: "Finally, I almost shouted at her that if she's not going to take my advice, she shouldn't bother to call and tell me about it!" He said that she then "shrieked at me," screaming, "Oh, listen to you! Now *you're* going to beat me up too!" The patient felt exasperated after this phone call, because he felt that his mother was acting as if he were abusing her, although he felt that she was abusing him!

He then sighed audibly, paused for a minute or so, and then returned in his associations to his sense of disappointment and anger about the woman who had stood him up. He said that he just could not understand why he still felt so angry, why he could not "just let it go and forget about it," and that he was still bothered by how he had been treated. Yet, as he recalled his friends' urgings for him to act, he said that he still did not feel that he could confront the woman, even though he wanted to and felt it would be reasonable to do so because her behavior had truly been abusive.

In my attempts to understand his current difficulties, I had reflected upon what I had understood from our previous analytic work. In the past he had often felt so unworthy (because of his experiences of emotional deprivation and abuse) that he simply did not feel entitled to ask someone why he was being treated badly, because he felt that he must be "deserving" of abuse. Although I did not think that that was what was happening at this time, I did ask him whether he felt that might be the problem. He said he did not think so, and emphasized that he felt angry *because* he now felt worthy of being treated better. But he said he still did not understand why he felt that he could not confront this woman, or even just tell her how he felt, or ask what had happened. When I began to ask him what he thought about it and why he might not be able to express his anger, I noticed that he became more passive, and seemed to behave more helplessly. Then I noticed, after several minutes of this kind of interaction, that *I* was beginning to feel frustrated by his helplessness and resignation, and was starting to feel helpless and impotent myself. I also became aware that he seemed to be getting angry at *me* for my questions, which he now was experiencing not as an attempt to help him, but as abuse! That's when I realized that I had begun to feel that I, too, was being "abused," in the sense that I felt that I had done nothing to deserve his anger.

I then began to wonder why this pattern was occurring, and what was happening at this specific moment. My thoughts returned to his description of the start of the interaction with his mother. She had not directly requested help from him, yet he had responded to her as if she had actually requested his help. Then it became clear to me that it was a request that his mother had made not in words but by the tone of her voice. He had done the same thing, I now surmised, with each of his three friends. He had not directly asked for their help, but had indirectly requested it. Then I recognized that he had done the same thing with me, and had indirectly requested my help, yet was now angry at me as if I were telling him what he "should" do, even though it had seemed to me that I was responding to his request to explore his stated problem with his anger.

So I then presented these observations and thoughts to him: I asked why he thought he had responded to his mother as he had; I wondered why he had tried to tell her what to do (to call his sister and tell his sister how she felt) since she was not actually asking for his help. He almost interrupted me as he quickly blurted out, "Yes, yes she was! Not by what she said, but by her tone. She definitely was asking me what to do! She doesn't ask directly, but by her sad, suffering, helpless tone, I know she's saying, 'Look, I have a problem, tell me what to do.' " I said, "So she asks you indirectly, rather than directly, and then when you try to help, she gets angry at you for telling her what to do, as if she had done nothing to engage you in the interaction." He replied, "Exactly! And I always take the

bait." "The bait?" I asked. "Yeah," he said, "she does this helpless sort of number on me, and I go for it, and I end up frustrated!" I then went on to interpret *his* similar behavior with
others: "So that's what you did with your friends, and here with
me too. You tell a story as if it's just a story, but it contains a
request for help, an invitation . . . the bait!" Now he began to
laugh, in an embarrassed, sheepish way, yet also became ani-
mated and excited, and said, "Wow! I can't believe that I do
that too! No wonder they get so pissed off at me!"

Now he could see that he did this so subtly, as his mother
had done with him, that it had not been recognized by others,
just as it had not been recognized by him with his mother. He
then started to chuckle and said, "It's really a neat way of doing
things. I can get other people to be angry, but then they really
can't be angry at me because I haven't done anything!" I then
interpreted that after he got someone to "take the bait," he
became increasingly helpless and would reject all suggestions
for help, while his "victim" became increasingly frustrated, and
then in the end, as his mother had done to him, he could
suddenly turn on the person and attack his victim for abusing
him by urging him to action. It was clear to him now that he
obviously had perfected this technique of provoking others to
action in order to make them feel as helpless as he had felt
when he was being abused. Further, and this was the "worst"
part to him, the part he now felt ashamed and guilty about,
he actually derived a certain pleasure from doing it. Thus he
accomplished a reversal of roles, so that the abused became the
abuser, but the entire process, and the motivations for it, had
remained unconscious.

In this case it was helpful to recognize my own response of
feeling frustrated and helpless, as I too initially took the bait.
But when I stopped doing that and instead began interpreting
his behavior, he could see what he had been doing. I began my
interpretation by reminding him that, at the beginning of the
session, I had observed that he had said that he felt angry and
"couldn't let go of it," but was not acting angry, or expressing
anger, but instead was behaving in a disappointed, hurt, defeated, and impotent manner. Although he had ignored my
observation then, he recognized it himself now, and so I then

went on to interpret that he seemed to need to feel impotent in order to avoid feeling angry. I then asked him why it was so important not to feel angry. He was silent for a moment, then grew visibly tense, and as he became angry and anxious, with his voice rising, and with his teeth and his jaws clenched tightly, he exclaimed that he was afraid to be angry because his anger would get out of control: "I might kill him—I mean her—I mean him, no, I mean both!" That is, he meant that he was afraid he might kill the woman "abuser," and the male "abusers," all of whom stood for his father—the original abuser.

From his further associations it became clear that what he also meant was that he needed to inhibit his anger because he was so afraid that if he felt angry he would *automatically* act upon it and become the violent, physically abusive man that his father was. He had learned to repress his anger and repudiate his unconscious identification with his abusive father by becoming a passive and impotent man, and yet one who (unconsciously) provoked others to abuse him as his father had done. In this way, he also played out the roles of both abused victim and abuser, in order to gain mastery over his helplessness, to turn passive into active, and to make others feel helpless too.

This pattern that I have described is a complex but, I believe, fairly common one in certain victims of abuse. Their need to repudiate their identification with the abuser, along with other motivations, can lead to such behaviors. From the countertransference standpoint then, at this point in the analysis it was important to be able to view his provocative behaviors as being designed both to express and to defend against still deeper conflictual issues. For example, earlier in the treatment, I did not feel angry when he described his inability to stand up to those who abused him. At that time his inability had been based primarily upon his sense of worthlessness, so that he did not feel entitled to fair treatment, and therefore, did not feel angry and could not defend himself. He felt he "deserved" to be abused, and was not allowed to complain about it. This pattern was similar to the way he had felt about his father's abuse, when, as a child, he would complain about the abuse to his mother, but his mother would not acknowledge it as abuse, and acted instead as if the patient had either provoked or deserved it, or wasn't supposed to complain—either way, it was his fault. But at this point in the therapy, when he did feel entitled to fair treatment, his inability to defend himself constituted more of a refusal, with additional motivations, as described above. His inability to demand to be treated better at the beginning of treatment was the result of his sense of not deserving anything better; his inability to demand to be treated better now was based upon his fear of his own murderous rage.

Although I had seen some of these patterns operating in his outside relationships, I had not been able to understand what actually happened until I "felt" it in my countertransference reactions. At first, I was not aware of why I felt the way I did, and just felt confused as to why he would say that he felt abused by me, when I was at that same moment feeling abused by him! It was only by carefully examining his actions and reactions, and my own, that I came to understand what was happening in the transference–countertransference relationship, and then I was able to interpret it successfully to the patient.

RECOMMENDATIONS FOR UTILIZING COUNTERTRANSFERENCE PRODUCTIVELY IN THE TREATMENT OF VICTIMS OF ABUSE

1. Monitor countertransference reactions closely. It is important to constantly pay attention to our own associations (thoughts, feelings, fantasies), including what might seem to be "stray thoughts," and to consider all of them as part of therapy—they are!

2. Try not to judge these reactions, but instead to analyze them, to understand their origins ("Why am I feeling this way now?"). We must pay particular attention to reactions that are recurrent or persistent, and must even be alert to what we do not feel, as described in the first clinical example. We must know our own blind spots, the areas where we may tend to either overreact or underreact, and recognize when these are playing a role, so that we can correct for them.

3. In regard specifically to treatment of victims of abuse, we must be particularly aware of the opposing tendencies, on the one hand, to either avoid, ignore, discount, or deny the abuse, and therefore, not see the patients as true victims, or, on the other hand, to rescue the patient and ally ourselves with the patient as "only" or "totally" a victim. This latter tendency can interfere with exploring and understanding the patient's deeper motivations, such as certain guilt-ridden wishes.

4. If our feelings become problematic, or the treatment is at an impasse, or when we just do not understand, it is a good idea to get help:

Talk with a colleague;
Get consultation or supervision;
Try ongoing group supervision, such as work or study groups. Consider treatment for ourselves if the issues seem to be predominately internal rather than stemming from our patients. Therapy can help us to better understand ourselves, and therefore, allow us to better help our patients.

REFERENCES

Burland, J. A., & Raskin, R. (1990), The psychoanalysis of adults who were sexually abused in childhood: A preliminary report from the discussion group of the American Psychoanalytic Association. In: *Adult Analysis and Childhood Sexual Abuse*, ed. H. B. Levine. Hillsdale, NJ: Analytic Press, pp. 35–41.

Cohen, Y. (1988), The "Golden Fantasy" and countertransference: Residential treatment of the abused child. *The Psychoanalytic Study of the Child*, 43:337–350. New Haven, CT: Yale University Press.

Freud, S. (1910), The future prospects of psychoanalytic therapy. *Standard Edition*, 11:141–151. London: Hogarth Press, 1957.

———— (1915), Observations on transference-love. *Standard Edition*, 12:159–171. London: Hogarth Press, 1958.

Greenson, R. R. (1967), *The Technique and Practice of Psychoanalysis*. New York: International Universities Press.

Heimann, P. (1950), On countertransference. *Internat. J. Psycho-Anal.*, 31:81–84.

Jacobs, T. J. (1986), On countertransference enactments. *J. Amer. Psychoanal. Assn.*, 34:289–307.

Kramer, S. (1987), A contribution to the concept of "the exception" as a developmental phenomenon. *Child Abuse & Neglect,* 11:367–370.

Krieger, M., Rosenfeld, A., Gordon, A., & Bennett, M. (1980), Problems in the psychotherapy of children with histories of incest. *Amer. J. Psychother.*, 34:81–88.

Levine, H. (1990), Clinical issues in the analysis of adults who were sexually abused as children. In: *Adult Analysis and Childhood Sexual Abuse*, ed. H. Levine. Hillsdale, NJ: Analytic Press, pp. 197–218.

Lisman-Pieczanski, N. (1990), Countertransference in the analysis of an adult who was sexually abused as a child. In: *Adult Analysis and Childhood Sexual Abuse*, ed. H. Levine. Hillsdale, NJ: Analytic Press, pp. 137–147.

Moore, B. E., & Fine, B. D. (1990), *Psychoanalytic Terms and Concepts.* New Haven, CT: Yale University Press.

Raphling, D. (1990), Technical issues of the opening phase. In: *Adult Analysis and Childhood Sexual Abuse*, ed. H. Levine. Hillsdale, NJ: Analytic Press, pp. 45–64.

Sandler, J. (1976), Countertransference and role-responsiveness. *Internat. Rev. Psychoanal.*, 3:43–47.

—— Dare, C., & Holder, A. (1973), *The Patient and the Analyst: The Basis of the Psychoanalytic Process.* London: Allen & Unwin.

Tyson, R. L. (1986), Countertransference evolution in theory and practice. *J. Amer. Psychoanal. Assn.*, 34:251–274.

Chapter 11

Illnesses, Failures, Losses: Human Misery Propelling Regression, Therapy, and Growth

John H. Hassler, M.D.

Emotional trauma is ubiquitous. No one lives without emotional pain and occasional feelings of victimization. There are an infinite variety of psychic responses to trauma (and for my purposes here I view emotional trauma, emotional pain, and loss—of other or self representations—as synonymous). On one extreme, we moan and wail and grieve and recover our pretrauma or preloss potentials without significant regression. Or we may suffer a period of reduced resistance to infections or reduced initiative. On the other end of the spectrum are torture victims who suffer permanent, severe emotional numbing and complex intrusive arrays of reenactment fantasies, feelings, or behaviors with loss of all prospective potential.

Most of our patients present for help in the midrange. They have suffered some trauma, often not obvious or recalled, where the degree of insult, real or symbolic, is sufficiently profound so that they have regressed to relatively restricted psychic functioning. Some feeling state is no longer tolerable, a self representation is not allowed, or some aspects of their world view have been distorted (usually by projections, or destructive reenactments).

In this paper, I will describe four examples of this process of trauma, regression to relatively fixed limitations of function, and recovery under dynamically focused therapy.

The primary psychoanalytic theory in this area of loss or trauma leading to growth includes Freud's seminal observations in "Mourning and Melancholia" (1917) and *The Ego and the Id* (1923) that loss may induce massive self-contempt and impoverished ego resources and that recovery includes new identifications (in situations of love or loss) and consequently options for self and ego expression. Mahler's observations on early childhood separation–individuation processes are also crucial to an understanding of loss and growth processes throughout the life cycle (Mahler, Pine, and Bergman, 1975). Through complex imitations and enactments and trial separations, toddlers internalize aspects of the mother representation into the self representation.

In more recent years, Horowitz (1976) delineated the array of clinical response patterns to loss. Some of these patterns reflect normative adult experiences (i.e., parent death, anticipating death of self) and are part of ultimately healthy adult development. Colarusso and Nemiroff (1981) have written broadly on these themes and have alerted the clinician to how often adult developmental challenges may become traumas leading to symptoms and suffering.

Throughout the literature, there is often a question of what is primary in causation of symptoms or regression. Is it internal trauma (oedipal fantasies at 5, fear of death at 40) or external trauma (seduction as Freud and Breuer first thought in hysteria, or death of a spouse)? In my patients, external traumas prompt internal development struggles (and either or both, for a time, may be outside the awareness of the patient and therapist).

Put simply, each of the following patients had two illnesses and two recoveries. Each had an adult trauma that included and led to multiple losses of developmental opportunity; and therapy had to focus on recovery from this trauma and grief over the subsequent losses. But each adult trauma also activated childhood and adult developmental themes; and so therapy also had to focus on resolving anew preoedipal or oedipal and postoedipal developmental struggles.

CASE PRESENTATIONS

While each of these cases, although disguised, are real, they also each represent a class of patients who form a significant part of clinical practice. Each then may reflect a suit in a deck of cards.

Case 1

Mr. Spade, a 50-year-old scientist, sought weekly psychotherapy for a writing block that had haunted him for ten years. He had creative approaches to difficult problems, but in recent years could not write them down. He would share his thoughts with friends or colleagues, who then by default would gain credit that he was blocked from earning. In dreams, other men would wear his clothes or sit at his mother's table, savoring her fresh pastries.

Mr. Spade initially credited the onset of his writing block to the failure of his marriage eight years before, but as he explored the nature of his marriage, and dreamt of another woman disrupting love making with his wife, he associated to new history: "I haven't mentioned it, it seemed minor, but about then my mother did move in with us, and she was demanding of attention for a few years before her death."

It wasn't loss of a wife so much as the intrusion of a mother and all she meant symbolically that left Mr. Spade blocked, as his subsequent history revealed.

Literate, cultured, and wealthy, his parents lived graciously in Chicago and Paris and spent endless hours (all recalled with great bliss) stimulating his curiosity and excitement with life. While father traveled on business away from the family, the patient would entertain mother with his enthusiasms. As a boy he had grown healthy enough to feel that he could triumph over his father at times while still loving him.

When he was 7, the family wealth and father's optimism crashed. For some time thereafter, the boy felt unsure of himself, unsure of his capabilities. "My two most poignant childhood memories were of shame as a 7-year-old offering my father the few pennies that I had saved so that he could pay the rent, and later of shame when he saw me enjoying my penis as a 10-year-old."

As reconstructed in therapy in the mind of a 7-year-old boy, his father's financial and emotional collapse had occurred because he had taken his father's manhood (a complex theft on multiple levels of prowess and identity). He had resolved and repressed this fantasy crime by young adulthood and enjoyed considerable success. But when his mother moved in when he was 40, he again feared that he would face retribution if he enjoyed his own prowess in too successful a way. For a time in the transference he had a fear that I would put him on the rack for his wish to take from me. As he examined his fear of my attack in response to his prowess, he began to write with progressively greater ease and clarity.

Case 2

Mrs. Heart, a 35-year-old manager, came to analysis with the pain of an empty marriage. She could feel no passion for her husband, whom she saw as controlling and demeaning. She also felt controlled and demeaned at work by male and female senior managers. Like Mr. Spade, she did not describe precipitating traumas or losses.

For the first few weeks of analysis she felt that I could not help her and dreamt of sexually provocative intruders prowling through her house. As her fear of her feelings for me and other males was identified and explored, she began to wear red "for the first time in years" and recall her envy of her older sister swimming with her father while she had to stay ashore with her mother.

As we explored what seemed like inhibitions in resolving standard childhood developmental challenges, new material developed out of a dream: "I'm thrown back and forth like the

Space Tours ride at Disneyland and I look past passengers all dressed in black to you as the pilot, but with Paul's face." She associated to a gondola trip up a mountain with her college boyfriend, Paul, at 20 before he died in an avalanche. "I feel here that I'm in that gondola, really scared." For fifteen years she had retreated from joyful intimacy out of a certainty that exuberant femininity would lead to death again. "I haven't skied since."

As with Mr. Spade, Mrs. Heart suffered from a form of survivor guilt. The death of her college boyfriend had broken her heart. She regressed to the doubts of an undeserving junior sister and set up scorning and heartless personal and professional intimacies. As with Mr. Spade, identifying the subjective consequences of the earlier traumatic experiences, felt as crimes leading to defensive inhibition and self-doubt, gradually allowed for a reintegration with preexisting and more exuberant self representations and levels of expression. She began to enjoy responses from her husband and other men, and to win promotions at work.

Case 3

Mr. Diamond, a 35-year-old businessman, unlike Mr. Spade and Mrs. Heart, remembered his precipitating trauma. He lost all his money—several hundred thousand dollars ("diamonds," as he called them)—that he and his friends had hoped would make them rich in a start-up business, five years prior to treatment. While he thought that he was generally satisfied with himself and his work since then, occasional, mild suicidal thoughts finally led him to therapy.

A careful review of his emotional states since the failure highlighted his psychic quandary. The humiliation of the business failure had pushed him into frequent dissociated states that reenacted memories of bliss with his boyhood mother. "I don't think about working for money, but only to please the patrons (even though my head tells me that I'm living on plastic). And of course I tell them (and my wife) whatever will make them like me."

Adult standards of honesty, and the adult empathy that would have protected him from the damage he was doing to his patrons, his family, and himself did not apply when he was in this dissociated psychological world. If good fortune (or his wife's hard work and budgeting) allowed him to get ahead financially, he would not fear humiliation; and he could temporarily pull free of his regressed dissociated state and react with engaging empathy, honesty, and great warmth toward all around him.

He only was corrupt when he feared humiliation (or more precisely the loss of love and self-love) in symbolically charged relationships. Then unbeknownst to himself or others he would operate in his safe world of a dutiful boy until the ultimate collapse of his real world (especially the terror of his wife) would bring him back to reality and mild suicidal remorse.

Therapy succeeded in identifying these two aspects of himself as he bobbed back and forth trying to avoid humiliations in the transference relationship with me as his preoedipal mother. As he began to see that he would not actually face humiliation (and associated losses of self) in therapy, he was able to explore the hierarchy of emotions that he feared when humiliation approached. Consequently the tendency to escape to boyhood magic generally diminished. Mr. Diamond could now go to work to look for diamonds instead of parent love, even when faced with debts and an anxious family.

His business trauma had induced the elaboration of this blissful but self-destructive escape, which had only been a potential option before. His dissociated states only presented after the adult humiliation. In the context of therapeutic exploration, it became obvious that childhood and marital dynamics allowed for elements of self-deception. His mother had doted on her "perfect" son, his wife also liked him best when he "protected" her from the insecurities of her childhood, and his father, out of pathological narcissism, undercut his son's many real personal and professional achievements.

Retreat to dissociated states after significant childhood or adult trauma is common. The recent literature is filled with case reports of defensive dissociated states evolving from severe physical or sexual abuse. As is clear with Mr. Diamond, lesser overt traumas (business failure) in a susceptible psyche also may bring dissociated states to expression.

Case 4

My final patient, Mrs. Club, was knocked down by illness. At 28 she had been trying for six years unsuccessfully to have a child. Now two months after surgery which opened her fallopian tubes, she was repulsed by "my husband's breeding program" and sought therapy "to give me the fortitude to be an architect." She reported that the surgeon was propositioning her and felt convinced that I certainly would—"Which is why I feel so trapped and brutalized, I can't even turn for help here."

For weeks she focused on the brutality of men in college and dreamt of graveyards ("guarded by suspicious old women"). She associated to her mother pushing her into closets as punishment for childhood pranks and reported that her parents disowned her when she moved in with her husband. As she gradually discovered that the therapist was not a punitive parent, and as she was able to gradually reexperience sexual pleasure with her husband (initially displaced from the erotic transference), she felt sufficient confidence to explore an unmentioned trauma: the death of her uncle soon after she began to want a child, six years before therapy.

"I can now feel with you the comfort I had with him on long walks in adolescence. He encouraged me to become an architect and even joked about marrying me if I weren't family." She then dreamt of having a little girl ("his, of course") and agreed with my interpretation and reconstruction that she feared that her wishes had killed her uncle. Her guilt and conviction of magical punishment were confirmed by her infertility and her recurrent dreads that she, her husband, or child would die. "It got worse before and after surgery. I knew the nurses and doctors were only pretending to help me."

As this material was explored and her guilt worked through, the patient revealed that, in fact, her parents were now extremely supportive of her marriage and possible career

("I'll be an architect after I'm a mother"). She realized that she and her husband were pretty good lovers and would be good parents.

Mrs. Club's working through of the trauma of her uncle's death allowed her to move from massive feelings of victimization (prompted by infertility, related marital frustrations, and the terror of surgery) to a confident game plan. Regression under chronic situational failure at pregnancy had activated previously resolved struggles with mother and dangerous incestuous fantasies with family males. When enacted in the transference, this regression, its causes, and the multiple representations of important players, were identified. Within months she regained an optimism that she had not felt since before her uncle's death, and was free of the erotic–paranoid world in which she lived during the months before and after surgery.

CONCLUSIONS

These four successful people were all playing with a full deck of reasonably integrated (i.e., neurotic) psychic structures and enjoyed considerable earlier life success and joy. But in each case life events, from modest to extreme in external intensity, led to significant regressions that were relatively fixed before therapy. They did not regress under vague chronic deficiencies of genetics, parenting, or adult opportunity.

Except for Mrs. Heart, who was seen in a three-year analytic effort, all these patients awoke from defensive retreats with less than two years of face-to-face exploratory psychotherapy. Not all of my patients have as much potential to start with or do as well.

There are several general therapeutic observations that are pertinent with this group of healthy but traumatized patients:

Rage

Anyone who has lost a lover to death or faced the humiliation of career failure is furious. Who is the murderer? Who is the thief? These patients, for any number of psychodynamic reasons, cannot neutralize the rage and self-contempt. External loss or trauma leads to anger and feelings of victimization that contaminate libidinal object representations and self-structures. For these patients, conflict with rage, in its various forms, is central to the initial regression; and an integration of rage into a caring world schema is central to recovery. The empathic therapeutic environment is essential to the gradual reemergence of the patient's belief in personal worth in a world where people may care.

Transference

Doubting the availability of caring others and of a generous, competent self representation is a presenting contaminant, and appears early and prominently in transference manifestations. "I doubt if I can trust you, and I'm not too sure of myself," quipped Mr. Spade during his first visit. "Why won't you want to rape me, all of the other doctors do," wondered Mrs. Club. The clinical adage that it is never too early to interpret a transference resistance is even more true than usual with this group of patients who protect such intense rage and arousal. Confront and interpret their transference distortions early and often!

A diagnostic warning also holds. The aura of mistrust that colors the initial transference, and the suspiciousness so often elaborated in the characterologic life-style of the patient, may mislead the therapist into doubting the patient's innate capacity for mature, integrated object ties. Here, as with other patients, seemingly borderline defenses may disguise neurotic potentials.

Grief

Anger, repression, and regression have kept these patients from grieving. Explicit reconstruction of the losses relating to and following the trauma is necessary to initiate the grieving and to allow for appropriate moves forward.

Oedipal Reworking

After the early transference projections and investments are interpreted and grieving is initiated and progresses, the exploration and resolution of the activated oedipal or preoedipal genetic material (or adult derivatives) is the major work of therapy. There is unusually little resistance to staying with this material; perhaps because these challenges have already been mastered once, and resolution achieved before the trauma and regression. Of equal importance for my patients was the rich, intimate, and elaborated object ties in the real world that allowed for renewed expression and repression.

REFERENCES

Colarusso, C., & Nemiroff, R. (1981), *Adult Development.* New York: Plenum Press.

Freud, S. (1917), Mourning and melancholia. *Standard Edition,* 14:237–260. London: Hogarth Press, 1957.

―――― (1923), The Ego and the Id. *Standard Edition,* 19:3–66. London: Hogarth Press, 1961.

Horowitz, M. (1976), *Stress Response Syndromes.* New York: Jason Aronson.

Mahler, M. S., Pine, F., & Bergman, A. (1975), *The Psychological Birth of the Human Infant.* New York: Basic Books.

Name Index

223

Subject Index